AF334994

Symbols in Life and Art

The Royal Society of Canada Symposium in Memory of George Whalley

---

Les Symboles dans la vie et dans l'art

La Société Royale du Canada Colloque à la Mémoire de George Whalley

edited by / rédigé par
James A. Leith, F.R.S.C.

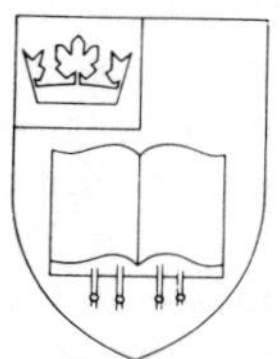

Published for the Royal Society of Canada
by McGill-Queen's University Press

ISBN 0-7735-0616-0
Legal deposit third quarter 1987
Bibliothèque nationale du Québec
Printed in Canada

The Royal Society of Canada Symposium
in Memory of George Whalley
was held on 26, 27, and 28 October 1984
at Queen's University.

Canadian Cataloguing in Publication Data

Main entry under title:
Symbols in life and art =
Les Symboles dans la vie et dans l'art

Text in English and French.
Held Oct. 26–28, 1984, at Queen's University, Kingston, Ont.
Includes bibliographical references.
ISBN 0-7735-0616-0
1. Symbolism – Congresses. 2. Signs and symbols – Congresses.
I. Leith, James A., 1931– . II. Whalley, George, 1915–
III. Royal Society of Canada. IV. Title.
N7740.S95 1987 704.9'46 C87-094017-1E

Données de catalogage avant publication (Canada)

Vedette principale au titre:
Symbols in life and art =
Les Symboles dans la vie et dans l'art

Textes en français et en anglais.
Tenu du 26 au 28 oct., 1984, au Queen's University, Kingston, Ont.
Comprends des références bibliographiques.
ISBN 0-7735-0616-0
1. Symbolisme – Congrès. 2. Signes et symboles – Congrès.
I. Leith, James A., 1931– . II. Whalley, George, 1915–
III. Société royale du Canada. IV. Titre.
N7740.S95 1987 704.9'46 C87-094017-1F

Contents/Table des Matières

Preface
vii

Acknowledgments
ix

Remerciements
xi

NORTHROP FRYE
The Symbol as a Medium of Exchange
3

ANTHONY STORR
Symbols of Unity and Integration
17

DOUGLAS JONES
Steel Syntax: The Railroad as Symbol in Canadian Poetry
33

BOGOMILA WELSH-OVCHAROV
Vincent van Gogh, Paul Gauguin, and Albert Aurier:
The Perception of Life in Death
52

ABRAHAM MOLES
La Fonction des Mythes Dynamiques dans la Construction de l'Imaginaire Social
66

WILFRED CANTWELL SMITH
Symbols in Religion
89

JAMES A. LEITH
Symbols in the French Revolution: The Strange Metamorphoses of the Triangle
105

EVA KUSHNER
Le Statut du Symbole dans la Poésie de la Renaissance
118

NORMAN MACKENZIE
Reflections
133

Organizing Committee / Comité d'Organisation
153

Illustrations
following 65 and 117

Preface

George Whalley, F.R.S.C., was for many years a distinguished member of the English Department at Queen's University, for eight of those years serving as Cappon Professor and Department Head. He was eminent in many fields – as critic, scholar, teacher, theorist, poet, biographer – the categories multiply. He was in fact a polymath whose keen and sensitive intelligence ranged widely. When the present symposium was first proposed, we were immediately aware of the enthusiastic interest that George Whalley would have had in such a project, so close to his central concerns. It is fitting, then, that this symposium should be dedicated to his memory.

John M. Stedmond, F.R.S.C.
Professor Emeritus of English
Queen's University

Acknowledgments

The Organizing Committee is grateful to the Social Sciences and Humanities Research Council of Canada, the British Council, the French Embassy, the School of Graduate Studies and Research at Queen's University, the Faculty of Arts and Science at Queen's University, and Principal David C. Smith for financial assistance which allowed us to bring speakers from six universities in four countries to participate in this colloquium, and to publish the Proceedings. Publication has also been funded by the Royal Society of Canada. The Organizing Committee would like to thank Professor Douglas Spettigue, Head of the Department of English, for his invaluable support, and Mrs Stella Gartland, Administrative Assistant in the same Department, for her generous help in preparing for the colloquium. In addition, the Committee is grateful to Mr Peter Dorn, Head of the Graphic Design Unit of Queen's University, for designing the handsome poster and program for the colloquium. Furthermore, we would like to express our appreciation for the help of Ms Marcia Jones, Program Assistant at the Donald Gordon Centre, and the rest of the staff of the Centre for their help in organizing and running the conference. Finally, we are grateful for the assistance of Mr E.H.P. Garneau, Executive Secretary of the Royal Society of Canada, and Professor John M. Robson, Honorary Editor of the Society, for their help and advice in preparing the Proceedings for publication.

Remerciements

Le comité organisateur tient à remercier le Conseil de Recherches en Sciences Humaines du Canada, le British Council, l'Ambassade de France, l'Ecole des études supérieures de l'Université Queen's, la Faculté des Arts et Sciences de l'Université Queen's, et le Principal David C. Smith, de l'aide financière qui a permis à des conférenciers venant de six universités et de quatre pays différents de participer à ce colloque. Cette aide a permis également la publication des Actes du colloque. Cet ouvrage a été publié grace à une subvention de la Société Royale du Canada. Le comité organisateur remercie le Professeur Douglas Spettigue, Directeur du Département d'Anglais, de son soutien précieux, et Mme Stella Gartland, Assistante administratrice dans le même Département, de son aide généreuse dans la préparation du colloque. Nous remercions en même temps M. Peter Dorn, Directeur du Département de Graphisme de l'Université Queen's, d'avoir préparé la belle affiche programme du colloque. Nous tenons aussi à exprimer nos plus vifs remerciements à Mme Marcia Jones, organisatrice des conférences au Donald Gordon Centre, et aux autres membres de l'équipe du Centre qui ont organisé et assuré le bon déroulement du colloque. Nous sommes très reconnaissants, enfin, à M. E.H.P. Garneau, Secrétaire exécutif de la Société Royale du Canada, et au Professeur John M. Robson, Directeur des publications de la Société, de nous avoir fait profiter de leur aide et de leurs conseils dans l'édition des actes du colloque.

Symbols in Life and Art

NORTHROP FRYE
University of Toronto

The Symbol as a Medium of Exchange

The word symbol is a term of such Protean elusiveness that my instinct, as a practical literary critic, has always been to avoid it as much as possible. However, the title of this conference, "Symbols in Life and Art," indicates, quite correctly, that it is a word of major importance in an aspect of criticism which has also been central to my interests, the linking of the arts, including literature, to other social phenomena, and the study of the place and function of the arts in social life. Symbol comes, we are told, from the Greek *symballein*, which means to put together, or, in many contexts, to throw together. A *symbolon* was a token or counter, something that could be broken in two and recognized again by the identity of the break. By an easy derivation it acquired the meaning of a ticket, say to a theatrical performance. Emily Dickinson writes:

I never spoke with God,
Nor visited in Heaven;
Yet certain am I of the spot
As though the checks were given.

"Checks" means railway checks, which validate the ticket and guarantee that one is going to the right place. The word is a symbol that takes us back to one of the most ancient and primitive senses of the term.

There is also a closely related masculine noun *symbolos*, which means an omen or augury, such as predictions made from entrails of birds or the positions of the stars. This brings us a little closer to the "throwing" meaning in *ballein*, the sense of something random or accidental which partly reveals something not fully understood. When Mallarmé tells us that a dice throw does not abolish chance, and ends his poem on the subject by saying "Toute pensée émet un coup de dés," he is using a symbol that takes us back to its other primitive sense. In these two Greek words we can see the beginning of a distinction in our conception of symbolism that has run all through its history. A *symbolon* is something that is not complete in itself, but needs something else, or another half of itself, to make it complete. A *symbolos*, in contrast, links us to something too complex or mysterious to grasp all at once.

In the chapter on "Symbol and Myth" in his book *Poetic Process*, George Whalley remarks that "a symbol, like metaphor, does not stand for a 'thing,' or for an idea; it is a focus of relationships." This is true of the literary context of the word symbol with which Whalley is concerned: it is not true of all its contexts. It is very common to use a symbol to stand for a thing or an idea: every noun in language represents a thing or idea in one of its aspects, and every verb an action or event. The relation between a word and the thing or event it represents is arbitrary, or more accurately fixed only by convention. But if we are going to use words in this way we must employ the words that convention has decreed to be the suitable ones. In medical diagnosis, for example, the doctor studies a set of symptoms and tries to find the verbal *symbolon* that unmistakably fits them. Such *symbola* of course need not always be verbal: in driving in traffic, red and green lights are symbolically related to actions that the driver must complete by performing.

But if we turn to other symbols, such as national flags, we find ourselves moving closer to *symbolos*, the omen or portent. A Greek flag on a ship may be a simple sign telling us that the ship is Greek in origin. But a nation is a very complex entity, and its flag can be used in any number of contexts with any number of possible responses. Here we are definitely in the area that Whalley describes as "a focus of relationships." Flags belong to a group of what may be called metonymic symbols: the symbol is *put for* a cluster of phenomena indicating what kind of social contract a certain body of people has been born into. If Joe Snitch the cat-burglar is on trial for stealing, his case is called Regina vs. Snitch. Everyone knows that the Queen has never heard of Snitch and has not the least awareness that she is going to law with him: the metonymy is there to show (among other things) that the Canadian social contract has a central British and monarchical strain in its cultural traditions. Similarly with religious symbols, like the cross in Christianity or the symbols that appear on the flags of Israel and Southern Korea.

When such symbols are simple visible or audible stimuli, like a flag or a slogan, they possess a tremendous condensing power. Their focusing of relationships can act as a burning glass, kindling a flame of response from the heat of a myriad social concerns that they draw together into a single impact. At the same time they are displacements of those concerns: they are not the concerns themselves, with all our conflicting and critical feelings about them. The words "condense" and "displace" remind us of Freud's conception of the dream symbol. And certainly there is something dreamlike about a social symbol of this kind. Like the dream image, it is a mirror of our own identity: it looms up out of a mass of vanished or submerged impressions, and speaks to us from a context of silence. Like the dream image, again, it bypasses all mental conflict. Once seen, it is to be accepted (or rejected, if it is a symbol of something hostile to our concerns), and accepted on a deep emotional and uncritical level. Such symbols may be essential to social unity, especially in a crisis, where their function is to stop debate and initiate action. But because of the uncritical element in the response to them, there are lurking dangers in their use. Such words as "flag-waving" express our awareness of these dangers.

Secular loyalties, however, have the built-in safeguard that they cannot be believed to have an ideal form. A sufficiently ferocious tyranny may prevent its citizens from expressing all criticism of it, but that merely makes it more obvious that such criticisms are possible. It is different with religious symbols. Take the symbol of the Christian church in a well-known hymn:

> We are not divided,
> All one body we:
> One in hope and doctrine,
> One in charity.

Anyone who had been, let us say, on an ecumenical action committee might well wonder how even a hymn-writer could bring himself to write this appalling blither. But such a perfectly unified church of pure love and compassion not only could conceivably exist in a spiritual world, but according to its own doctrine it does. Hence it is possible to define the church in a way that would have, to a visitor from Mars, not the slightest discernible connection with that building on the corner advertising a rummage sale. This fact has in the past given a peculiarly venomous quality to disputes over religious symbols, and it is all the more essential to keep in mind that a spiritual church, so far as ordinary experience is concerned, is the same thing as a dream church in a dream world.

One of the best known discussions of symbolism occurs in Carlyle's chapter on symbols in *Sartor Resartus*. The chapter begins with a praise of silence and secrecy as the atmosphere in which all creative work takes shape, and goes on to say "in a Symbol there is concealment and yet revelation: here therefore, by Silence and by Speech acting together, comes a double significance." I have tried to show that this is true of the metonymic symbols I have been discussing, and why it is true. Carlyle then goes on to distinguish extrinsic from intrinsic symbols: symbols without value in themselves, like the flags mentioned above, and symbols that have inherent value. These latter include, first, works of art, and, secondly, charismatic personalities, heroes, leaders, prophets, and finally Jesus of Nazareth. The implication is fairly clear that the intrinsic symbol is the reality to which the extrinsic symbol points.

It seems to me that in this conception of an intrinsic symbol Carlyle made the fatal misstep that sent him on the way to becoming a prophet of fascism. A human personality, whether of Jesus of Nazareth or of our local member of Parliament, is not a symbol but a presence. Certainly some persons, like the Queen or the Pope, incorporate many symbolic attributes, but the symbolism is still extrinsic to them so far as they are persons. In the title of Kantorowicz's great book, the king has two bodies: if they are not separable, we have a human leader who claims a more than human authority, which I think is one of the things that the New Testament means by Antichrist.

In his inclusion of works of art among intrinsic symbols, again, it seems clear that Carlyle thinks of the work of art as essentially its creator's personal rhetoric, a by-product of the artist's life. It is true that in poetry, at least, there is a constant association of the poem with the poet speaking. But this is a literary convention based on the fact that the poem is being referred back to an original performance. If we ask a poet what his poem means (or, in still clumsier language, what he meant by it), the only truthful answer he could give would be to recite the poem. The poets themselves, from the authors of the Homeric Hymns invoking the deity they were celebrating to T.S. Eliot invoking a catalyzer in a chemical laboratory, have insisted that their poetry was not their personal rhetoric but something that seemed to emerge with an origin of its own. The poet, then, like the king, has two bodies, one a maternal body where the poems are gestated and born, the other the person who is, in Yeats's phrase, the bundle of contradictions that sits down to breakfast.

We have now to turn to the question of symbols in works of art, and the obvious art to begin with is literature. Every word is a verbal symbol with two contexts. First, it is half of a *symbolon* which must be matched up to its other half, its conventional meaning, in memory or in a dictionary. Second, it is a *symbolos*, with a meaning related to its context which will give us one more clue to the sense of the whole verbal design of which it forms part. What makes a word a word is its difference from all other words, but what makes verbal arrangement, or syntax, possible is the opposite: a prehensile quality that words have of linking up with one another. To speak in the romantic idiom of early theories of social contract: no sooner has a noun discovered its identity as a word apart from all other words than it also discovers that it is in fact a subject, and must go off looking for a predicate. The predicate meanwhile has been searching for an object; adjectives and adverbs leap in to extend the world of things and actions into a world of qualities and universals and values, and so on until finally an articulated verbal society takes shape. But in, say, a poetic structure, where the bonding of words is so concentrated, there is a second level of linking up which may co-operate with the syntactic links or may override them. This is the level of metaphors and other figures of speech.

The double nature of the symbol, as something completed both by its context and by its relation to something outside the world of words, still remains: as long as it continues to use words, literature can hardly become as abstract, as removed from all direct representation of what is external to itself, as painting or music can. We see this in a late development of the theory of symbols, Eliot's conception of an "objective correlative": "The only way of expressing emotion in the form of art is by finding an 'objective correlative'; in other words, a set of objects, a situation, a chain of events which shall be the formula of that *particular* emotion; such that when the external facts, which must terminate in sensory experience, are given, the emotion is immediately evoked." There are many things wrong with Eliot's conception: it contains an unnecessary mechanical metaphor (the words "automatically" occurs in a sentence following the quotation), and it is a theoretical principle invoked to rationalize a bad value judgment. It occurs in an essay on *Hamlet* in which Eliot asserts that *Hamlet* is an artistic failure because Hamlet's personal disgust and nausea is in excess of the "correlative" it is projected on, namely his mother. But the excess of Hamlet's feeling is precisely what the play is about, and the hinge on which the tragedy turns. None the less the conception is a useful one, and is closely related to such metonymic images as the flag and the dream symbols that we have just been looking at.

We most frequently find such correlatives in the titles of works of fiction, where a central symbol conveys what the author feels his book is "about," what its main theme is. The Canadian novel *White Narcissus*, for example, tells the story of a young man whose love for a young woman is frustrated by the latter's parents, who are emotional vampires: for some reason they have quarrelled and have retreated into a mutual sulk in which they communicate only through their daughter, while the mother spends her energies raising white narcissi. Clearly the flower, with its sickly-sweet smell, funereal colour, and mythical affinities conveys the sense of psychological deadlock more clearly than any description would do.

We may take the metaphor, perhaps, the statement or pseudo-statement that A is B, as the basic form of verbal figure, perhaps the essential figure of which all the others are variants. Let us look at the following verse from Isaiah (55:12): "For ye shall go out with joy, and be led forth with peace: the mountains and the hills shall break forth before you into singing, and all the trees of the field shall clap their hands." Passing over for the moment the rhythm of parallelism which makes the whole verse poetic, we can accept the first part of it as a more or less conscious syntactic statement. The concluding part seems to come from a less conscious part of the mind which is none the less linguistically structured. Our normal response to such a statement as "the trees of the field shall clap their hands" is something like "Of course we can't take this literally, but –." What follows the "but" is usually some qualification that turns the response into "This doesn't makes sense, or appear to make sense, and yet it does make its own kind of sense." What we have to do with such a metaphor is look into the empty space between what it appears to be saying and what is obviously untrue about what it is saying. What we find in that empty space is, first, a *symbolon*, the counter or other half of the first or more conscious part of the total statement. Second, it is a *symbolos*, a portent or augury of a state of existence in which nature is totally humanized and responsive to human life.

Syntactic and metaphorical meanings, the meaning conveyed by statements or quasi-statements and the meaning conveyed by the sequence of imagery, have long been distinguished. Gerard Manley Hopkins speaks of them as "overthought" and "underthought." In very ironic structures the stated meaning can even be a disguise for the figurative one, or, in Eliot's phrase, a piece of meat thrown by a burglar to keep a watchdog quiet. The watchdog in this case is the anxiety of a reading or listening public. If we listen to the opening scenes of

Shakespeare's *Henry V*, for instance, we hear, superficially, what the original audience wanted to hear, the patriotic nobles of England urging a heroic king to invade France and clean up on a lot of foreigners. If we listen more closely to the metaphorical imagery, we hear something much more ominous and foreboding. England, says the Archbishop of Canterbury, a century earlier sent the King of Scotland a prisoner to Edward III, then fighting in France:

To fill King Edward's fame with prisoner kings,
And make her [England's] chronicle as rich with praise
As is the ooze and bottom of the sea
With sunken wrack and sumless treasuries.

It is also generally recognized that the metaphorical texture is less under the control of the conscious will than the syntactic one. Ever since Aristotle's *Poetics* it has been said that the ability to think metaphorically is the distinguishing mark of the poet, what he must be born with, and is the one thing that he cannot learn from others.

If we examine these two levels of meaning in a major poet, we usually find that the syntactic meaning is infinitely varied and flexible, but that the metaphors used are much less so. They tend to cluster around certain repeating images, as though they were building up a kind of structure based on recurring units. Let us look at a sonnet by Sir Thomas Wyatt, written in the reign of Henry VIII:

My galley chargèd with forgetfulness
Thorough sharp seas, in winter nights doth pass
'Tween rock and rock, and eke mine enemy, alas,
That is my lord, steereth with cruelness;
And every oar a thought in readiness,
As though that death were light in such a case.
And endless wind doth tear the sail apace
Of forcèd sighs and trusty fearfulness;
A rain of tears, a cloud of dark disdain,
Hath done the wearied cords great hinderance;
Wreathèd with error and eke with ignorance.
The stars be hid that led me to this pain;
Drownèd is Reason, that should me comfort;
And I remain, despairing of the port.

This poem is based on a sonnet of Petrarch, and is sometimes said to be a translation, though "paraphrase" is more accurate. I think it a tighter and more completely realized poem than Petrarch's. It was first published, not in Wyatt's lifetime, but fifteen years after his death in an anthology known as Tottel's *Miscellany*. The Tottel editor provides the poem with a fancy title: "The Lover Compareth his State to a Ship in Perilous Storm Tossed on the Sea." This suggests that the poem is an allegory, a narrative illustrating a concept. Perhaps it is: it certainly uses allegorical techniques, such as personification ("Wreathèd with error and eke with ignorance"). But I should prefer to think of the controlling design as analogical metaphor. Two vivid pictures, of a despairing lover and a foundering ship, are set up facing each other, each reflected in the other, with occasional points of coincidence such as the "lord," who is both the master of the ship and the god of love, and the hidden "stars," which are both the concealed stars of a stormy sky and the averted eyes of an indifferent or absent lady.

The narrative of the sonnet proceeds straight ahead, glancing at a great variety of entities on its way. But its metaphorical meaning, its underthought, is totally absorbed into this single structure of two reflecting pictures. We note that the specifically poetic features in the sounds of the poem reinforce the metaphorical rather than the syntactic organization. Rhyme emphasizes recurring and echoing sounds; metre recurring and echoic movement. There is also an unobtrusive imitative harmony, as "'Tween rock and rock, and eke mine enemy, alas," where the *k*'s stick up like rocks, or "Thorough sharp seas," where the sibilants hiss like wind in sails. The relation between words and the things they describe is arbitrary: the effect of these devices is to minimize the arbitrariness, to suggest an incantation with some hidden link between what is said and the objective world it is, so to speak, said *at*. Modern free verse may dispense with formal devices like rhyme or metre, but its discontinuous rhythm breaks up the syntactic structure into meditative fragments. Instead of a suggestion of a magical connection between words and the world, it suggests, not exactly that reality is verbal, but that our only possible contact with reality must be verbal or something closely related to the verbal, such as the pictorial or the musical. In modern poetry, reality is absorbed into what Wallace Stevens calls "a world of words to the end of it."

One inference from all this is familiar to students of literature. Poetry speaks the totality of language, the language of the subconscious as well as the language of consciousness; the language of emotion as well as the language of intelligence. The units of this language, whether words or images or even letters, are symbolic in relation both to their own verbal context and to the external entities they represent. The

Romantic poets, beginning with Blake, adapted the word "imagination," which previously had usually the general sense of hallucinatory vision, to express this linguistic union of conscious and unconscious, the language of reason united to the language of feeling. One principle that emerges here is that every conscious verbal construct, such as a metaphysical system, is founded on less conscious metaphorical ones, usually diagrams of some kind. The other is that criticism cannot deal with literature unless it recognizes the creativity of metaphor in poetic language, and recognizes also that metaphor cannot be described except by another metaphor.

Sometimes such a metaphorical understructure of thought changes without notice. The Romantic critics put metaphorical above syntactic language, a "higher" against a "lower" reason. In this post-Freudian era, aware of the connection of creative power with repression and dream states, we tend to put it below. In between came the *symboliste* movement, which put them side by side, with their backs turned to each other. It is common knowledge that *symbolisme* was a development mainly in French literature, influenced by Wagner and Baudelaire, and, through Baudelaire, Edgar Allan Poe. *Symbolisme* emphasized how words made their own kind of reality, and were not merely servomechanisms calling up non-verbal elements of experience. It reacted against rhetorical poetry, and often seemed hermetic and puzzling, because it insisted that the reader should think metaphorically, instead of regarding metaphor as "poetic licence," a concession to immature intelligence.

Earlier critics, such as Edmund Wilson, had an easy way of writing off this movement: they described it as a movement of almost total subjectivity, where reality consists of one's own moods and perceptions, which have to be indirectly suggested or evoked rather than described. Certainly the subjectivity is there, to a degree that is occasionally funny or grotesque. For example, Des Esseintes, the hero of Huysmans's *A Rebours*, who admires Dickens, decides to take a trip to England. He packs his bags, takes a train to Paris, and a taxi to Galignani's, buys a guide to England, and visits a restaurant that caters to English tourists, where he eats an English meal surrounded by people he identifies with characters from Dickens. Then he goes home. He does not have to get sick on a channel crossing, endure any more English weather (it is pouring rain in Paris), or eat any more English food. He has had all the pleasure and none of the trouble of a trip to England, and to follow this symbolic journey with a real one would be most pedestrian and literal-minded.

In Villiers de l'Isle Adam's dramatic romance, *Axel*, there is a somewhat grislier version of the same principle. The hero is sitting on top of a vast treasure: he goes down to it and finds the heroine about to plunder it–how she got there would take too long to explain. She tries to kill him, but they fall in love instead. The hero decides that, again, they have had the one moment worth living for in their lives, and to go on to consummate their union, or, worse still, go on the extended honeymoon that the heroine proposes, would be simply anticlimax. So the hero proposes mutual suicide: "as for living," he says, "our servants will do that for us." It is not said what the surviving servants are to live on.

The conception of "peak experiences," as they have come to be called, is found in other writers too, notably Pater. Such experiences are symbolic, and reflect our two traditional meanings of symbol: they are portents or auguries of what life could be, and it is worth any amount of commonplace life to purchase one of them. But *symbolisme*, the movement that produced Mallarmé and Laforgue and Valéry and Rilke, is very much more than merely a paradoxical cult of introversion, and it gives the conception of "symbol" a new dimension.

The earlier poetry of Rilke, for example, the poetry of the *Neue Gedichte* of 1907–8, is a poetry full of "things," of emotions let loose in a world of Eliot's "correlatives" ready to respond to and complete them. The main influences on him at that time, Rodin's sculpture and Picasso's blue-period painting, are representational, even to some degree realistic. Rilke then fell into a long period of silence, and at the end of it came two works, the *Duino Elegies* and the Orpheus Sonnets, almost simultaneously. According to a long letter he wrote at the time, the world of things had to be interiorized, the visible world transmuted into the invisible, before the later poetry could take shape. Man's spiritual evolution has to proceed in the direction of moving from a physical into a symbolic world. In the Elegies the symbol of the "angel" appears, representing the kind of being for whom this transcendence has been accomplished, and of course Orpheus is pre-eminently the artist who can transform his physical environment at will. Rilke emphasizes that his conception is not Christian, but it is clearly religious in most senses of the term, an almost Neoplatonic or Gnostic effort to find through words, and through the symbolic relationships of words, a more intense mode of life and experience.

In Mallarmé it is clearer that what Rilke calls an invisible world is a verbal world created in a certain way. In one place Mallarmé speaks of "transposition" and "structure" as characteristic of the poetic process. The poet has to use the same words that everyone else uses, but as they do not belong in ordinary syntactic structures, words in poetry become as distinct from their everyday use as the tones of a violin are from noises in the street. The verbal world is the form for which external reality supplies the material. But there is a single verbal or symbolic world, not just a pile of poems, and this symbolic world, or "supreme fiction" as Wallace Stevens calls it, is forged in defiance of external reality. The world of reality dies into nothing; the symbolic world is born from nothing, for a symbol to begin with is nothing apart from the context that forms around it and completes it.

So although Mallarmé speaks of God as an old scarecrow whom he has at last overcome, he also speaks in his letters of a symbolic death and resurrection that he has attained through his search for a pure poetry, and speaks also of the poet who creates in the teeth of *the* creation, so to speak, as though he were the vehicle of a holy spirit. "Man's duty," he says, "is to observe with the eyes of the divinity, for if his connection with that divinity is to be made clear, it can be expressed only by the pages of the open book in front of him." He also describes himself, in a letter to Cazalis, as "one of the ways the Spiritual Universe has found to see Itself, unfold Itself through what used to be me."

Mallarmé's monologue drama, or whatever it is, called *Igitur*, depicts a man (though he is said to be a young child) descending to the tombs of his ancestors, where he blows out his candle, throws dice, and lies down on the ashes of his ancestors. A throw of dice does not abolish chance, Mallarmé says, but it is a gesture of defiance against the totality of chance: it defines a world where chance and choice are one, in Yeats's phrase. So the ashes may be phoenix ashes after all. Igitur does not commit suicide (if he does) merely because, like the lovers in *Axel*, he is afraid that the rest of his life will be an anticlimax. He has entered the world of nothingness because it is there that everything has to renew itself.

Mallarmé's symbolic world, then, is not a Platonic world above the physical one, nor a world of buried treasure below it, nor a private world inside it. It is the world where human creation comes to be, where meaning is, where chance is not abolished but where a world that within itself is not chance has taken shape. It is not a subjective world, because, as Rilke says, all poets are manifestations of the same Orpheus. Symbols intercommunicate: they are not, like dream symbols, parts of a code to be interpreted by unknown or repressed desires within a dreamer. So although we have become increasingly aware, in the last century, of the close connection between dreaming and the poetic process, it seems to me that Keats's principle that "The poet and the dreamer are distinct" still holds up.

It should be becoming clearer that a symbol is a unit of meaning, that is, an image *plus*. If someone knowing nothing of physics examines the traces left in an atom-smashing cloud chamber along with a physicist, or if someone knowing nothing of geology goes for a walk with a geologist and sees a mountainside exposing a series of rock strata, the two see the same images, but only the trained eye sees them symbolically, as units meaning something in a context of knowledge. Freud became one of the great pioneers of contemporary thought as soon as he realized that dream images were dream symbols, in the subjective context I just mentioned. On the other hand, there is probably no human society that has not attached some kind of symbolic value to dream images. So perhaps the ability to see the image as a symbol, as a unit to be completed by an understander or by a context, may be, as Cassirer among others suggests, the distinctively human element in consciousness.

The word symbol enters the English language in the fifteenth century in the sense of a dogma, or articulated doctrine of religion. We find "the credo and symbol of our faith" in Caxton. This meaning of the word is a late derivation of *symbolon* through Latin. Since then, the meanings of symbolism and faith have widely diverged: symbolism now means to us something that may or may not suggest a belief, but by-passes belief, and does not commit us to acceptance of any specific body of values. It is in their doctrines or conceptual languages that religions disagree: symbols form part of a universal language. And yet a historical religion does establish a framework of understanding that confers symbolic meanings on images, and such a framework may persist unconsciously, however strongly repudiated by the consciousness. In studying poets who have talked about symbolism, I find those who, like Mallarmé and Rilke, explicitly repudiate the association with doctrinal Christianity most useful, because it is in them that the historical Christian shape of the framework organizing their conceptions emerges most clearly, more clearly than it does in, say, Claudel or Auden. It is not surprising in any case to find that the whole program of nineteenth-century *symbolisme* was anticipated in the seventeenth century by Andrew Marvell, the Puritan member of Parliament for Hull, in the familiar lines of "The Garden":

Meanwhile the mind, from pleasure less,
Withdraws into its happiness:
The mind, that ocean where each kind
Does straight its own resemblance find.

Yet it creates, transcending these,
Far other worlds, and other seas,
Annihilating all that's made
To a green thought in a green shade.

I have now come within sight of my title, "The Symbol as a Medium of Exchange." The basis for the title is an aphorism of Heraclitus: "There is exchange of all things for fire and of fire for all things, as there is of wares for gold and of gold for wares." Heraclitus is concerned with the perennial theme of the one and the many, the world of "all things" and the sense of unity that the mind constantly struggles for, which emerges in some form in practically every effort to make sense of a pluralistic world. Heraclitus's teaching appears to include some metaphorical conception of a ladder of elements. Earth, wet mud, and water are at the bottom of this ladder: people with undisciplined emotions and undeveloped intelligence are soggy and moist. As they rise in the scale of being they become drier and warmer, and capable of sharing in the common light of experience that Heraclitus calls the *logos*. On the top level of fire, where there is dryness and light, we begin to experience the unity of things instead of simply their plurality. But unity, the oneness of things, cannot be expressed except by such a symbol as the word fire provides. Heraclitus apparently does not think that we go up to an "other" world where, in Yeats's phrase again, we stand indefinitely in God's holy fire. Sooner or later the descent back to the world of things takes place, and we begin to sink from the dry light of fire to the mud-vision of the dreaming ego. Perhaps everything consists of these two movements: of death passing into nothingness, of new life coming to birth from the same nothingness. We live each other's deaths and die each other's lives, he says: we move from "all things" to the unity they symbolize, and find that the symbol of unity, the fire, is also the symbol of all things. If so, then the illustration of buying wares with gold is to be taken seriously: we may have one or the other, but not both.

And yet, it is possible that he is speaking of an interchange rather than simply an exchange. "All things" are wholes, yet surely every one of them must have something of what Heraclitus symbolizes by fire in it. What he calls fire, on the other hand, is a whole which may illuminate "all things" rather than causing them to disappear. Let us go back to the early English meaning of symbol as dogma. One of the central dogmas in Christianity is that of the Eucharist, which develops from Paul's conceptions of both being in Christ and of having Christ in himself. Christ is a whole of which we are parts, and at the same time we as individuals are wholes of which Christ is a part. The rite of the Eucharist expresses this paradoxical interchanging of part and whole, the world of fire and the world of all things. The Reformation did not change this doctrine, so far as its symbolism is concerned, but it put more emphasis on another aspect of it. We exist in Christ as the Word of God; as individuals reading the Word of God in the Bible, we are wholes of which the Word is part, so part and whole interchange again.

These are statements of belief, because they are attached to the centre of a specific religion. They could be loosely or vaguely attached, as in Edgar Allan Poe's cosmological essay *Eureka*, which ends in the contemplation of "this Divine Being, who thus passes his Eternity in perpetual variation of Concentrated Self and almost Infinite Self-Diffusion." Poe puts in the word "almost" because he will not concede the infinity of the universe. But they could be stated with no such attachments at all, and then they would cease to be statements of belief, or gestures toward it like Poe's, and become simply statements of experience. The teachings of Zen Buddhism have been summarized in the formula: "First there is a tree and a mountain; then there is no tree and no mountain; then there is a tree and a mountain." First, simple images, then a state of enlightenment in which particulars vanish, and finally a return to the world of images, now not the less images for having been transformed into symbols of enlightenment. Whatever the English word "enlightenment" may translate from Sanscrit or Japanese, the word itself is clearly not far away from Heraclitus's "fire." Every creative achievement is an invention, and to invent something is, subjectively, to construct it, and, objectively, to find it. A scientist discovers something new in his science, alone, or, more likely nowadays, with the help of forty or fifty colleagues, collects his Nobel Prize, and adds something to the total structure of the science in his time. Before long the entire world-picture of which that scientific structure forms part begins to change, in the manner set out in Thomas Kuhn's now classical study, *The Structure of Scientific Revolutions*. I have only to add that no scientific revolution is confined to science: there are invariably parallel and closely related revolutions going on in all other areas of culture, even though they may come at slightly different times. Whenever they come, that curious union of thing and meaning that we call a symbol shows once more that it is neither static nor arbitrary, but part of the continuing presence of our own becoming and being.

ANTHONY STORR
Oxford University

Symbols of Unity and Integration

The psychology of symbols is a vast subject. I have therefore given this lecture a subtitle, "Symbols of Unity and Integration," in order to indicate that I can only comment upon a small part of the subject. Perhaps the best way of beginning is to ask why we use symbols at all? What is the place of symbols in the mental economy of human beings? What function do symbols serve? It is clear that symbolization belongs with the higher reaches of human mentation; with conceptualization and abstraction rather than with reflex responses or emotional outbursts. Although higher animals may well be capable of appreciating or forming symbols in the same way as they are capable of dreaming, it is difficult to believe that the capacity to symbolize is found very far down the evolutionary scale. I believe that the development of the capacity to use symbols is closely linked with the development of intelligence and thinking, and with the development of what we may call an "inner world" of the psyche which does not necessarily correspond very closely with the reality of the external world.

Let us imagine an animal which is more or less perfectly adapted to its environment. The food it needs for survival is plentiful and easily obtained. There are sufficient mates in the neighbourhood for reproduction to be assured, and no serious threat from predators against which it need take precautions. For such an animal to survive and prosper, all that is required is that the environment remain constant. So long as this obtains, the animal's behaviour can be governed by pre-programmed, automatic responses. It does not have to think or plan, let alone make use of symbols. As we know from observation of insects, quite complex sequences of behaviour, like those concerned with catching prey or digging burrows, are built into the creature's nervous system. At first sight, some of these patterns of behaviour are so elaborate that it is difficult to believe that they are not governed by conscious deliberation. Yet, if the sequence is interfered with experimentally, the rigidity of the pattern is made manifest. The animal has to "go back to the beginning." It cannot vary the pattern. More importantly, it cannot adapt it if circumstances change. Such animals are very much at the mercy of the environment. Koala bears live on the leaves of the eucalyptus tree. No doubt their internal economy is perfectly adapted to digesting eucalyptus leaves. But, suppose a blight hits the eucalyptus. The koala may well be wiped out. This can even happen in man. In the eighteen forties, when Ireland suffered from a blight which destroyed the potato crop, the peasant population died in their thousands in spite of the fact that the seas around the island were teeming with fish. If the peasants had been sufficiently educated to make use of their human potential, instead of being exploited and ignorant, the Great Hunger need never have happened. Behavioural rigidity is the enemy of survival, except in a world in which the environment remains entirely stable. This may occur in the Isles of the Blessed, but is not a feature of the world as we know it.

The success of the human species is in part due to behavioural flexibility. Konrad Lorenz calls man "The specialist in non-specialization." We are not rigidly programmed for adaptation to one particular environment or to one particular type of food. Because of this, man has been able to survive both at the Equator and in the Arctic; to live at the level of the Dead Sea, or high in the peaks of the Andes. We can exist on a diet which is largely protein or on one which is mostly vegetable. Although man is limited by certain basic needs, for oxygen, water, and protection against extremes of temperature, the limits imposed by Nature are wide indeed.

It can, however, be argued that the price of flexibility is a less than perfect adaptation to the external world, and hence some degree of dissatisfaction. Consider the more or less perfectly adapted animal which I asked you to imagine. So long as the environment remains constant, all its needs are met. Satisfied, content, and at peace with itself and the world, the animal, we may suppose, lives in a condition of Boeotian bliss. For man, however, such peace belongs to fantasy rather than to reality. "Call no man happy till he dies," said Solon, according to Herodotus. Although we may experience moments of utter content, such moments are always transient. The achievements of man are based upon a restless hunger which drives him to seek new conquests, to search for new ways of living, to entertain Utopian fantasies, to range even beyond this planet through the fearsome expanses of space.

The fact that there is no close fit between man and his environment has been one factor determining the development of human imagination. "Ah, but a man's reach should exceed his grasp, Or what's a heaven for?" is Browning's acknowledgment of human imaginative capacity. The development of an inner world of the imagination and the development of symbolization march hand in hand. Since the inner world of the imagination and the external world are discrete entities, bridges between the two are needed if man is to be able to relate one with the other. One function of symbols is to form such bridges. Let me give you a simple example. The late Donald Winnicott, a British psychoanalyst of considerable originality, made a study of what he called "transitional objects." Many very young children develop powerful attachments to inanimate objects from which they are very reluctant to be parted. Such objects may be teddy bears or dolls, but can equally well be blankets or even towelling nappies. Because such an object provides comfort and security for the child, it is invested with such emotional significance that he or she may be unable to sleep without it. It is clear that such an object has become a symbol. It symbolizes what the mother provides and therefore acts to some degree as a substitute for her. This kind of object cannot be dismissed as merely imaginary, for it does have a real existence in the external world. Yet, the child's imagination is what renders it significant. In this way a symbolic object acts as a bridge between the child's imagination and the external world. It belongs wholly to neither world, but partakes of both.

Because symbols bridge the gap between subjective and objective, they give meaning to the external world. Symbols and symbolic activities can transform one form of psychic energy into another. In "Symbols of Transformation," C.G. Jung gives as an example the fertility rites of the Wachandi of Australia. When spring comes, they dig a hole in the ground, shaping it and setting it round with bushes so that it looks like the female genitals. Then they dance round the hole all night, thrusting their spears into the hole, shouting, "Not a pit, not a pit, but a cunt." By means of these symbolic gestures, they convert the primitive sexual drive into energy directed toward agriculture, and give meaning to an activity which might otherwise seem no more than exhausting toil. Jung also notes the old custom of the "bridal bed" in the field, to make the field fruitful. He comments: "As I make this woman fruitful, so I make the earth fruitful. The symbol canalizes the libido into cultivating and fructifying the earth."[1]

When the symbolic function fails, or the gap between inner and outer is too wide to be bridged, the external world loses all significance. Something of this kind appears to happen in schizophrenia. In some varieties of this mental illness, the sufferer turns away from an external reality which has brought him no satisfaction, and retreats into his own inner world of fantasy. Because this inner world is no longer linked with reality through the symbol, it becomes less and less comprehensible to others. We begin to call the sufferer "mad." We do not yet understand what causes schizophrenia, but it is interesting to note that, in many cases, it is possible to demonstrate that the patient's capacity to use language in a metaphorical or symbolic way is defective. Thus, if one asks a schizophrenic the meaning of a proverb – "A rolling stone gathers no moss" – for example, the chances are that he will reply: "If a stone is rolling down hill, there isn't time for moss to grow upon it." If one is tied to the literal, one cannot make use of symbols. In some cases of schizophrenia, the patient reports dreams of being in a colourless, featureless, perhaps ice-bound landscape. This aptly reflects his inability to invest the external world with his own feelings. Schizophrenia is also characterized by loss of cohesion within the personality. In chronic cases of schizophrenia, cohesion is so severely impaired that the person no longer seems to exist as an entity, but appears to the observer as a series of disconnected egos, each governed by the emotion of the moment, with nothing to connect one with the other.

But all men are, to varying extents, "divided selves." We are creatures of conflict, the prey of impulses and wishes which are often incompatible with each other. I suggest that this is something to do with the flexibility with which Nature has endowed us. Our imaginary, perfectly adapted animal would be at peace with itself as well as at peace with its environment. Perhaps, at times, there might be temporary conflict – for instance, between its reproductive urge and its need for food. One cannot imagine, however, that such an animal would suffer from such conflict for very long. When one need was satisifed, it would turn to seek fulfilment for the other. Man, or at least Western man, seldom seems able to find entire fulfilment. Freud once wrote: "It is my belief that, however strange it may sound, we must reckon with the possibility that something in the nature of the sexual instinct itself is unfavourable to the realization of complete satisfaction."[2] If this is so, it is not surprising that men seem compelled to seek a fusion or unity which perpetually eludes them. Plato, in the *Symposium*, assigns to Aristophanes the speech in which it is supposed that men are merely halves of original wholes, which were of three sexes, male, female, and hermaphrodite. Because of their *hubris*, they were bisected by Zeus. Every man is therefore compelled to seek for his lost half, in order to regain his pristine unity. Love is "the desire and pursuit of the whole." Aristophanes says: "the way to happiness for our race lies in fulfilling the behests of Love, and in each finding for himself the mate which properly belongs to him; in a word, in returning to our original condition."[3] The conciseness with which this myth expresses a truth about human nature in symbolic language points to another function of the symbol. Because the meaning of symbols is not precise, but diffuse, they can convey ideas with an economy which prosaic statements cannot rival.

The desire and pursuit of the whole can be sought in other ways than in physical unity with a beloved person. The psychologist who has paid most attention to the quest for unity is Jung. Whereas, in the *Symposium*, Aristophanes conceives of unity in terms of union with another person, Jung postulates a quest for integration within the psyche of the single individual. Jung called this quest "the process of individuation"; and the greater part of Jung's later work is devoted to exploring this process and the symbols in which it is expressed. In the course of his clinical practice, Jung encountered a number of patients who were not suffering from a definable neurosis, but from a sense of emptiness and futility. Many of these patients were conventionally successful. Most were in the second half of life. The majority had had some sort of psychological treatment before seeking help from Jung. Jung treated such patients chiefly by dream analysis. He looked to the patients' dreams not only to reveal what was actually wrong, but also to point the way to a solution. He found that, if he could get the patient to experiment with his own nature, a process of self-exploration and psychological development could be initiated which went far beyond conventional, reductive methods of psychotherapy. This is the process of individuation, and the goal toward which the patient is striving is that of integration and unity.

Jung found that, as the patient progressed, his new-found unity was expressed in symbols which assumed the form of a circle. Jung encouraged his patients to paint and draw these circular forms, as he himself had done when passing through the intense period of mental distress which followed upon his break with Freud. He called these circular forms "mandalas," a Sanskrit term applied to similar forms which were used in the East for meditation. Jung wrote: "As psychological phenomena they appear spontaneously in dreams, in certain states of conflict, and in cases of schizophrenia. Very frequently they contain a quaternity or a multiple of four, in the form of a cross, a star, a square, an octagon etc."[4] For Jung, the quaternity was also a symbol of wholeness. The fact that mandala forms tend to appear spontaneously both when the patient is making progress toward a new unity and in the fragmented condition of schizophrenia may appear paradoxical. In fact, I think the phenomenon illustrates something important about symbols. Symbols both express states of mind and also tend toward inducing them. The patient who is progressing toward integration produces these symbols as evidence of a new attitude of mind. The schizophrenic produces them as desperate attempts to recapture the integrated state of mind which is eluding him. The same dual function can be discerned in those symbolic statements which we call "works of art." A work of art, unless it is merely a detailed commission undertaken to satisfy a patron, necessarily expresses something of the inner world, the state of mind, of the artist. But when we contemplate the artist's work, we are ourselves affected by whatever order or harmony he has imposed upon his material. Harrison Gough, in his paper "Identifying the Creative Man," writes: "The work of art, for example, reorders and brings into balance the tensions of form and space, and in so doing moderates the inner tensions of the observer, giving him a sense of encounter and fulfilment."[5]

Mandalas occur in various cultures, and date back at least to the palaeolithic. They also occur spontaneously in the drawings of children. Between the ages of two and three, according to Rhoda Kellogg, children begin to superimpose forms one upon the other, thus creating what Kellogg calls "combines." One of the most frequent combines is a circle enclosing other forms like squares or triangles. In his book on children's drawings, *Artful Scribbles*, the Harvard psychologist Howard Gardner writes: "Mandalas are the examples, par excellence, of a combine. Not only are mandalas visible in many combines but, more important, mandalas seem to represent a central tendency of 'combining behavior': the simplest and most balanced diagrams, when combined with one another, produce mandala-like forms."[6]

What Howard Gardner inelegantly calls "combining behavior" seems to me to be characteristic of man. It is a process which goes on both subjectively and objectively. The recurrent synthesis of opposites which Jung described as going on within the personality as a process of individual development, is also characteristic of the creative process, whether in the arts or in the sciences. At an earlier point in this paper I referred to one function of symbols as providing bridges between the inner world of the imagination and the outer world of fact. When, one afternoon in 1865, Friedrich August Kekulé von Stradonitz, Professor of Chemistry in Ghent, was dozing in front of the fire, visions of atoms combining in various structures played before his eyes. He wrote:

> My mental eye, rendered more acute by repeated visions of this kind, could now distinguish larger structures, of manifold conformation; long rows, sometimes more closely fitting together; all twining and twisting in snake-like motion. But look! What was that? One of the snakes had seized hold of its own tail, and the form whirled mockingly before my eyes. As if by a flash of lightning I awoke ... Let us learn to dream, gentlemen.[7]

Kekulé's vision enabled him to formulate the structure of the benzene ring, and thus lay a foundation of modern organic chemistry. It also happens that the snake eating its own tail is an ancient symbol, the uroboros, which, according to Jung, is often found coiled about the centre of mandalas painted by patients.[8] This is another instance of a symbol partaking of both worlds: the world of the psyche and the world of external reality.

The process of creation in both the arts and the sciences is often characterized by finding a new synthesis between ideas which had previously appeared to be distinct or widely separated. Solutions to problems, whether artistic or scientific, come about by discovering how apparently discrepant themes or facts can be linked to form greater wholes. I am not asserting that making a scientific discovery and creating a work of art are exact equivalents. As Leonard Meyer has pointed out, scientists discover something which is already there, like the structure of the benzene ring, or the double helix, while artists create something which has never previously existed.[9] But the sciences and the arts share the aim of seeking order in complexity, and unity in diversity. The intense pleasure, described as the "Eureka" experience, which scientists enjoy when they have made a new synthesis, is surely paralleled by the pleasure described by painters and musicians upon solving an aesthetic problem. Each type of solution has both an external and an internal validity. Nature has so framed our mental processes that we rejoice in bringing together things which have previously appeared to be incongruous or widely separated. The "desire and pursuit of the whole" is not confined to love.

Perhaps what I am saying demands examples. I shall use two that I have used elsewhere because, to my mind, they are particularly telling. My first example is that of Newton's discovery of the law of universal gravitation, sometimes described as the greatest generalization achieved by the human mind. The Newtonian synthesis was based upon the discoveries of Kepler, who had been able to describe the motions of the planets round the sun, combined with those of Galileo, who had described the laws of motion of objects upon the earth. Until Newton, these two sets of laws had appeared to be quite separate. But when Newton made the leap of the imagination which led him to suppose that gravity was a universal which acted at enormous distances, he combined the discoveries of Kepler and Galileo in such a way that the motions of bodies upon earth and bodies in the heavens could be proved to obey the same universal laws. Newton's leap of the imagination had, of course, to be subjected to mathematical proof before it could be accepted by other scientists or, more importantly, by himself. Newton first demonstrated that the path of the moon around the earth could be accounted for by the interaction of the gravitational force upon it which he supposed the earth to be exerting, together with the centrifugal force of the moon, the formula for which had already been discovered by Huygens. Newton then computed the sun's attraction on the planets, and demonstrated that their orbits, which Kepler had described but could not explain, complied with the same laws. Newton actually left behind a diagram which anticipates the possibility of artificial satellites by showing that increasing the velocity of a projectile will eventually result in its circling the earth at the same velocity for ever.

This is surely a classic example of scientific discovery being based upon the union of two sets of ideas which had hitherto been unconnected. Kepler's laws and Galileo's laws were both reconciled and superseded by a principle which comprehended both. I am no physicist, but I am told that we are still awaiting a unified theory which will cover all the forces of nature at once. It is a problem which defeated Einstein.

My other example of the union of apparently discrepant ideas is taken from one of Beethoven's late quartets. The so-called "Grosse Fuge" was originally written as the last movement of the quartet in B flat major, Opus 130. Because of its length and power, Beethoven's publisher offered to publish the movement as a separate work if Beethoven would agree to write another final movement for the quartet. Martin Cooper, in his book *Beethoven: The Last Decade*, writes: "The Grosse Fuge is unique ... What grips the listener is the dramatic experience of forcing – for there is frequently a sense of violence in this mastery – two themes which have, by nature, nothing in common, to breed and produce a race of giants, episodes or variations that have no parallel in musical history."[10] The Grosse Fuge is an extreme example of combining and transcending discrepant themes; but even the simplest kind of music is composed of contrasting elements. A single line of melody, for example, leaves the tonic, ventures forth, and then returns home whence it came: two steps in opposite directions, brought together by the form of the melody. Music, it seems to me, is par excellence a symbolic activity. It is often declared to be the most abstract of the arts. Perhaps this is why Walter Pater wrote his famous sentence: "All art constantly aspires towards the condition of music." Music has no obvious biological utility. It is possible to argue that drawing and painting, by sharpening man's perception of the external world, were originally adaptive rather than purely aesthetic activities. No such claim can be made for music. We may suppose that literature derives from the art of the primitive story-teller: that, by passing on to his listeners a tradition of their origins, he was enhancing their sense of identity, and, by providing a framework of conventional ways of behaviour, was aiding their adaptation to the world. It is impossible to regard music in a similar light. Although some music imitates natural sounds, like the song of the cuckoo or the surge of the sea, musical sounds are not very common in nature, and most music is not representational. Even the origin of music is disputed. Herbert Spencer believed that music was developed from speech: Darwin that speech was derived from music. But biological and linguistic theories fail to explain the pleasure that we get from music and why we feel great music to be so important. Some musicians maintain that music has no meaning outside itself. Stravinsky, for example, says that "Music expresses itself." He describes music as "supra-personal and supra-real and as such beyond verbal meanings and verbal descriptions." Although he agrees that a composition has its origins in the feelings of the composer and may therefore be considered as symbolizing them, he goes on to state: "More important is the fact that the composition is something entirely *beyond* what can be called the composer's feelings ... A new piece of music *is* a new reality."[11] Formalists, like Stravinsky, not infrequently compare music with mathematics. They believe that the meaning of music is to be found in the perception of the musical relationships within a particular work, and that such appreciation is primarily intellectual rather than emotional. No one with any understanding of either music or mathematics will deny the beauty of pattern and structure. But, as G.H. Hardy pointed out in his book *A Mathematician's Apology*, "Music can be used to stimulate mass emotion, while mathematics cannot."[12] It is clear that the appeal and the effects of music cannot be entirely cerebral.

While still accepting that music is non-referential, and that its meaning is to be sought solely within the work of music itself, other theorists admit that particular musical relationships excite emotion rather than a purely intellectual response. However, whether these emotions are genuine is open to question. Hindemith, for example, states: "The reactions music evokes are not feelings, but they are the images, memories of feelings."[13] Hindemith denies that music expresses the composer's feelings, and affirms that the composer is simply a skilled manipulator of the feelings of others. "Here is what he really does: he knows by experience that certain patterns of tone-setting correspond with certain emotional reactions on the listener's part. Writing these patterns frequently and finding his observations confirmed, in anticipating the listener's reaction he believes himself to be in the same situation."[14] Hindemith goes on: "Thus a composer can never be absolutely sure of the emotional effect of his music on the listener when using complex material, but by experience and clever distribution of this material, moreover with frequent references to those musical progressions that evoke the uncomplicated feeling-images of sadness or gaiety in an unambiguous form, he can reach a fairly close approximation to unanimity of all listeners' reactions."[15] Perhaps it is arrogant of a mere listener to take issue with the statements of a distinguished composer, but I confess that I find Hindemith's theories unconvincing. To my mind, although he recognizes that "Music touches both the intellectual and the emotional parts of our mental life,"[16] he underestimates the compelling power and satisfaction which a symbolic union between these two different aspects of our being affords us. Man's greatest intellectual achievements depend upon being able to separate intellect from emotion. Perhaps his greatest satisfactions come from being able to reunite them. Perhaps, also, composers are not so much skilled manipulators, as Hindemith supposes, but rather individuals who are particularly skilled at making new syntheses within their own psyches. I suggest that such gifted people command our admiration because they have been able to realize, in their own achievements, what we would all like to be able to do; to make a coherent whole out of our experience and personality.

In his recent biography of Elgar, Jerrold Northrop Moore expresses exactly what I mean. He prefaces his biography by deploring the traditional division between "life" and "works." As he rightly says: "A creative life can have no general significance apart from its works, and works have no cumulative significance outside the worker's life. What I wanted was some means of combining the two modes, so that each new adventure in theme and form could be understood as a chapter in the spiritual biography of the whole man." Moore goes on:

> The artist, like the rest of us, is torn by various desires competing within himself. But unlike the rest of us, he makes each of these desires into an element for use in his art. Then he seeks to synthesise his elements all together to form a style. The sign of a successful synthesis is a unified and unique style plain for all to recognize. So it is that a successful style can seem to an audience full of indefinably familiar things – and at the same time invested with godlike power of "understanding" that is far indeed from the daily round. The process by which a man has forged such a style is the most profound and most exalted of human stories.[17]

So style, in the case of the creatively gifted, is the element which holds the differing parts of the personality together, and which makes manifest to others the unity which the artist has achieved. It is interesting that we value this evidence of individuality so highly. Works "in the style of" count for far less, both aesthetically and in the market-place, than those which are recognized as authentic products of a single individual.

A painter's or a composer's style may be easily recognizable without any implication that the artist himself feels that an ultimate goal of unity has been reached. Aaron Copland, in his Harvard lectures on *Music and Imagination* wrote:

> The serious composer who thinks about his art will sooner or later have occasion to ask himself: why is it so important to my own psyche that I compose music? What makes it seem so absolutely necessary, so that every other daily activity, by comparison, is of lesser significance? And why is the creative impulse never satisfied; why must one always begin anew? To the first question – the need to create – the answer is always the same – self-expression; the basic need to make evident one's deepest feelings about life. But why is the job never done? Why must one always begin again? The reason for the compulsion to renewed creativity, it seems to me, is that each added work brings with it an element of self-discovery. I must create in order to know myself, and since self-knowledge is a never-ending search, each new work is only a part-answer

to the question "Who am I?" and brings with it the need to go on to other and different part-answers."[18]

There are close parallels between what Aaron Copland wrote about the creative process and what Jung says about the development of personality. Jung writes: "The achievement of personality means nothing less than the optimum development of the whole individual human being. A whole lifetime, in all its biological, social and spiritual aspects is needed. Personality is the supreme realization of the innate idiosyncrasy of a living being."[19] This, of course, is an ideal which no human being attains. In another paper, Jung writes: "The new attitude gained in the course of analysis tends sooner or later to become inadequate in one way or another, and necessarily so, because the constant flow of life again and again demands fresh adaptation. Adaptation is never achieved once and for all."[20]

Perhaps I can now explain why I referred to music as the symbolic activity par excellence. First, music is a temporal art. The patterns of music exist in time, and require time for their development and completion. Susanne Langer, in *Feeling and Form*, refers to music as "an image of subjective time."[21] Although painting and architecture and sculpture make symbolic statements about relationships, these relationships are static. Music, like life, is in constant motion. Second, music symbolizes typical patterns in human life. Leonard Meyer, in his book *Emotion and Meaning in Music*, suggests that "Music activates tendencies, inhibits them, and provides meaningful and relevant resolutions."[22] It is, I think, obvious to anyone reared in the Western diatonic tradition that the resolution afforded by the return to the tonic is analogous to "returning home," "winding safe to sea," or, at a more mundane level, to bodily patterns of need or desire followed by fulfilment. As Meyer points out, one of the ways in which composers arouse our emotions and our interest is by postponing completion and return. Meyer gives as an example the fifth movement of Beethoven's C sharp minor quartet, Opus 131. Beethoven denies the listener's expectation by the progressive fragmentation of the rhythmic and melodic pattern. "But at the very moment when rhythm, harmony, texture, and even melody in the sense of pattern seem all but destroyed, the little figure which opens the movement and the first phrase raises our hopes and redirects our expectations of completion and return. Now we are certain what is coming."[23] Meyer's description is very close to the theory of music advanced by Hans Keller. Keller contrasts what he calls "background" and "foreground" in a piece of music. "The background of a composition is both the sum total of the expectations a composer raises in the course of a piece without fulfilling them, and the sum total of those unborn fulfilments. The foreground is, simply, what he does instead – what is actually in the score." According to Keller,

> musical meaning ... depends for its sheer existence on the clearly implied conflict between that which you hear and that which is being contradicted by what you hear. It is this tension, varying in intensity according to the structural juncture a composition has reached, between what the composer does and what he makes you feel he was expected to do that constitutes musical logic. The clearer the tension, the more logical the music – and the clearest tension is that which combines a maximum of contradiction with a maximum of unity between the contradicting elements.[24]

Once again, in a different context, we encounter the notion that combining elements which are widely separated or discrepant is a profound and satisfying experience.

This is not the only way in which music can be described as a form of "combining behavior." Music integrates a variety of differing elements to form a whole. As Yehudi Menuhin put it: "Music creates order out of chaos; for rhythm imposes unanimity upon the divergent; melody imposes continuity upon the disjointed, and harmony imposes compatibility upon the incongruous."[25] Music, therefore, symbolizes man's attempt to make sense out of existence by discovering or imposing order upon it: and, because music is, for the most part, non-representational, it is "purely" symbolic in a way which the other arts are not. This is why Schopenhauer regarded music as the direct expression of the Will and wrote: "The composer reveals the innermost nature of the world, and expresses the profoundest wisdom in a language that his reasoning faculty does not understand." After detailing various analogies between human emotions and different types of music, Schopenhauer goes on: "But we must never forget when referring to all these analogies I have brought forward that music has no direct relation to them, but only an indirect one; for it never expresses the phenomenon, but only the inner nature, the in-itself, of every phenomenon, the will itself."[26]

Schopenhauer here touches upon another feature of music which Susanne Langer explores in *Philosophy in a New Key*. To express the essence of feelings, rather than the feelings themselves directly, requires abstraction. Aaron Copland, discussing his need to compose, referred to "self-expression." But, as Langer observes: "*Sheer self-expression requires no artistic form.*"[27] We can all abreact our feelings of grief by howling. To reach the essence of grief, as does Purcell in Dido's Lament, requires not only the skill of transmuting feelings into music, but the capacity to stand back from such feelings, and, by imposing form upon them, universalize them. The notion of "psychical distance" elaborated by Edward Bullough, and used by Langer, is, I believe, significant. So long as a composer is possessed by an emotion, he will not be able to symbolize it in music. Psychical distance, the ability to detach oneself from immediate experience, is characteristically human. Without this capacity, there would be no scientific discoveries, no mathematics, and, though this is not always appreciated, no works of art. Wordsworth said that poetry "takes its origin from emotion recollected in tranquillity." Charles Lamb wrote that it was a mistake to attribute uncontrolled feelings of exaltation to the poet. "The true poet dreams being awake. He is not possessed by his subject, but has dominion over it."[28] It is only when psychical distance has been achieved that symbolization can occur, and what we admire about the works of great composers and other artists is not only the evidence they provide of the artist's capacity for deep feeling, but also the proof which they afford of the artist's power to master and integrate such feelings.

I have repeatedly referred to man's quest for integration and unity as an inescapable part of the human condition. Because of its ability to make a whole out of contrasting elements, music is the art which most aptly symbolizes this quest. It is interesting that so many scholars have reached the same conclusion. For example, Susanne Langer, in her chapter "On Significance in Music," quotes a sentence by Hans Mersmann: "The possibility of expressing opposites simultaneously gives the most intricate reaches of expressiveness to music as such, and carries it, in this respect, far beyond the limits of the other arts."[29] Edmund Gurney writes of music as seeming

> like a fusion of strong emotions transfigured into a wholly new experience, whereof if we seek to bring out the separate threads we are hopelessly baulked: for triumph and tenderness, desire and satisfaction, yielding and insistence, may seem to be all there at once, yet without any dubiousness or confusion in the result; or rather elements seem there which we struggle dimly to adumbrate by such words, thus making the experience seem vague only in our own attempt to analyse it, while really the beauty has the unity and individuality pertaining to clear and definite form.[30]

Zuckerkandl, in his massive two-volume work, *Sound and Symbol*, discussing the function of music as opposed to language, writes: "Words divide, tones unite. The unity of existence that the word constantly breaks up, dividing thing from thing, subject from object, is constantly restored in the tone." In another passage, he states: "Musicality is not an individual gift, but one of man's basic attributes; man's very nature predisposes him to music. In music, man does not give expression to something (his feelings, for example), nor does he build autonomous formal structures: he *invents himself*. In music, the law by which he knows himself to be alive is realized in its purest form."[31] If there be anyone who doubts the importance of symbolism, let him meditate upon this sentence.

NOTES

1 C.G. Jung, *Collected Works*, 5 (London, 1956), paras. 213–14 and n. 22.
2 Sigmund Freud, *Standard Edition*, 11 (London, 1957), 188–9.
3 Plato, *Symposium*, trans. W. Hamilton (Harmondsworth, 1951), 65.
4 C.G. Jung, *Collected Works*, 9i (London, 1959), paras. 713–18.
5 Harrison Gough, "Identifying the Creative Man," *Journal of Value Engineering*, 2, no. 4 (1964), 5–12.
6 Howard Gardner, *Artful Scribbles* (New York, 1980), 41–3.
7 A. Findlay, *A Hundred Years of Chemistry*, 2nd ed. (London, 1948), 36–8.
8 C.G. Jung, *Collected Works*, 9i (London, 1959), para. 646.
9 L.B. Meyer, "Concerning the Sciences, the Arts – *and* the Humanities," *Critical Inquiry*, 1, no. 1 (1974), 165.
10 M. Cooper, *Beethoven: The Last Decade* (Oxford, 1970), 388.
11 I. Stravinsky and R. Craft, *Expositions and Developments* (London, 1962), 101–2.
12 G.H. Hardy, *A Mathematician's Apology* (Cambridge, 1940), 26.
13 P. Hindemith, *A Composer's World* (New York, 1961), 45.
14 Ibid., 42.
15 Ibid., 51.
16 Ibid., 48.
17 J.N. Moore, *Edward Elgar: A Creative Life* (Oxford, 1984), vii.
18 A. Copland, *Music and Imagination* (Harvard, 1972), 40.
19 C.G. Jung, *Collected Works*, 17 (London, 1954), para. 289.
20 C.G. Jung, *Collected Works*, 8 (London, 1960), paras. 142–3.
21 S. Langer, *Feeling and Form* (London, 1953), 118. 22 L.B. Meyer, *Emotion*

and Meaning in Music (Chicago, 1956), 23.

23 Ibid., 155.

24 "Towards a Theory of Music," *Listener*, 11 June 1970, 796.

25 Y. Menuhin, *Theme and Variations* (New York, 1972), 9.

26 A. Schopenhauer, *The World as Will and Representation*, trans. E.F.J. Payne, 1 (New York, 1969), 260–1.

27 S. Langer, *Philosophy in a New Key* (Cambridge, Mass., 1960), 216.

28 C. Lamb, *Essays of Elia and Last Essays of Elia* (London, 1977), 219.

29 Quoted in Langer, *Philosophy in a New Key*, 243.

30 R. Gurney, *The Power of Sound* (London, 1880). Quoted in T. McLaughlin, *Music and Communication* (London, 1970), 101–2.

31 V. Zuckerkandl, *Sound and Symbol*, Vol. 2: *Man the Musician*, trans. N. Guterman, Bollingen Series XLIV (Princeton, 1973), 350.

DOUGLAS JONES
Université de Sherbrooke

Steel Syntax: The Railroad as Symbol in Canadian Poetry

The train, the railway, has marked Canadian life politically, economically, sentimentally. It has shaped and coloured Canadian space; it has structured time.[1] As the Canadian Pacific became one of the world's great transportation empires in the earlier twentieth century, many Canadians could easily identify the life of the country with the life of the railroad.

Indeed, the two were intimately linked from the beginning. As Susan Mann Trofimenkoff says, for some of the liberal politicians of Quebec in the nineteenth century, the whole idea of Confederation appeared to be merely an excuse to build railroads.[2] Pierre Berton notes that "By 1871, there were fifty-two men in the House and the Senate with vested interests in railroads."[3] Despite the cynicism of the Quebec *rouges*, Sir John A. Macdonald saw Confederation primarily as a means to ensure a transcontinental dominion against American expansion. In Berton's words, it was Macdonald's intention "to defy nature and fashion a nation in the process. His tool, to this end, would be the Canadian Pacific. It would be a rare example of a nation created through the construction of a railway."[4]

Here the romance of technology is joined to the epic theme of the founding of a nation to produce a national myth. It becomes articulate as such when the most prominent Canadian poet of the first half of the twentieth century, E.J. Pratt, as the climax of his career, writes *Towards the Last Spike* (1952). For Pratt, the CPR is not merely a railroad but "Three thousand miles of *Hail* from port to port."[5] It is a symbol of national community. Its mythical status is reinforced and popularized by Pierre Berton's two-volume history of the building of the road, especially when the televised version, *The National Dream*, was broadcast to a national audience by the CBC in the early 1970s.

Here, then, is one reason why the railroad moves from being a fact of life to being an imaginative symbol in Canadian culture. In verse, in prose, on film, the accomplishment of such men as Macdonald and Cartier, Smith and Stephen, Van Horne and Fleming, plus a host of ordinary labourers, becomes identified as that of the nation. Their virtues are our virtues: vision and daring, technical prowess and ingenuity, determination, a willingness to give one's all, to risk one's life and fortune for a large and seemingly impossible goal – with little popular support and in the face of organized political opposition "to build a Road over that sea of mountains,"[6] thus transforming a wilderness into a civil order, a collection of divided states into a single nation.

As Berton says, the example of a nation created through the building of a railway is rare. So is the example of the railroad as a significant symbol in art and literature, above all poetry.

Though the first passenger trains develop in England in the 1820s, spreading to France, Germany, North America, India, and Australia during the next two decades and practically altering the lives of millions of people, they have little impact on poetry except in a negative sense: we see the disappearance of "Diana and her train," "thoughtless pleasure and her train," and a variety of other such poetic trains.

In a recent introduction to comparative literature, Professors Brunel, Pichois, and Rousseau ask, "Du côté des techniques, n'y a-t-il pas une littérature des chemins de fer, comme de la navigation à voile ou à vapeur ...?" Yes, they reply, but it is only represented by "une production romanesque de basse qualité," a literary dung heap that may hide the odd pearl but is otherwise only interesting to sociologists.[7]

Though Emily Dickinson wrote, "I love to see it lap the miles / And lick the valleys up,"[8] the train has made little progress in American poetry–even if the U.S. boasts the most complex rail system in the world and Americans are supposed to have an eye for these things. And while France may boast *le train à très grande vitesse*, it remains too pedestrian for *la poésie pure* from Mallarmé to Yves Bonnefoy. T.S. Eliot did make use of London's Underground, but most British or Irish poets practically ignore it. Rilke and his angels do not appear to have considered it worthy of translation into their articulate heaven. (Eliot's hippopotamus fares better.) Generally, that noisy concatenation of locomotives, boxcars, mobile salons, not to mention the caboose, has no great attraction for the twentieth-century muse.

Except in Canada.

And here one must be discriminating and say, except in English-speaking Canada. For the Québécois poets remain closer to *la poésie pure*. They go in for *la navigation à voile*, rarely *à vapeur*. The reader may sometimes find them taking a canoe, or simply swimming, even walking, on occasion, over or under the sea. But the reader would be hard pressed, until very recently at least, to catch a train or plane or even a bus in Quebec verse.

This difference may suggest a general point. Whether some feature of everyday life becomes a symbol in the artistic or imaginative life of the society is determined less by its practical importance in human affairs than by its capacity to find a functional role in the symbol system or cultural code. The traditional cultural code of Quebec and its poetic sub-codes have little place for trains or the various forms of mechanical transport.

Bluntly, since the early nineteenth century, when we see the beginnings of Quebec and Canadian literature, the two cultures have developed in opposite directions. In Harold Innis's terms, Quebec focused primarily on the control of time, ensuring a certain continuity between past and present, more radically, between temporal and eternal. English Canada focused primarily on the control of space, ensuring a certain continuity between centre and periphery, the domestic and the imperial, or, as Robert Kroetsch puts it, between "space" and "place."[9] The one concentrates on articulating a largely symbolic or ideal "reality," the other on articulating a largely material "civil space." The result is two different symbols systems or encodings of "reality." (In the case of the Québécois writer, the general cultural code was reinforced by the poetic codes of the High Romantic, the Symbolist, and various forms of the Modern, in which the aspirations towards pure painting, pure poetry, are informed by a certain philosophical idealism.)

Within the cultural code of Quebec, then, space by itself, without connection to the glorious past or to some timeless idea, becomes meaningless. Roads, the mere organization of space and movement from place to place, these have no ultimate significance. Saint-Denys-Garneau writes:

> On a cet élan pour éclater dans l'Au-delà.

He would break out of the relative to arrive at some absolute. But our terrestrial roads merely shift us about on the surface:

Et l'on connaît bientôt la surface
Du globe tout mesuré inspecté arpenté vieux sentier
Tout battu.[10]

Le voyage is a pervasive motif in Quebec poetry, but if the images of roads and travelling are not ironic, as in the above example, they symbolize an essentially vertical or metaphysical movement. One does not set out for Montreal, or France, or the Far East, but rather:

Comme un bateau que prend la mer
Pour un voyage au bout du vent.[11]

Technological innovations in transport are irrelevant. The Massawippi Valley Railway Company, the Montreal and Atlantic Railway Company, even the CN and CP cannot help the traveller here.

Within the cultural code of English Canada, however, to use a phrase of Dennis Lee's, "space is primal."[12] And for the Canadian writer, the general cultural code is reinforced by a poetic code first defined by an eighteenth-century, pre-Romantic literature, whose representational mode, descriptive, discursive, and narrative elements, Canadians have been very reluctant to abandon. Much of the poetry and painting of the late eighteenth and early nineteenth century is topographical. Certain nineteenth-century narrative poems threaten to turn into mere itineraries, inventories of North American space. The hero of half a dozen long poems, from Adam Burwell's *The Talbot Road* (1820) to Isabella Valancy Crawford's *Malcolm's Katie* (1884), is the pioneer axeman, and his central project, clearing land, building a house, making paths and roads, is to transform a "wilderness of trees,"[13] or "trackless solitudes,"[14] into human community or civil space. And the main argument that emerges more and more explicitly in the course of the century is an argument between two conceptions of civil space or of what one may call a pastoral and imperial vision of one's relation to space.

This was an argument posed by Oliver Goldsmith's eighteenth-century pastoral elegy, "The Deserted Village," which lamented the destruction of traditional village life as a result of England's new imperial economy, urban and industrial society. The Canadian Oliver Goldsmith confidently reversed his great uncle's theme in "The Rising Village" (1825), which shows the New World community, its houses, church, and mill, harmoniously rooted in the environment, among the fields, orchards, woods, and sparkling streams. Yet his poem ends with an ambiguous, if not contradictory, celebration of imperial England. And in William Kirby's *The U.E.: A Tale of Upper Canada* (1859) we may see something of the same ambiguity developing around the image of the road.

The earliest roads in North America were the waterways, and it is by travelling up the St Lawrence to the end of Lake Ontario that the hero of Kirby's poem arrives at his land to build his own house. Though house and family provide the initial and final focus of the narrative, there is a long intervening section in which the narrator inventories the resources of different points along the route, and, especially as he takes stock of the port of Montreal, its varieties of shipping, its wealth of goods and talents, it becomes apparent that what he calls "the great highway"[15] is as much an instrument of political and commercial empire as it is of domestic exchange.

The CPR extended the great highway into the West; it also extended the ambiguous symbol of the road and the arguments between the pastoral and the imperial vision into twentieth-century Canadian writing. For if the new railroad carried settlers into the prairies, it also carried the 10th Grenadiers, the York Rangers, the Governor-General's Foot Guards, and the Queen's Own Rifles, the troops that put down the North-West (Second Riel) Rebellion in 1885.

The ambiguity of the road is evident in a passage that Pierre Berton cites from Macdonald's speech to the House that same year.

> Late events have shown us that we are made one people by that road, that that iron link has bound us together in such a way that we stand superior to most of the shafts of ill-fortune, that we can now assemble together, at every point which may be assailed, or may be in danger, the whole physical force of Canada by means of that great artery, against any foreign foe or any internal insurrection or outbreak.[16]

Can an iron link become an artery? What is the normal condition of people bound by an iron link?

The ambiguity is less immediately apparent in Pratt's *Towards the Last Spike*, but the poem is informed by a similar rhetoric, the same suggestion that the embattled spirit will use whatever force is necessary to impose its order on a refractory world, whether in forging a road or forging a dominion from sea to sea. For Van Horne, we read, it is a job "To lead, then build a highway which men claimed / Could not be built."[17] For Donald Smith it is an opportunity to work miracles, to rival Moses:

To smite the rock and bring forth living water,
Take lead or tin and transmute both to silver,
Copper to gold, betray a piece of glass
To diamonds, fabulize a continent.[18]

For the narrator it becomes an exploit in which "cliffs delivered up their features / Under the civil discipline of roads."[19]

Throughout Pratt's work there is a tendency to equate speech and the material syntax of communication with any human and civilized order. Most of his major poems focus on dramatic challenges to maintaining or extending transportation or communication lines. And though Pratt may often focus on the heroic sacrifice made by individuals, the reader must be impressed by the agonistic character of the world, by the often military character of the action or the tropes, and by the essentially imperial character of the collective orders involved. The bugles may be Roman or archangelic, may call out the soldiers of king and country or the soldiers of Christ – or a civil army of workers – but it is all much the same. Men as well as cliffs must deliver up their features to the civil discipline of roads.

Thus, in the midst of winter, Van Horne contemplates the first stage of his task, five hundred miles of track from Oak Lake to Calgary. It may not be possible within the allotted time. He then casts off his doubts and swings into action:

An order from him carried no repeal:
It was as final as an execution.
A cable started rolling mills in Europe:
A tap of Morse sent hundreds to the bush,
Where axes swung on spruce and the saws sang,
Changing the timber into pyramids
Of poles and sleepers. Clicks, despatches, words,
Like lanterns in a night conductor's hands,
Signalled the wheels: a nod put Shaughnessy
In Montreal; supplies moved on the minute.
Thousands of men and mules and horses slipped
Into their togs and harness night and day.
The grass that fed the buffalo was turned over,
The black alluvial mould laid bare, the bed
Levelled and scraped. As individuals
The men lost their identity; as groups,
As gangs, they massed, divided, subdivided,

Like numerals only – sub-contractors, gangs
Of engineers, and shovel gangs for bridges,
Culverts, gangs of mechanics stringing wires,
Loading, unloading and reloading gangs,
Gangs for the fish-plates and the spiking gangs,
Putting a silver polish on the nails.[20]

Here the text descends, comically, to the mules, who are presumably too stupid to share a vision and so know when it's time to quit.

Pratt, like Macdonald, sees in the building of the road the creation of a national community, but there is nothing here of the settler's vision, of Goldsmith's pastoral vision. The settler creates a domestic centre, an intimate individual space; Pratt's heroes drive an imperial line across the continent.

The pastoral vision may also be embodied in the nomadic hunter, the prairie Métis and Indian. Just as it would betray glass into diamonds, it would betray these local Manitobans into Canadian citizens – or turn them under like buffalo grass. Rudy Wiebe's novel, *The Temptations of Big Bear* (1973), focuses on this collision, and one of his characters, Edgar Dewdney of the Department of Indian Affairs, is eloquent on the symbolism of the road. Dewdney is himself a man of two minds. Writing to Macdonald he evokes the awe the land can inspire, its fertility, its vast curving lines, and the fact that such apparently "unresisting and unchecked space" can drive a small man to madness. As a kind of reflex of self-preservation he is led to celebrate the CPR, that project to order and control such space – though it is also followed by a recognition that the Indian's quite different approach may provide a better defence against his essentially metaphysical anxiety. Dewdney writes:

To control, to humanize, to structure and package such a continent under two steel lines would bring any engineer headier joy than the lyric prospects of heaven. The man you find who can do it will be a man indeed and I envy him, as certainly every engineer will after, but Old Big Bear has lived into his own understanding of that land and sometimes while I was out there his seemed the more beguiling prospect; it may in the end last much longer than steel.[21]

Wiebe's novel as a whole is less ambiguous in implying that the imperial control of space does not breed communion with the land or one's fellow man or with the divine. What Pratt saw as three thousand miles of "Hail," others may see as simply three thousand miles of rail, or, worse, a technological extension of Babel. As Karen Blixen puts it in an unexpected remark in *Out of Africa,* "When the first steam engine was constructed, the roads of the races of the world parted, and we have never found one another since."[22] The sentiment finds an echo in Hugh Maclennan's *Seven Rivers of Canada* (1961).

"Space," says Maclennan in his introduction, "much of North American art and literature has been obsessed with it." But in growing older, in returning to the rivers, the original arterial roads of the continent, one discovers time, "that mysterious companion of space," without which things or people have no history, identity, personality. "But in Canada," he says, "the time-sense of the people was abruptly fractured when the railway age began." Air travel only fractured it further, with the result that "This modern Canadian life has not grown out of us; it has been imposed on us by technology. That may be why the nation seems almost to have out-travelled its soul."[23]

Here the symbolism of the train is clearly reversed. The age of the railways did not create, it destroyed a community. And Maclennan reminds us that tradition, history, continuity in time were implicit values in the pastoral vision of the nineteenth-century poets, though often eclipsed by the more dramatic emphasis on the transformation of space.

With this concern for time, Maclennan moves closer to the Quebec writer. We can see other examples of such an *approchement* – as well as of the initial difference in cultural coding – if we look at the symbolism of the tree.

For Quebec poets from Alfred Garneau to Anne Hébert the tree symbolizes continuity in time, between the ancestral dead and the living present and, especially with a bird in its branches, between heaven and earth, the temporal and eternal. If the tree dies or is felled, it symbolizes a break with the past, a separation from the divine, an exile in meaningless space.

For many early Canadian poets, the tree is part of the waste, the wilderness, and its gloomy shades, until it is cut down and transformed into a log cabin, a corduroy road, or Pratt's "pyramids of poles and sleepers" that become the railroad. A good tree is a dead tree, is really lumber.

However, as the split between pastoral and imperial becomes more pronounced, we find twentieth-century poets like Earle Birney, Al Purdy, or Irving Layton taking the side of the tree against the road builders and entrepreneurs. Birney praises the hands of the cedar which work no bombsight.[24] Purdy writes of a "nurse log" in the BC forest, which, though fallen, witnesses to the past and serves as a seed bed to future generations.[25] Layton writes in "Mount Rolland," "Pitiless towards men, I am filled with pity / For the impractical trees climbing the exhausted hillside." They are monks, or disciples of Tolstoy; one with enormous boughs "might have remembered Absalom." They are Gardes Civiles of a silence "made for primeval birds."

Nevertheless the Lilliput train trivializes
The tolerant monk, the trees, and this whirlpool of silence,
Though it fling over its side like a capitalist's bequest
A memorial row
  Of blossoming cherry trees.[26]

The train, or the capitalist order with which it is identified, may in its munificence make an ironic gesture towards pastoral, but it is a mortuary garden, a memorial as it were to the space it has exploited, to its vanished life. The train saves time, and kills the past. It has no time to contemplate the impractical.

Contemplation rather than action, stillness rather than motion, silence rather than speech flesh out the paradigmatic opposition in Layton's poem and is a register of the difference between many of his texts and Pratt's. None the less, in this respect Layton's poem is not novel to Canadian poetry, but part of what might be called a mini-genre. The same set of oppositions is implicit at least in what may be the first example of the train as a demonic symbol, Archibald Lampman's sonnet, "The Railway Station" (1888). The octave may be all we really need.

The darkness brings no quiet here, the light
    No waking: ever on my blinded brain
    The flare of lights, the rush, and cry, and strain,
The engine's scream, the hiss and thunder smite:
I see the hurrying crowds, the clasp, the flight,
    Faces that touch, eyes that are dim with pain:
    I see the hoarse wheels turn, and the great train
Move labouring out into the bourneless night.[27]

The railway station concentrates all the features of the urban world that in another short poem Lampman ironically calls "Reality": noise and commotion, aggression and alienation. And it anticipates the sort of automated ironfoundry that Lampman envisages in "The City of the

End of Things." For Lampman, the rising village has been transformed into a metropolitan power centre for the modern politician, the modern millionaire, the power brokers of commercial and industrial empire. It has betrayed the pastoral vision. Like other Confederation poets, he thus abandons the city, the highway, for the stillness of a half rural, half wilderness world. There within the limits of his individual horizon, he rediscovers an intimate relation to place, its personality as Maclennan would say, and the pulse of its life. It is the song of the white-throat registered on silence, note by note, not the clamour of the Grand Trunk or the Irondale, Bancroft, and Ottawa Railway, that inspires Lampman's best poems.

D.C. Scott had more stomach for violence and cultural collisions than his friend Lampman, but one late poem, "En Route" (1935), provides a quiet counterpart to "The Railway Station." Part of the point of "En Route" is that the speaker is no longer, in a conventional sense, *en route*.

> The train has stopped for no apparent reason
> In the wilds;
> A frozen lake is level and fretted over
> With rippled wind lines;
> The sun is burning in the South; the season
> Is winter trembling at a touch of spring.
> A little hill with birches and a ring
> Of cedars – all so still, so pure with snow –
> It seems a tiny landscape in the moon.

This is an ostensibly absurd moment. The meaningful movement of the train from a to b had been inexplicably arrested, leaving the speaker in the middle of nowhere. Yet it is precisely because the train is still that his eye can wander from the track to discover other tracks. It is precisely because the landscape has been partially stilled by winter that it can register and reveal this delicate network to the speaker, the life-lines of things and creatures; "wisps of shadow from the naked birches," emerging cedar roots, traces "of wild things in the snow." This is in fact the privileged moment in a Lampman poem, where an intimate communion with each particular of one's immediate environment becomes possible. And here the speaker does develop a certain empathy for the life he perceives – like him in transit, like his transitory. But partly, too, his elegiac mood, the unexpected autumnal drift of the last lines, springs from the fact that the speaker is incorrigible. He discounts his own experience. In part, at least, he maintains the perspective with which he began, that meaning lies in those publicly recognized directions and directives symbolized by the train. The movements of wind and snow, trees, animals and birds, is meaningless. Unlike the steel tracks, these traces and those of his own sensuous and emotional life find themselves dismissed as mere vagaries.

They're going fast where all impressions go
On a frail substance – images like these,
Vagaries the unconscious mind receives
From nowhere, and lets go to nothingness
With the lost flush of last year's autumn leaves.[28]

Margaret Avison's "Perspective" (1980) is more witty and explicit in its enlargement of the theme and its dramatization of the speaker's own ambiguity. Associated with the train is the new scientific or, more narrowly, linear perspective that once gave Mantegna's painting such freshness and power but now seems a jaded convention for packaging continents. The speaker protests that her eye must be a sport, a freak of nature, though also more fun, since it doesn't see that way – it doesn't chasten the world into some "small tapering design" and reduce it to a *punkt*. More bluntly she declares, "Your seeing is diseased / That cripples space."

Do you not miss the impact of that fierce
Raw boulder five miles off? You are not pierced
By that great spear of grass on the horizon?
  You are not smitten with the shock
    Of that great thundering sky?

It is a Cartesian world without secondary qualities, emotional content, personality. Why? Like Edgar Dewdney she suggests that "fear has eaten back / Through sockets to the brain / And made of it a sifty habitation." Because clearly such a picture of the world is an illusion:

Your law of optics is a quarrel
Of chickenfeet on paper. Does a train
Run pigeon-toed?

And yet, she admits, this madness has its method, its power to generate technology, to order and control space.

I took a train from here to Ottawa
On tracks that did not meet. We swelled and roared
Mile upon mightier mile, and when we clanged
Into the vasty station we were indeed
Brave company for giants.

She too wavers between two perspectives, telling her interlocutor to keep his eyes, he will have a safer return, and admitting that his fear is contagious, she too may end up producing "dwindling vistas from / The massive flux massive Mantegna knew."[29]

Avison herself goes on to proclaim the beauty of the unused, the consequence of the inconsequential. In *sunblue* (1978), she gives us a series of sketches from train windows ("CNR London to Toronto," "Leamington to Windsor"), richly textured, empathetic, in which the train, effectively, disappears.

While the positive symbolism of the railroad may loom large in Pratt and Berton, the negative symbolism is more typical of Canadian writing for nearly a century following Lampman.

The simplest satirical identification of train and nation can be found in Bill Bissett's "The Canadian," where the transcontinental train becomes the symbol of a compartmentalized society, provinces that separate rather than join the passengers, where few ever get to the dining car.

Perhaps its most nightmarish elaboration appears in John Flood's *The Land They Occupied*, a series of poems that views the history of the north as one of imperial invasion and rape. "Night Train" proclaims that

To move on the night train
is to whistle down the night mare
room of steel rail
blind and disfigured
toward a discovery that is not
a destination.

We are on Bissett's train, moving into Lampman's bourneless night. A man may try to get out, or off, but

... if he falls under
the wheels of the train,
the broken pieces of his body will wave
    like the corpse of a dead god,

a lethal germ once
inhabited life,
at the passengers
whose pathology is that of ravens
rummaging through the waste
between the steel rails.[30]

One of the subtlest is b p nichol's "Trans-continental," where the train-ride across a continent tends to become pure syntax, the passing scene reduced to letters and ciphers. The articulation of space is literally the folding and unfolding of the alphabet. Section 16 reads:

hornpayne to armstrong
h to a

ha!

ah ah ah ah
t
u v m l k
r s p

stops

s to s

bless this.[31]

One might see this poem as highly positive in so far as it alerts Canadians to the fact that a civil space might well be a linguistic space – perhaps even more than pre-Cambrian rock or paved throughways. Still, if we can also judge from another of nichol's poem called "Continental Trance," the symbolism of the train remains largely negative. The latter text begins with a harvest of minuses, the speaker heading out of Vancouver for Toronto,

minus the ALL ABOARD
minus my father waving
minus the CN logo
minus my mother waving
minus seventeen years of my life.[32]

I presume that nichol is being pointedly literal when he refers in this poem to his "train of thot," when he asks, "where is this poem going?" and answers, "Toronto."[33] It suggests that many of us have been inclined to share what William New terms "the inability of modern man to distinguish the passage of imagination from the movement of commercial transport."[34] Pratt comes close to this confusion, not least in his celebration of the building of the CPR.

But perhaps there are two imaginations or imaginative visions at work here. From Jules Verne to *Space Odyssey 2001*, from Stephenson's "Rocket" or Ford's Model-T to NASA's "Challenger," the Western imagination has focused heavily on the conquest and exploitation of space. In fiction or fact it tends to take the form of a competition, a race against time, an imperial struggle for dominion. Much of modern art from the Romantics to the present can be seen as a reaction to the main bias of the culture. But Canadian poets were loathe to turn their backs on the general culture, were as suspicious as Dr Johnson of any purely ideal reality, were much too interested in having biblical knowledge of the domestic space ever to say with Villiers de L'Isle-Adam, "As for living, our servants will do that for us." Keeping their feet on the ground, they rooted their opposition in the traditional vision of Edmund Burke and the eighteenth-century poets–later Wordsworth and Arnold or, on the American side, William Carlos Williams and Charles Olson, poets who cultivate an almost physical relation between language and place. When a poet like Dennis Lee goes so far as to draw upon European idealist philosophy, he at least goes to Heidegger, who writes of "Building Dwelling Thinking" and insists on the radical importance of dwelling in place.[35]

In Canada, then, though it may be stretching a term, the opposition to the main drift of Western culture may not inappropriately be dubbed the pastoral vision. One may suggest that it embodies the aspirations of many of the early settlers, small farmers and landholders, and it inspires much of the literate culture of the society. However, the imperial vision, to which Pratt is rather more sympathetic, is equally a reflection of that society, though normally less literate in the expression of its values. For while the farmers, editors, civil servants, and poetic sons of ministers were busy articulating their traditional pastoral vision, the retiring members of the fur trade, the rising representatives of the lumbering and mining business and, of course, of the transportation industry were busy forging their own vision of the land, what F.R. Scott calls "the steel syntax ... of its exploitation."[36] When the historian W.L. Morton describes the basic duality of Canadian life as a division between hinterland and baseland, his own highly spatial terms somewhat disguise an essentially ideological division, one entailing an imperial, the other a domestic economy–both, of course, formulated in the baseland, both, uneasily, sustaining the existence of an independent Canada.

When Morton remarks that the period of agricultural dominance appears to have been an aberration and that in becoming urban Canada appears to be returning to its normal state, he partly explains the increasingly elegiac note in the writers who speak for the pastoral vision. Though Ralph Gustafson, in his poem "Quebec Winter Scene," balances the "far horizontals" of the mail train, its poised pistons, its loud warning as it pulls past, with a farmer's footprints, frozen snake-fence, and the answer of "the local heart"[37] – though Al Purdy rejects the train's "violent anapest," the "steel's dream," in his poem "Winter Walking"[38] – by mid-century the train had clearly outstripped the pedestrian farmer. Pratt was English Canada's most representative poet, and few failed to welcome the invasion of American capital and culture– except the new generation of conservative historians. George Grant's *Lament for a Nation* (1965) warns that traditional Canadian culture, and all local cultures, will be homogenized by an American, and increasingly global, liberal technological culture, whose imperial design is simply to exploit the universe. Dennis Lee's "Civil Elegies" (1968, 1972) sees Toronto, indeed the whole country, as a twentieth-century version of "The Deserted Village." As traditions are forgotten, neighbourhoods founder like marriages, and Canada becomes a branch plant of the U.S., an "outpost of empire," the speaker is found saying goodbye to "the grainy sense of place," "the quirky particulars," the Muskoka lakes, and the Shield with its "terminal vistas" of spruce.[39] The past, the very land itself is being carried off before his eyes.

> ... and now what
> races toward us on asphalt across the Shield –
> by truck, by TV minds and the ore-bearing flatcars –
> is torn from the land and the mute oblivion of
> all those fruitless lives, it no longer
> stays for us, immemorial adversary, but is shipped and
> divvied abroad though wrested whole from the Shield.[40]

In this argument between pastoral and imperial in Canadian culture, it is partly because both share something of the same spatial vocabulary, partly because both have at times shared the symbolism of the road, and partly because the railroad looms so large, historically, that the train, depending on its valency, becomes an important symbol functioning to discriminate a significant difference in two visions of civil space, of meaningful communication and community. And the debate continues, even if the flatcar, and other forms of what Brian Fawcett calls "aggressive transport,"[41] appear to have the last word.

That may be an illusion. If the agrarian base of the pastoral vision has largely disappeared, many of its values find new support in the feminist movement, the concern for the local and global ecology, the resurgent holistic philosophies. And the continuing technological innovations have again shifted the bias of communications, from hardware to software, from the steel track to the electronic highway. And as the railroads adjust and find a more modest role in the economy, the train itself may be cherished as part of the past, the make-up of memory. Dorothy Livesay, in a recent article entitled "All Aboa-r-rd" recalls her experience of trains with positive fondness; for the child, she suggests, the train-ride could both open new horizons and recover a familiar foetal feeling; for the adult it could become sexual arousal.[42] George Amabile's "Railroad Switching Yard" gathers up boxcars, coalcars, gondolas, tankers, "and sometimes a bright caboose," to conclude:

> They wear insignia like veterans
> of our ancient war with space
> and bring to our windows and backyard gates
> contagious distances
> in the names of towns whose legendary ways
> died into history
> before the engineers
> in their puffed caps and coveralls
> had learned to roll their first Bull Durham.[43]

But, since Amabile was born in New Jersey, perhaps he doesn't count. One may end, then, with Erin Mouré, born in Calgary, herself a veteran railroader, who writes an elegy as it were, for a train. It is something missed, she tells us in "Super-Continental, 1955–1981," "Our craving, nearly sexual" – at least for those who have once been intimate with its "metal / skin and bolts holding it together, steampipes / dirty as ever, / generators humming under the floor." It is as if she had failed it, human society let it down, like an extinct species.

I love its ugliness as a thing with soul,
as a possible human painted blue,
as a transport to destinations
we dream of, its cars bring us,
courtesy & service,
the myth of strangers meeting
as words jump from their shoulders like desire
& now sorrow,
the Super-continental unheard, voted down
in parliament
The crossings and mailine empty of it,
the talk of the passengers, their outbursts of
love, a muteness, unheard.[44]

NOTES

1 Time was affected all over the world in so far as it was an equivalent of the Universal Day proposed by Sir Sandford Fleming, Engineer-in-chief for the CPR, that was adopted at Greenwich, England, in 1885. See Pierre Berton, *The National Dream and The Last Spike* (Toronto, 1974), 438.

2 *The Dream of Nation: A Social and Intellectual History of Quebec* (Toronto, 1982), 108.

3 *The National Dream and The Last Spike*, 23.

4 Ibid., 22.

5 E.J. Pratt, *Collected Poems* (Toronto, 1958), 388.

6 Ibid., 360. (The phrase is that of Edward Blake, leader of the Liberal opposition in the House, and one of the few phrases Sir John A. Macdonald finds disturbing.)

7 *Qu'est-ce que la littérature comparée?* (Paris, 1983), 90.

8 "The Railway Train," *Poems* (Cleveland, 1948), 138.

9 "Space and place are not quite able to find equation." Kroetsch makes the comment in his "The Fear of Women in Prairie Fiction: An Erotics of Space," *Essays: Open Letter*, Fifth Series, No. 4 (Spring 1983), 54. Kroetsch notes that in a number of prairie novels, American and Canadian, the women take over the house and leave the men at a loss as to how to approach them. The men find roles as orphan, cowboy,

outlaw, and end up making love with the whores, or the horse, or the iron horse, some spending a good deal of time on trains. "Travel," says Kroetsch, "is possibly the true intercourse in these prairie novels: a frenetic going back and forth, up and down, in and out" (53–4). More shunting, as Dorothy Livesay might say (see n. 42).

10 *Poésies complètes* (Montréal, 1949), 79.

11 Ibid., 89.

12 *Civil Elegies* (Toronto, 1972), 39.

13 Oliver Goldsmith, "The Deserted Village," *Nineteenth-Century Narrative Poems*, ed. David Sinclair (Toronto, 1972), 3.

14 Alexander McLachlan, "The Emigrant," *Nineteenth-Century Narrative Poems*, 126.

15 *Nineteenth-Century Narrative Poems*, 102.

16 *The National Dream and The Last Spike*, 488.

17 E.J. Pratt, *Collected Poems*, 365.

18 Ibid., 362.

19 Ibid., 375.

20 Ibid., 367–8. Reprinted by permission of University of Toronto Press.

21 *The Temptations of Big Bear* (Toronto, 1973), 114–15.

22 *Out of Africa* (Harmondsworth, 1982), 186.

23 *Seven Rivers of Canada* (Toronto, 1977), vii-viii.

24 "Hands," *The Collected Poems of Earle Birney*, 2 vols., I (Toronto, 1982), 67.

25 "The Nurselog," *The Stone Bird* (Toronto, 1981), 60–1.

26 Irving Layton, *Collected Poems* (Toronto, 1965), 15–16. Used by permission of the Canadian Publishers, McClelland and Stewart, Toronto.

27 *The Poems of Archibald Lampman* (Toronto, 1974), 116.

28 *The Oxford Book of Canadian Verse*, ed. A.J.M. Smith (Toronto, 1960), 104.

29 Ibid., 356–7.

30 *The Land They Occupied* (Erin, Ont., 1976), 50.

31 *love: a book of remembrances* (Vancouver, 1974), n.p.

32 *An Anthology of Canadian Literature in English*, ed. Donna Bennett and Russell Brown, 2 vols., II (Toronto, 1983), 603.

33 Ibid., 604.

34 *Articulating West: Essays on Purpose and Form in Modern Canadian Literature* (Toronto, 1972), 264.

35 Martin Heidegger, *Poetry, Language, Thought*, trans. Albert Hofstadter (New York;, 1975), 145–61.

36 "Laurentian Shield," *The Collected Poems of F.R. Scott* (Toronto, 1981), 58.

37 *The Moment Is All: Selected Poems, 1944–1983* (Toronto, 1983), 21.

38 *Poems for All the Annettes* (Toronto, 1968), 90.
39 *Civil Elegies*, 47, 43, 41, 35.
40 Ibid., 40.
41 *Aggressive Transport* (Vancouver, 1982).
42 *Canadian Literature*, No. 100 (Spring 1984), 200–3.
43 *The Penguin Book of Canadian Verse*, ed. Ralph Gustafson (Harmondsworth, 1984), 288.
44 *Wanted Alive* (Toronto, 1983), 105–6.

BOGOMILA WELSH-OVCHAROV
University of Toronto

Vincent van Gogh, Paul Gauguin, and Albert Aurier: The Perception of Life in Death

In writing about Vincent van Gogh in the inaugural issue of *Le Mercure de France* which appeared January 1890, Albert Aurier, while not overlooking the painter's roots in traditions of Realism, could nonetheless describe him as "a symbolist who feels the continual need to clothe his ideas in precise, ponderable, tangible forms ..."[1] This characterization is sometimes challenged as the imposition of an aesthetic foreign to the artist by a leading Symbolist critic, but the astuteness of Aurier's perceptions is being steadily reinforced in recent literature on van Gogh, where his affinities with Symbolism and especially with the art of Paul Gauguin are regularly emphasized. This paper will thus examine several manifestations in Vincent's *oeuvre* of the twin themes life and death in the light of Aurier's definition of him as an artist who loved material reality "only as a kind of marvelous language destined to render the Idea." Without the existence of these idealistic tendencies within his naturalistic art, a large part of the work we are considering would remain poorly understood.

Let us hear then the words with which Aurier explained the basic approach to iconography by Vincent in reference to the critic's emerging definition of Symbolism in art:

As for the brilliant, radiant symphonies of color and line, no matter what the importance may be for the painter, in his work they are merely simple expressive *means*, simple *methods* of symbolization. Indeed if we refused to acknowledge the existence of these idealistic tendencies beneath his naturalistic art, a great deal of the work we are examining would remain completely incomprehensible ... how could we explain the *Sower* without thinking of that fixed idea haunting his brain, of the necessary advent of a man, a messiah, a sower of truth, who would regenerate the decrepitude of our art and perhaps of our imbecilic and industrialist society? And how could we explain that obsessive passion for the solar disk he delights in blazing forth from the conflagration of his skies, and at the same time for the other sun, for that vegetable star, the splendid sunflower which he repeats tirelessly, like a monomania, if we refuse to accept his persistent preoccupation with some vague and glorious heliomythic allegory.[2]

Two aspects of Vincent's subject matter are here identified by Aurier. First, his figural content such as that of the *Sower* (Fig. 1) transcends in meaning such a previous usage as that of J.-F. Millet's *Sower* (Fig. 2), in which the action, no matter how heroically conceived, remains basically on a narrative level. In contrast, Vincent's *Sower* in its equation with a life-giving force, symbolized in the presence of a disk-like sun functioning simultaneously as the figure's halo, transforms the literal action into a quasi-iconic representation. In Vincent's many representations of *Sunflowers* (Fig. 3), according to Aurier, even figural content is unnecessary for the presence of essentially the same heliomythic allegory. Later in St Rémy, Vincent painted a *Raising of Lazarus* (Fig. 4) after the famous etching by Rembrandt (Fig. 5) from which he deleted the figure of Christ found in his source but added an overt symbol of "a yellow sunrise." This object, in its contrast to "the blue hills" in the background, was meant to suggest "the same thing which the *chiaroscuro* of the etching expresses" (L 632).[3] Of course Vincent's use of this age-old symbol of life-giving force goes back in North European Art to early calendar representations of the seasonal changes as found in the *Très Riches Heures de Duc de Berry* in which scenes of sowing (Fig. 6) and reaping are prominently featured.

Moreover, when in St Rémy Vincent chose to depict *The Wheatfield behind St. Paul's Hospital with a Reaper* (Fig. 7), he introduced a further degree of complication in meaning. Whereas one might here have expected the traditional parable of the reaper as symbolic of death, Vincent's own words show that something more was intended:

I see the reaper [as] an indeterminate form, who hacks away in the sweltering heat like a devil, in order to finish his work. I see in him the image of death in the sense that humanity is the grain which he cuts down. It is therefore, if you will, the opposite of the *Sower* which I attempted earlier. However this death has nothing sad about it, it occurs in the bright daylight under a sun which inundates everything with a delicate golden light ... It is an image of death such as the great book of nature speaks to us of it – but what I sought is the "almost smiling." (L 604)

This ironic comment to the effect that the symbol of death is nonetheless reassuring of life may have its final reverberation in the equally famous *Wheatfield with Crows* (Fig. 8) from the Auvers period, a painting sometimes interpreted as a harbinger of the artist's own death by suicide. Such a negative interpretation is rendered dubious by the presence in Vincent's *oeuvre* of so many other depictions of wheatfields that exude a sense of sun-drenched abundance. As early as 1887, with the Paris period *Wheatfield with Lark* (Fig. 9), Vincent clearly had associated the earth's fecundity with an appropriately accompanying bird (the lark as celebrant of spring and summer) to produce a confirmation of the life-giving force of nature. There is no clear reason to doubt that the same force constituted one expressive meaning retained in the *Wheatfield with Crows* as well.

Even if one admits some degree of psychological unrest with the latter painting, it is necessary to recall Vincent's own words in describing during his Brabant period the seemingly funereal image of the crumbled *Old Church Tower at Nuenen* (Fig. 10), a structure situated behind his father's vicarage:

I wanted to express how those ruins show that for ages the peasants have been laid to rest in the very fields which they dug up when alive – I wanted to say what a simple thing death and burial is, just as simple as the falling of an autumn leaf. And now these ruins tell me how a faith and religion mouldered away, strongly founded though they were, and how the life and death of the peasants remain forever the same, budding and fading regularly, like the grass and the flowers growing there in that churchyard ground. *Les religions passent, Dieu demeure,* is a saying of Victor Hugo's whom they have recently brought to rest. (L 411)

That this underlying content was not accidental to the choice of subject matter in the *Old Church Tower* is proven by a similar significance which can be attached to another work of the Nuenen period, the *Public Sale of the Crosses of the Cemetery at Nuenen* (Fig. 11); namely, life goes on despite the physical destruction of this particular Christian church and structure and its environs. The hard life of the Brabant peasant is ameliorated by the discarded wood crosses, which originally provided spiritual sustenance and now are to engender physical warmth from the family hearth. This is another application for Vincent's quotation from Hugo: "*Les religions passent, Dieu demeure,*" in this case in the faith of the devout Brabant peasantry.

Clearly the same preoccupation with the life/death continuity survived into Vincent's later French periods, as exemplified in such well-known paintings as *The Starry Night* (Fig. 12) and *Road with Cypress and Star* (Fig. 13).

It is first of all relevant that in both paintings the cypress tree is equated with vertical man-made structures, either the Gothic church spire seen in the middle distance of *The Starry Night* or the Egyptian obelisk form, which Vincent recalls in one of his letters to Theo:

> The cypresses are always occupying my thoughts, I should like to make something of them like the sunflowers, because it astonishes me that they have not yet been done as I see them. It is as beautiful of line and proportion as an Egyptian obelisk. (L 596)

In either instance the cypress is a symbol not only of faith by pointing upwards towards the heavenly regions, but also of death, since in another letter Vincent associates it with funereal significance, presumably because the tree occurs in southern countries and is related there to the cemetery and the idea of death (L 541). Significantly, it was not long after his arrival in Arles that he stated: "I must also produce a starry night with cypresses" (L 474), which implies an immediate preoccupation with this iconographic conflation and the concept of life in death.

An additional and more revealing interpretation of his Starry Night theme is given when Vincent writes to Theo from Arles:

> Perhaps death is not the hardest thing in a painter's life ... the stars always make me dream ... Why I ask myself shouldn't the shining dots of the sky be as accessible as the black dots on the map of France? Just as we take the train to get to Tarascon or Rouen, we take death to reach a star. (L 506)[4]

He returns to the theme shortly thereafter:

> I have just read Victor Hugo's *Année Terrible*. There is hope there but ... that hope is in the stars. I think it is true and well told and beautiful, and indeed I should be glad to believe it myself. But don't forget that this earth is a planet too, and consequently a star or celestial orb. (L 511)

Neither should it be imagined that Vincent's preoccupation with the cyclical themes of life and death was limited or even primarily embodied in his landscape depictions, since they are equally recurrent with paintings devoted to either still life or figural subjects. Good examples of the former genre are *The Skull* (Fig. 14) of the Paris period and the *Death's Head Moth* (Fig. 15) of 1890. Skull imagery is traditionally associated with *vanitas* themes, of which Vincent was well aware from his knowledge of seventeenth-century Dutch precedents, such as the engraving *Vanitas: The End Crowns the Work* (Fig. 16) by Hendrick Hondius. Typical seventeenth-century lowland *vanitas* representations, as in the Hondius engraving, often include more than one object, such as books, candles, precious objects, and other symbols of earthly existence; yet, the skull is the most easily recognizable *vanitas* symbol for life's transience. Sometimes, as in *A Cranium* by Hercules Segers (Fig. 17) the skull is shown in stark isolation as in Vincent's example, whether or not a *vanitas* theme was indicated. What differentiates Vincent's conception is the luminous yellow background, which colour here is as suggestive of life as it is in his sunflowers and wheatfield depictions or the *Raising of Lazarus*. And Vincent himself not only identified the "death's head" in the *Moth* (L 592) but also expressed regret that this beautiful creature had to be killed to be painted. Both the skull and moth image thus involve the theme of physical mortality as concentrated in a microcosmic symbol, contrasting with the more elaborate, literary approach to symbolism found in traditional *vanitas* still-life paintings.

An additional significance to the skull is the implication of its presence in Vincent's *Self Portrait: Dedicated to Paul Gauguin* (Fig. 18), in which there is a comparable ambiguity in reference to the symbolic representation of life versus death. Here, too, there were occasional lowland prototypes, for example, the skull in a simulated niche (Fig. 19), which appears on an external panel of the Louvre diptych by Jan Gossaert representing on the inside panels the Portrait of *Jean Carondelet* and a *Madonna and Child*. This image was part of a double portrait, which can be taken to imply the sitter's awareness of his own mortality.[5] At the least, this type of precedent provides assurance that Vincent either did know or might have known the possibility of conflating self-portraiture with *vanitas* skull imagery. In Vincent's *Self Portrait: Dedicated to Paul Gauguin*, his well-known reference to a Bonze or Buddhist initiate with shaved head implies an asceticism which in oriental religions, of course, contributes to the search for an ultimate state of Nirvana, the triumph over an otherwise unending cycle of life, death, and reincarnation.[6]

Some months previous to the execution of the "Bonze" portriat, Vincent had imparted a similar "symbolic death head" association to his Paris period *Self Portrait before the Easel* (Fig. 20), by means of its almost clean-shaven, thus skull-like, physiognomy. Vincent in this instance referred to Frederick van Eeden's book, *Kleine Johannes*, at the same time stressing his primary purpose to produce a portrait which transcended the limits of photography. He stated:

> The figure against a grayish-white wall. You will say that this resembles somewhat, for instance, the Face of Death – in Van Eeden's book or some such thing – all right, but it is a figure like this – and it isn't an easy job to paint oneself – at any rate if it is to be different from a photograph. (LW 4, June-July 1888)

When Gauguin, the recipient of the "Bonze" Portrait, depicted Vincent painting his symbolically laden sunflowers (Fig. 21), he gave him a gaunt countenance, which Vincent himself recognized as reflecting his state of physical ill-health and psychological tension during the days immediately preceding the self-mutilation and Gauguin's hasty departure from Arles (L 605). Certainly Gauguin, as the owner of one or more sunflower depictions by Vincent, was aware of their heliomythic symbolic significance, as he was equally aware of Vincent's ascetic personal habits. Thus, in an essay on the artist published in 1894, Gauguin associated his own *Van Gogh Painting Sunflowers* with the time of their common residence in Arles.[7] On another instance Gauguin in his memoirs, *Avant et après*, recounted that Vincent interpreted this portrait as, "It is I all right, but I gone mad."[8] As for Vincent, he subsequently chose to combine the sunflower paintings with figural content (L 574) although not in a self-portrait but rather with the *Berceuse: Madame Augustine Roulin* (Fig. 22), the postman's wife at Arles, whose identification with the maternal lullaby theme makes her, as Aurier once implied, a modern, secular Madonna.[9] Thus, in wishing to display the *Berceuse* flanked by two sunflower paintings (for example, Fig. 23), Vincent was creating a modern equivalent of such traditional Christian triptych forms as that of Hugo van der Goes' *Portinari Altarpiece*. Symptomatically, on the eve of Gauguin's arrival at Arles, Vincent had described himself as being on the brink of madness by referring to a similar illness in his earlier lowland compatriot.[10]

Despite the variety of images employed, we may thus surmise that Vincent's use of still-life and figural subjects, especially self-portraits, was permeated with thoughts of life and death and of the tenuous physical state of the artist.

As indicated above, the meaning of Vincent's landscape paintings is informed by his repeated use of symbolic colour. This usage, too, is alluded to in the 1890 article by Aurier, who writes:

No doubt like all the painters of his race, he is very much aware of the importance and beauty of the pigment, but even more often, he only considers this bewitching pigment as a kind of marvellous language defined for the translation of the Idea. He is almost always a symbolist. Not at all a symbolist like the Italian primitives, those mystics who hardly felt it necessary to dematerialize their dreams, but rather a symbolist who feels the continual need to clothe his ideas in precise, ponderably tangible forms, in intensely sensual and material envelopes.[11]

Aurier's observations emphasize two aspects of Vincent's art that deserve to be noted. First, he seems to have been aware of Vincent's antagonism against the use of traditional modes of symbolic or allegorical painting in the late mediaeval tradition to which, over his objections, both Gauguin and Emile Bernard by late 1889 had to some extent returned. Second, despite his paraphrase of the famous dictum stated in the 1886 Symbolist Manifesto of Jean Moréas, namely the "aim to clothe the *Idea* in symbolic form," Aurier stresses Vincent's determination to retain a high degree of Realist canons of form while still implying symbolic content, including that achieved by the use of colour.

A good example of Vincent's approach to the issue of form versus content is provided by his several landscape representations, sometimes in series, in which he wished to depict changes of season according to appropriate colour combinations.

The most important early instance of this usage was embodied in his planned series of six paintings of the seasons as commissioned by an acquaintance from Brabant named Hermans, for his dining room. Whereas the patron originally had wished to decorate the room with compositions of various saints, Vincent advised Hermans to alter this plan, as he recalled to Theo:

I begged him to consider whether the appetite of the worthy people who would have to sit down at that table would not be more stimulated by six illustrations taken from peasant life in the Meierij [local district] – at the same time symbolizing the four seasons – than by the mystical personages mentioned above. (L 374, from early 1884)

Just two months earlier Vincent had formulated an idea for a cycle of paintings devoted to the seasons, but which also would involve a sequential contrast of the four sets of complementary colours. As he explained:

Spring is tender, green young corn and pink apple blossoms. Autumn is the contrast of the yellow leaves with violet tones. Winter is the snow with the black silhouettes. But now, if summer is the contrast of blues with an element of orange in the golden bronze of the corn, one could paint a picture which expressed the mood of the seasons in each of the contrasts of the complementary colours (red and green, blue and orange, yellow and violet, white and black). (L 372, from early June 1884)

The Hermans commission of six paintings did not allow for an exact realization of Vincent's colour series of four contrasts, but in two of the extant realized examples, *The Plower,*[12] a spring subject, and *The Woodgatherers* (Fig. 24), the final member of the series depicting Winter, there is evidence that Vincent's symbolic concept was present. *The Plower*, for example, seems to include some element of the tender greens versus red colour appropriate for Spring while *The Woodgatherers*, with its stark white snow in contrast to the black figures outlined against the horizon, is an even clearer expression of the winter season depicted. These colour usages differ appreciably from their likely models, such as *The Faggot Carriers* (National Museum of Wales) by Vincent's idol, J.-F. Millet, and the thematically related *The Poor Women of Ornans* (Private Collection) by Gustave Courbet, both of which feature the customary earth tones of Realist tradition. *Woodgatherers* once again illustrates how Vincent could build upon Realist narrative conceptions, yet, as Aurier states, how he could clothe the Idea in a more appropriate sensual and material envelope.

Naturally it is doubtful that Aurier would have been aware of such an early anticipation of full-blown Symbolist art in Vincent's Brabant works, since his own appreciation of Vincent's thinking relates to the later French periods, especially Arles and St Rémy. It is thus instead to such archetypal harvest scenes as *The Mowers: Arles in Background* (Fig. 25) that his own descriptive analysis relates. One may nonetheless deduce that in this and in many related examples of summer landscape paintings the stark contrast between the resonant blue sky and the yellow/orange hues of the ripened grain field embodied in Vincent's thinking a complementary contrast, initially posited during his days in Brabant. Here too we can see that Vincent's conception involved a non-narrative, thus oblique symbolic rendering which contrasts, for example, with the most obvious historical antecedent, Pieter Breughel's *The Harvesters* (Fig. 26), a painting which figured in a six-part series of calendrial depictions. A further example of Vincent's fundamental usage of complementary colour juxtaposition is contained in *Les Alyscamps* (Fig. 27), in which he plays off yellow and orange leaves against lilac tree trunks (L559).

By way of contrast, in *The Red Vineyard: Montmajour* (Fig. 28), Vincent seems to have selected the dominant red colouration as symbolic of the wine itself and perhaps also of the red sunset ("Abendroth," according to Goethe's colour theory). This hypothesis is substantiated by the hyperbolic language of a Belgian critic who in 1890 described this painting in the following terms:

> If one assumes an ordinary point of view in judging this painting, what does one say of the irradiating light, the diffusion of flaming rays, the vineyard in blood-drenched colors, and the orgy of warm and intense tonalities in which blood and fire appear to have usurped the place of colour? ... Van Gogh has wished in his *Vineyard* to show us the ferment and the intoxication, the maddening warmth and effervescence of wine. And the abandonment in his color suggests the senseless orgies of which the vineyard can be considered the singular promoter and primary source.[13]

Much of the symbolic content must have been known to Gauguin during his stay with Vincent in Arles when he chose to follow Vincent's example in depicting a similar setting in his *Grape Gathering* (Fig. 29) of November 1888. As widely noted, Gauguin's use of symbolic figural content, namely the brooding woman in the centre foreground and the crone shrouded in black at the left, symbolic of death, justify the alternative titles *Misères humaines* or *Poverty* that Gauguin assigned to this painting. The two stooping figures centre above, however, clearly paraphrase one or more of those found in the thematic counterpart by Vincent, and even Gauguin's brooding figure, although now known to have derived from an image of a Peruvian Mummy (Fig. 30), may also reflect Gauguin's knowledge of similarly posed women and men in such images of sorrow and despair as Vincent's *Sorrow: Sien* (Fig. 31) and *Old Man*, dating from as far back as 1882 during the Hague period.[14] At the same time it must be recognized that such types build upon a wealth of similarly posed figures from the Renaissance-Baroque allegories of Melancholy, as embodied in such symbolic figures as the well-known engraving *Melancolia I* (Fig. 32) by Dürer.

In Vincent's case the broad span of this involvement with the theme extends from his very beginnings as an artist to the end of his career. Thus the drawing *Sorrow: Sien* derives pictorially from a mid-nineteenth-century English illustration from the *Illustrated London News* by H.B. Roberts called *Homeless*, which Vincent owned.[15] Yet the meaning of the image was enriched both by his formal involvement with the model, a pregnant prostitute named Sien, whom he took from the streets as a living companion, and by a reading of the French novelist Jules Michelet, an early champion of women's rights, who supplied the quotation that the artist placed beneath the drawing: "How is it that on the earth there can be a lonely, forsaken woman?"

The final embodiment of this theme in Vincent's career is seen in his *Portrait of Dr. Gachet* (Fig. 33), executed in 1890 in Auvers and based upon a number of precedents such as Delacroix's *Tasso in the Madhouse* (Fig. 34). The theme of melancholy also derives from the fact that the sitter had produced a thesis on the subject of Melancholy for the University of Montpellier and that Vincent recognized a certain kinship between the doctor and himself in terms of psychological depression and mental instability.[16]

It is significant that Vincent described this portrait as containing "the heartbroken expression of our time" and compared it in intention with Gauguin's *Christ in the Garden of Olives* (Fig. 35) of 1889, of which he otherwise disapproved for its allusion to an overt religious narrative (L 614).

Vincent would have been less, if at all, aware of how central to Gauguin's art in 1889, after the latter's departure from Arles, had become the Peruvian Mummy – the Melancolia image first found in the *Misères humaines*. This was first displayed at the so-called Café Volpini exhibition of painters, "Impressionists and Synthetists," which figured as a virtually overlooked part of the Universal Exposition held in the summer of 1889 in Paris. The figure, now transformed and Christianized into an image of the fallen *Eve* (Fig. 36), appears in isolation, except for the symbolic tree and serpent included in a watercolour version exhibited in the Café Volpini. It also occurs in the title page *Aux roches noires* (Fig. 37) of the catalogue for this same exhibition, but there situated, albeit without a serpent, against a black rock of the Breton coast and next to a female seen from the rear hurling herself against the waves. The latter figure was also present at the exhibition as a painting entitled *In the Waves* (Fig. 38), but later renamed, by Gauguin himself, *Undine*. Although this latter figure has been described as an image of death, indeed a watery suicide, the present writer has interpreted it in less lugubrious terms, as symbolic of procreation, according to the so-called Venus of the Sea and Undine mythologies.[17] Another painting, now in Egypt, includes the Eve-Woman against a Black Rock along with another bather, in this case drying herself after her presumed immersion in the sea. It is of some importance that the hair of the latter figure is of the same intense red as that of the *Undine*, which allowed for her identification by a note to a critic as "the life part of the La Vie et La Mort" title which Gauguin assigned to this painting when first exhibited.[18] This same essential confrontation between the forces of life and those of death is continued in two other examples.

One of these, *Portrait of Meyer de Haan: Nirvana* (Fig. 39) of 1889, shows Gauguin's follower and financial benefactor, the Dutchman Meyer de Haan, situated in front of the Eve and Undine figures, presumably meditating upon the cycle of life/death and perhaps reincarnation implied in the Oriental religious reference of the title. The second elaboration of this iconography occurs in the 1890 painted wood relief entitled *Be Mysterious* (Fig. 40), which shows the Undine figure once again, apparently turning away from a shrouded female figure on the left, towards another head, possibly androgynous, which has been identified as the symbol of disembodied mysticism.[19] That this Undine figure did in fact signify for Gauguin the principle of life rather than death is further substantiated by the recent discovery of a previously unidentified figure in the upper-right background of a *Self Portrait of Gauguin* (Fig. 41), a work generally dated 1888. This figure can now be identified as a reverse or mirror-image rendering of the Undine figure, as contained in the oil version present at and executed shortly before the Volpini exhibition.[20] What is often considered the unusually self-confident mien of Gauguin's facial features in this portrait might well be explained by his atypically optimistic outlook at the time of the execution of the *Self Portrait*, that is, just following his departure from Arles, when he had emerged as the leader of the "Synthetist-Symbolist" movement in painting, but before he had experienced the disappointing lack of attention the exhibition was actually to encounter.

In the light of this identification, we must now redate this portrait from Gauguin's period of collaboration with Vincent in Arles to approximately half a year later. At that time, to be sure, Vincent was not included, as one might have expected, in the Volpini exhibition. The Gauguin *Self Portrait* nonetheless provides further evidence of the close relationship in approach to treating the themes of Life and Death by the two artists, despite equally significant differences in their choice of imagery.

Hence, as noted by Aurier, Vincent chose not to include specific traditional religious iconography in his subject preferences. He nevertheless impregnated much of his *oeuvre*, whether landscape, still-life, or figural, with suggestions of symbolic content which imply the inevitable concern of all religions with the problem of human mortality versus transcendent survival. Gauguin, in contrast, despite a variety of subtle and oblique references to traditional religious themes, employs subjects and titles that relate to traditional Christian or other mythological allegories.

Albert Aurier ultimately was to identify Gauguin in 1891 as the leader of the Symbolist movement in painting, most particularly in reference to paintings to which the artist had given titles with Christian references. Yet a year earlier he had chosen to treat Vincent as an artist deeply concerned with symbolic or ideational content, as he stated in summary of Vincent's achievement: "Vincent Van Gogh is thus not merely a great painter enraptured by his art, his palette and nature; he is also a dreamer, a fanatical believer, a devourer of beautiful Utopias living on ideas and dreams."

NOTES

1 Aurier's pioneering article first appeared in "Les Isolés: Vincent van Gogh," *Mercure de France*, 1:1 (January 1890), 24–9, and was reprinted in *Oeuvres posthumes* (Paris, 1893), 257–65. For the English translation of a major segment of this article see Linda Nochlin, *Impressionism and Post-Impressionism, 1874–1904* (Englewood Cliffs, N.J., 1966), 135–9.

2 Nochlin, 137. The interpretation of van Gogh's work by Aurier is examined in B.M. Welsh-Ovcharov, *Vincent van Gogh and the Birth of Cloisonism* (Toronto and Amsterdam, 1981), 53–5.

3 This and subsequent letter references follow the standard numeration as found in *The Complete Letters of Vincent van Gogh*, 3 vols. (Greenwich, Ct., 1958).

4 For interpretation of *The Starry Night* see: Meyer Schapiro, "On a Painting of Van Gogh: Crows in the Wheatfields," *View: The Modern Magazine*, 7:1 (October 1946), rpt. in B.M. Welsh-Ovcharov, *Van Gogh in Perspective* (Englewood Cliffs, N.J., 1974), 166, n.3; Sven Loevgren, *The Genesis of Modernism: Seurat, Gauguin, Van Gogh, and French Symbolism in the 1880s* (Bloomington, Ind., 1971), 159–91; Albert Boime, "Starry Night: A History of Matter and a Matter of History," *Arts Magazine*, 4:3 (December 1984), 86–103. Laurea Soth, "Van Gogh's Agony," *Art Bulletin*, 68 (June

1986), 301–13; Charles Whitney, "The Skies of Vincent van Gogh," *Art History*, 9:3 (September 1986), 351–62.

5 I should like to express my appreciation to Prof. Joaneth Spicer, University of Toronto, for relevant suggestions on *vanitas* themes. The inscription on the ledge, "Matura" (Maturity or Ripe), can be seen as an ironic reference to the sitter's own physical mortality. For a *vanitas* discussion in van Gogh's art see Hope B. Werness, "Some Observations on van Gogh and the Vanitas Tradition," *Studies in Iconography*, 6 (1980), 123–36.

6 On *The Self Portrait: Dedicated to Paul Gauguin* see Tsukusa Kodera, "Japan as Primitivistic Utopia: Van Gogh's Japonisme Portraits," *Simiolus*, 4 (1984), 189–208; Vojtech Jirat-Wasiutynski *et al.*, *Vincent van Gogh, Self Portrait Dedicated to Paul Gauguin*, Center for Conservation and Technical Studies, Harvard University Art Museums (Cambridge, Mass., 1984), 3–9.

7 Paul Gauguin, "Natures Mortes," *Essais d'Art Libre*, 4 (January 1894), 273–5. For the English translation see Welsh-Ovcharov, *Van Gogh in Perspective*, 42–3.

8 Welsh-Ovcharov, *Van Gogh in Perspective*, 47.

9 Aurier, "Les Isolés," English translation in Nochlin, 138. For the *Berceuse* as a modern madonna, see Welsh-Ovcharov, *Vincent van Gogh and the Birth of Cloisonism*, 148–9.

10 The *Portinari Altarpiece*, Uffizi Gallery, Florence, was probably known to van Gogh from reproductions. Van der Goes and his tragic personality were compared to that of van Gogh's own haggard physical and mental condition in Arles (L 514) when he referred to a painting of 1872, *The Madness of Hugh Van der Goes* by Emile Wauters, which he had known since 1873 (L 10).

11 Nochlin, 137.

12 J.B. de la Faille, *The Works of Vincent van Gogh* (Amsterdam, 1971), 99, F 172; *The Plower*, executed at Neuen (August 1884) and now at the Von der Heydt Museum der Stadt Wupperthal, Wuppertal.

13 Ernest Closson, "Peinture Symbolique," *Impartial Bruxellois*, 22 March 1891; for the English translation see Welsh-Ovcharov, *Van Gogh in Perspective*, 52–3.

14 De la Faille, 368, F 997: *Old Man with His Head in His Hands*, Rijksmuseum Vincent van Gogh, Amsterdam.

15 *Illustrated London News*, 30:865 (20 June 1877), 614. For a discussion and illustration see Charles Chetham, *The Role of Vincent van Gogh's Copies in the Development of His Art* (New York, 1976), 100, pl. 67a.

16 For an extensive analysis on Dr Gachet see Evert Van Uitert, *Vincent van Gogh in Creative Competition: Four Essays for Simiolus* (Amsterdam, 1983), 56–66, and Welsh-Ovcharov, *Vincent van Gogh and the Birth of Cloisonism*,

163–6. Another possible source for the pose is Rembrandt's *Old Woman Reading*, an image that appeared in fact in an issue of the *Gazette des Beaux Arts* in 1887, and combines a head-in-hand pose with the idea of interest in learning.

17 Welsh-Ovcharov, *Vincent van Gogh and the Birth of Cloisonism*, 204–5. However, an interesting compromise solution to the life or death dilemma of the Undine or woman in waves figure has been offered by Vojtech Jirat-Wasiutynski in "Paul Gauguin's Self Portraits and the Oviri: The Image of the Artist, Eve and the Fatal Woman," *Art Quarterly*, 2:2 (Spring 1979), 172–4, a study unfortunately not known to the present writer when preparing this lecture.

18 For this identification see M. Bodelson, "The Wildenstein-Cogniat Gauguin Catalogue," *Burlington Magazine*, 108 (January, 1966), 37.

19 Wayne Anderson, *Gauguin's Paradise Lost* (New York, 1971), 116–17.

20 This identification was made by Jirat-Wasiutynski in "Paul Gauguin's Self Portraits and the Oviri," 174.

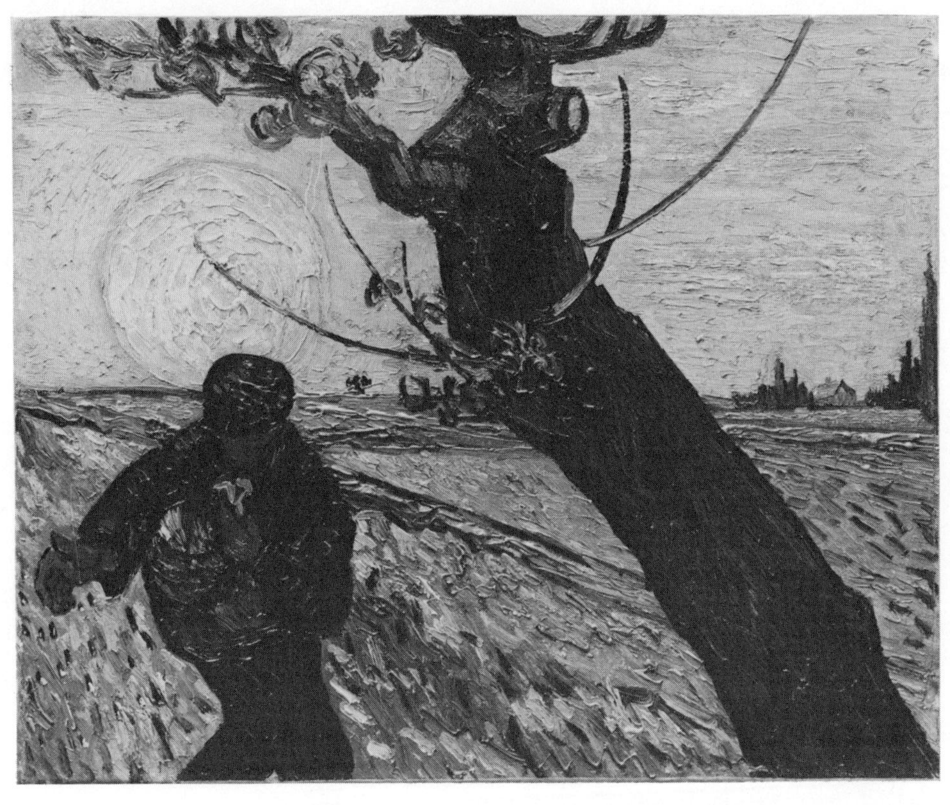

Fig. 1 Vincent van Gogh: *The Sower*, Arles (1888). Rijksmuseum Vincent van Gogh, Amsterdam.

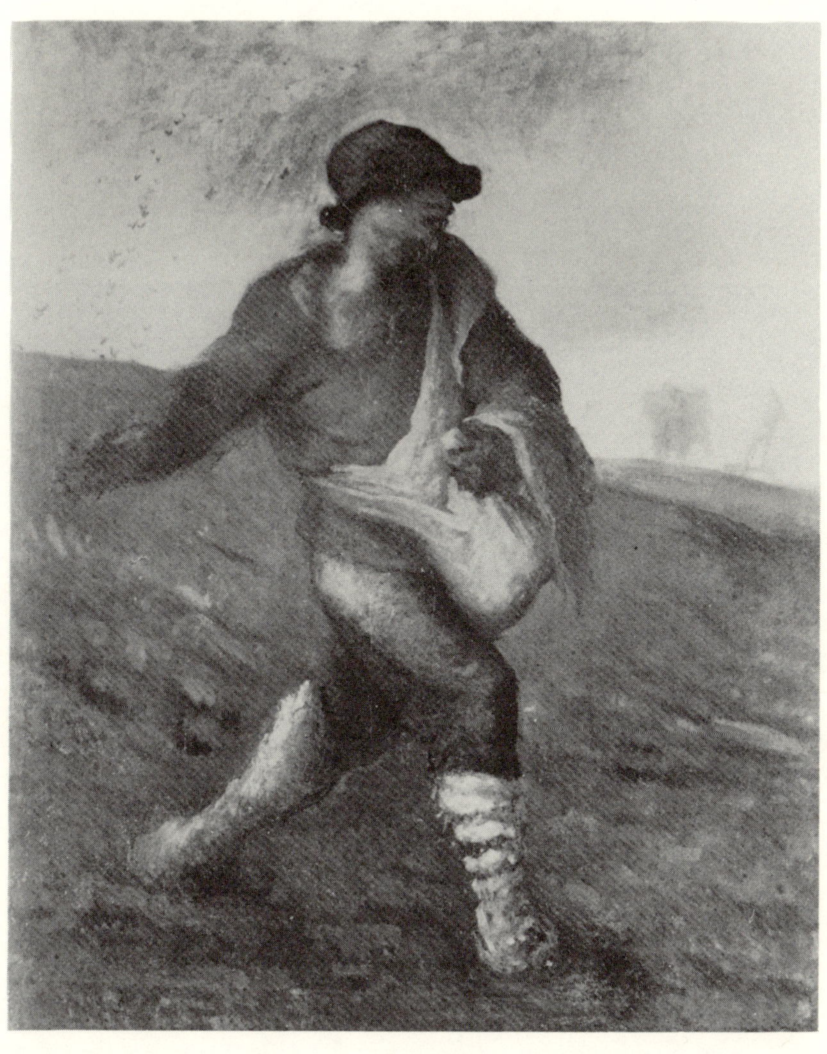

Fig. 2 Jean-François Millet: *The Sower* (1850).
Provident National Bank, Philadelphia.

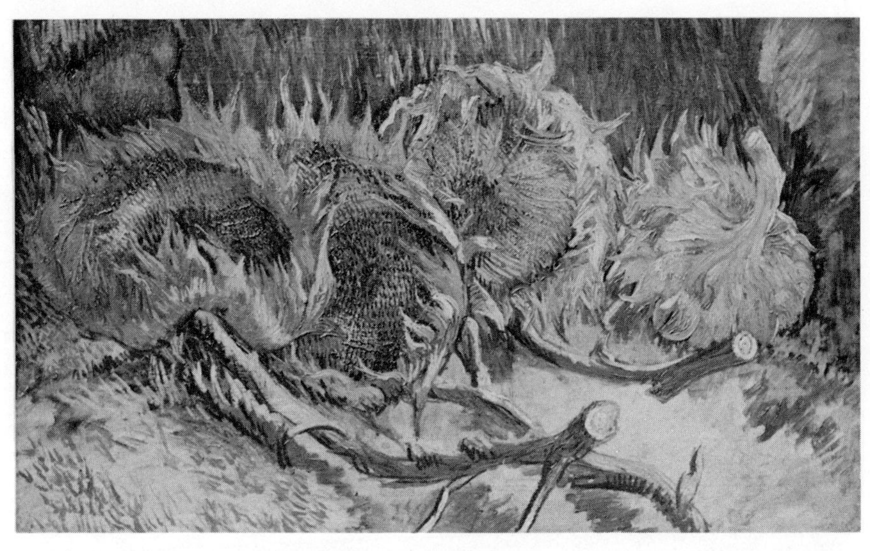

Fig. 3. Vincent van Gogh: *Sunflowers*, Paris (1887). Rijksmuseum Kröller-Müller, Otterlo.

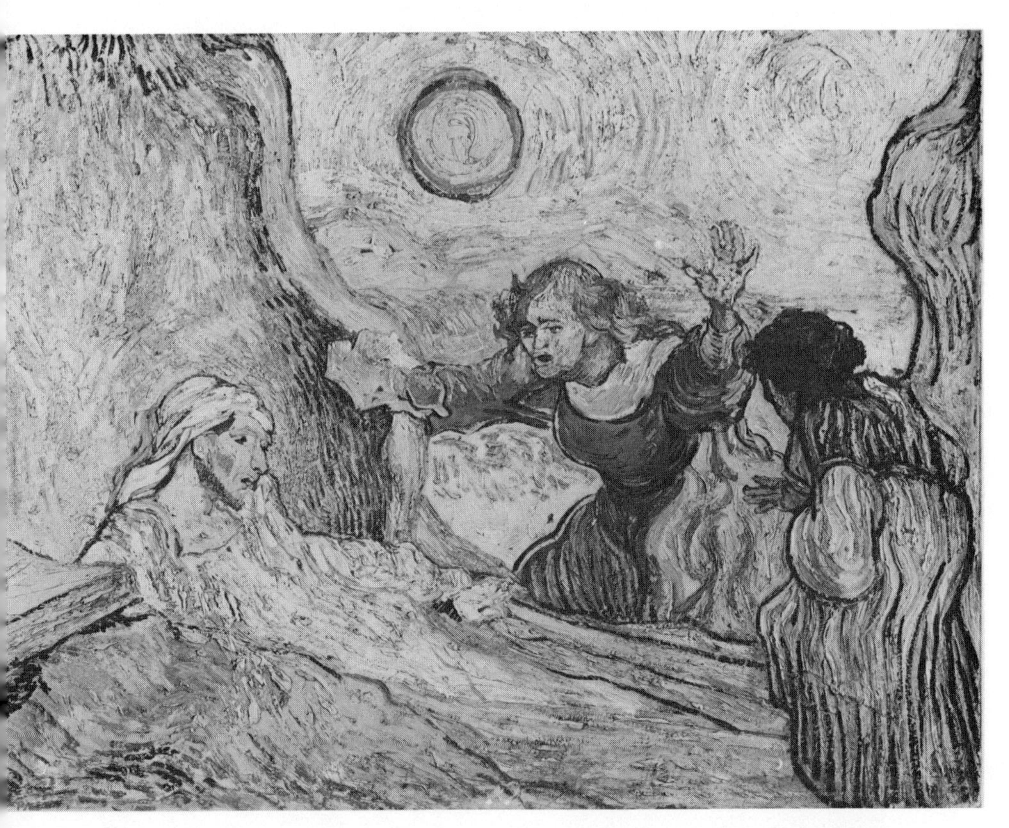

Fig. 4 Vincent van Gogh: *The Raising of Lazarus* (after Rembrandt),
Saint-Rémy (1889).
Rijksmuseum Vincent van Gogh, Amsterdam.

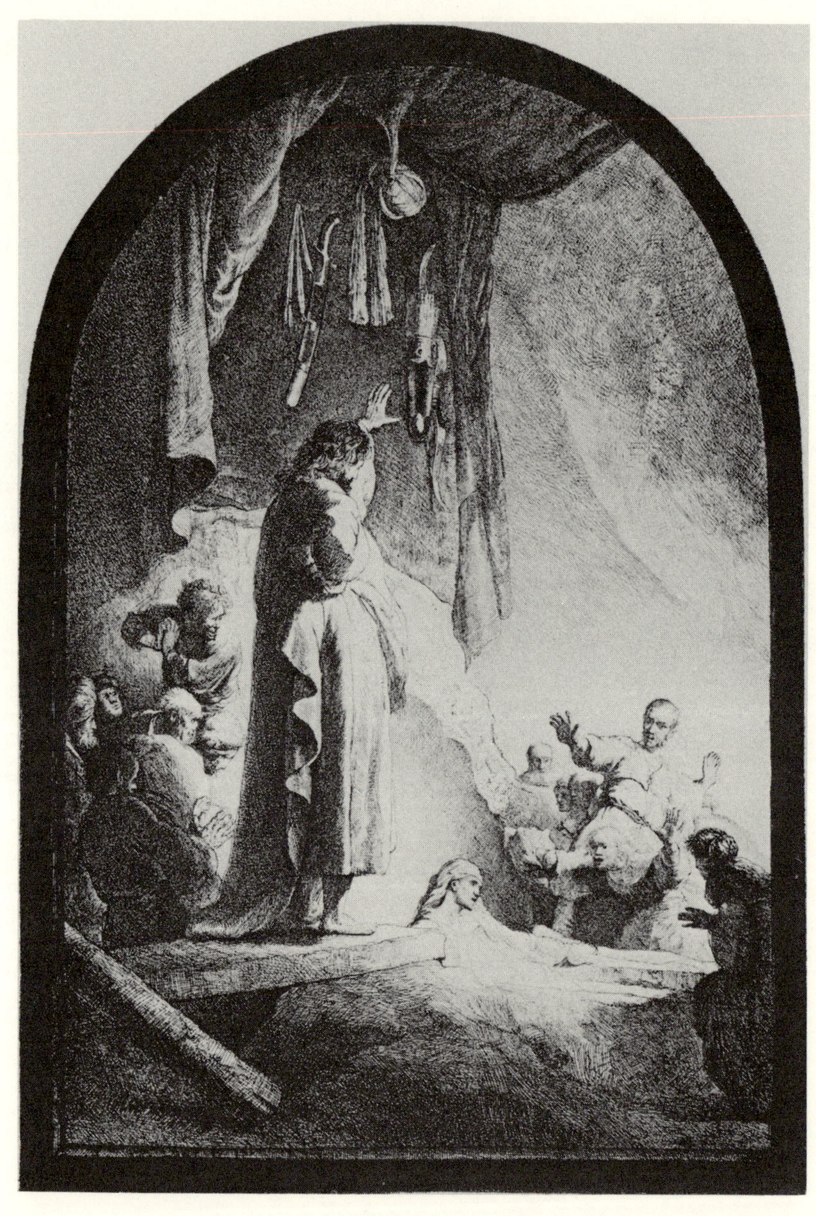

Fig. 5 Anonymous (after Rembrandt): *The Raising of Lazarus*, etching.
After fifth state of Rembrandt's etching (c. 1632).
Rijksmuseum Vincent van Gogh, Amsterdam.

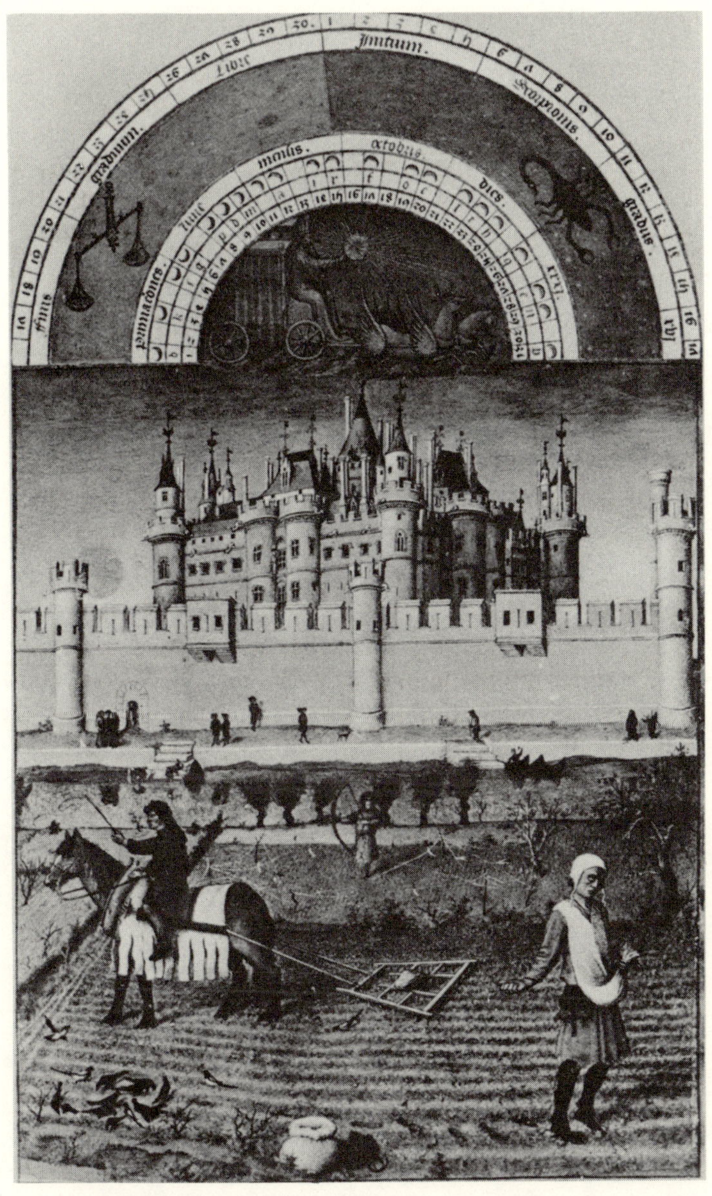

Fig. 6 Pol de Limbourg: *Sowers in Front of the Louvre* (1411–1416).
Très Riches Heures du Duc de Berry.
Musée Condé, Chantilly.

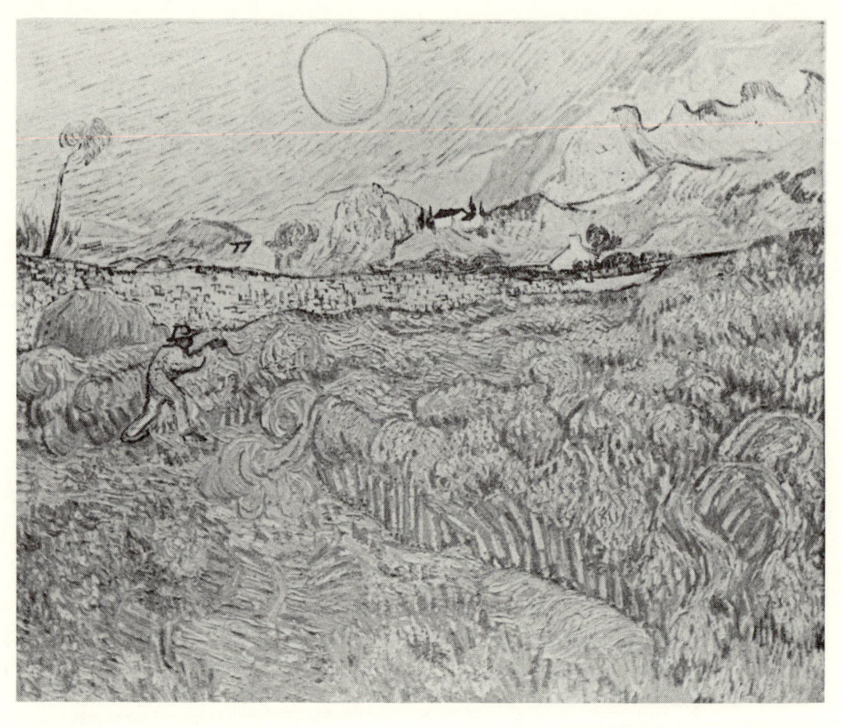

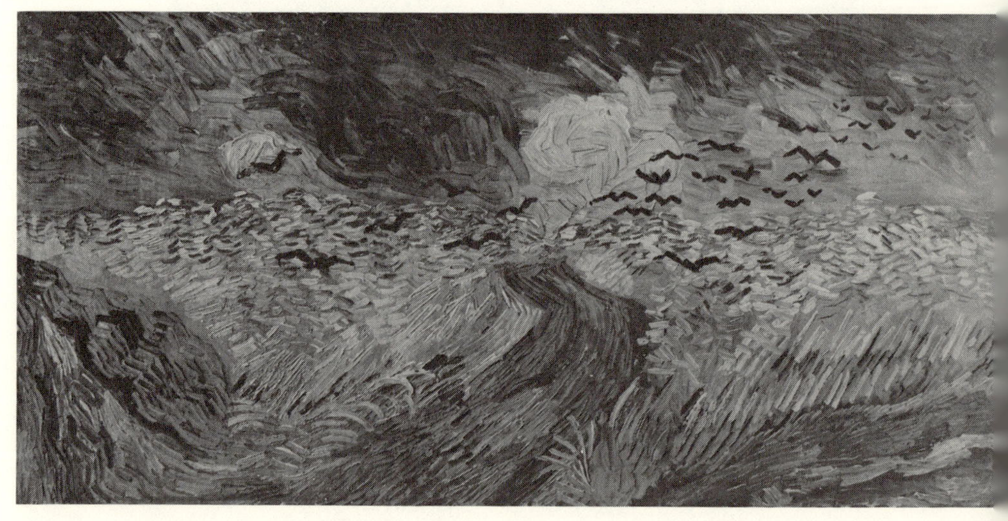

OPPOSITE

Fig. 7 Vincent van Gogh: *The Wheatfield behind Saint Paul's Hospital with a Reaper*, Saint-Rémy (1889).
Museum Folkwang, Essen.

Fig. 8 Vincent van Gogh: *Wheatfield with Crows*, Auvers (1890).
Rijksmuseum Vincent van Gogh, Amsterdam.

Fig. 9 Vincent van Gogh: *A Wheatfield with a Lark*, Paris (1887).
Rijksmuseum Vincent van Gogh, Amsterdam.

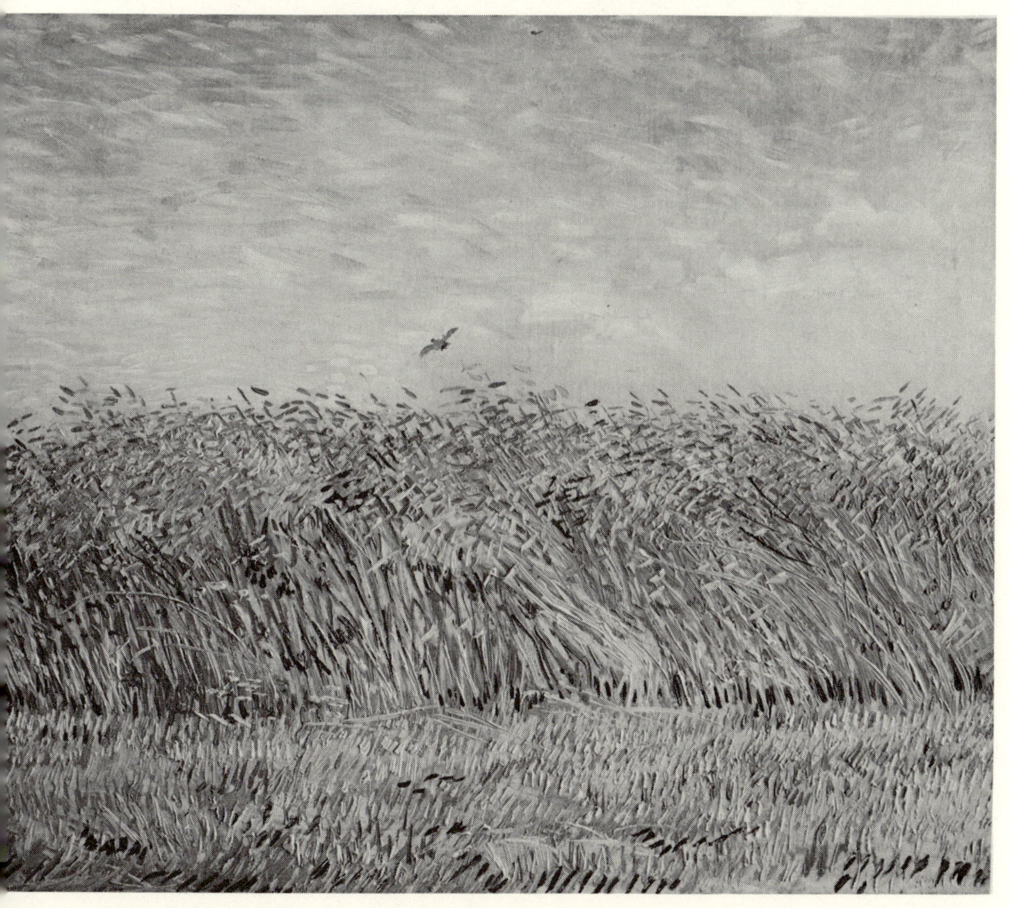

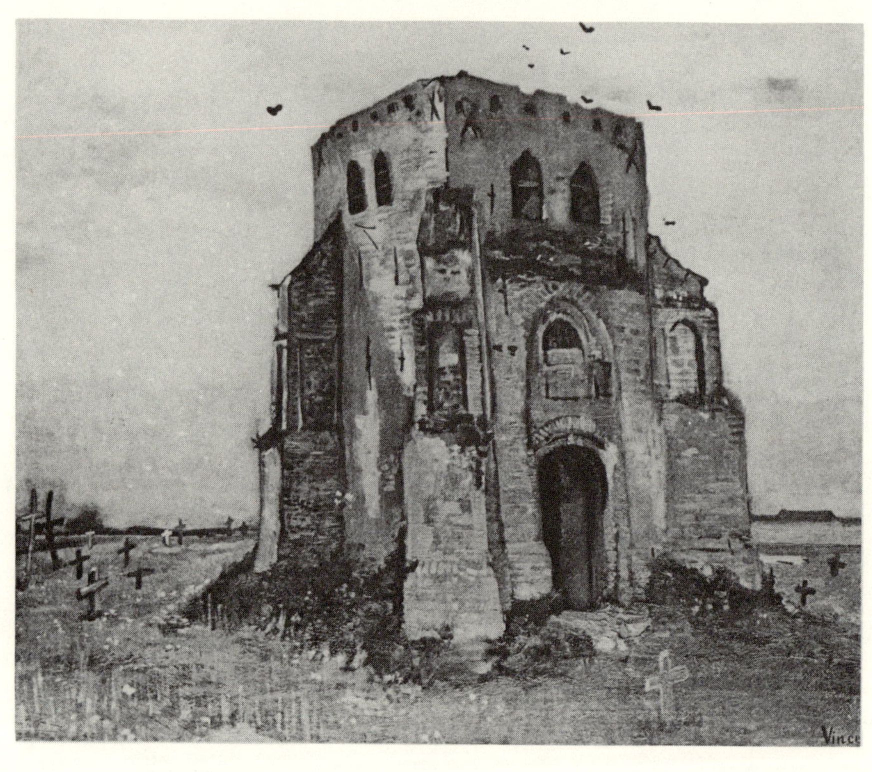

Fig. 10 Vincent van Gogh: *The Old Church Tower at Nuenen*, Nuenen (1885). Rijksmuseum Vincent van Gogh, Amsterdam.

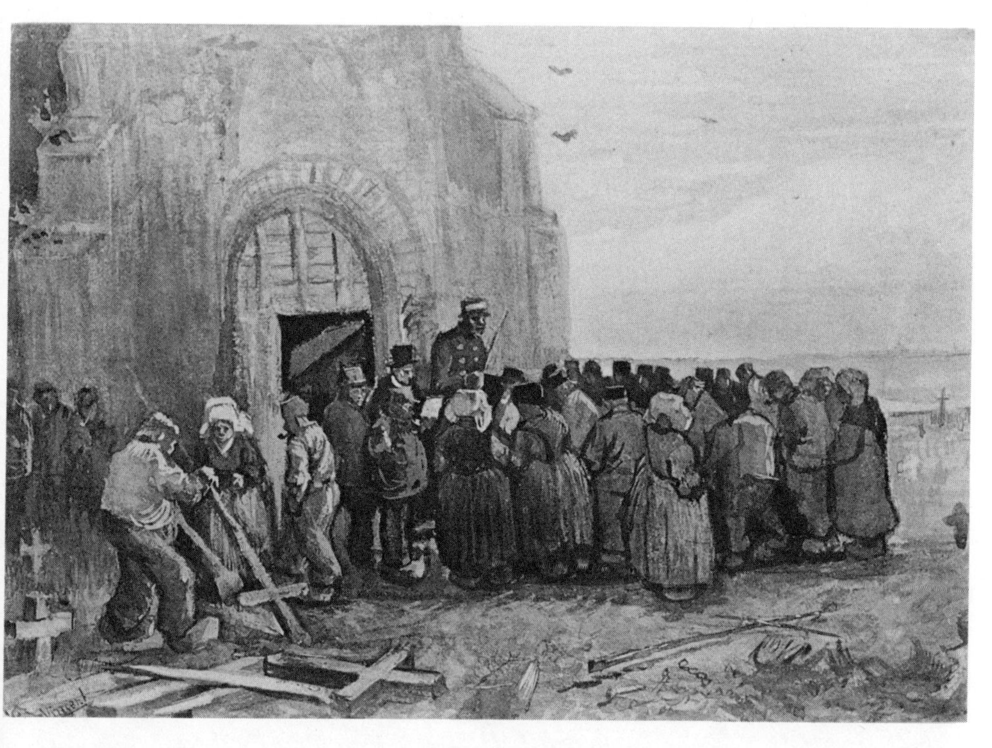

Fig. 11 Vincent van Gogh: *Public Sale of the Crosses of the Cemetery at Nuenen*, Nuenen (1885).
Rijksmuseum Vincent van Gogh, Amsterdam.

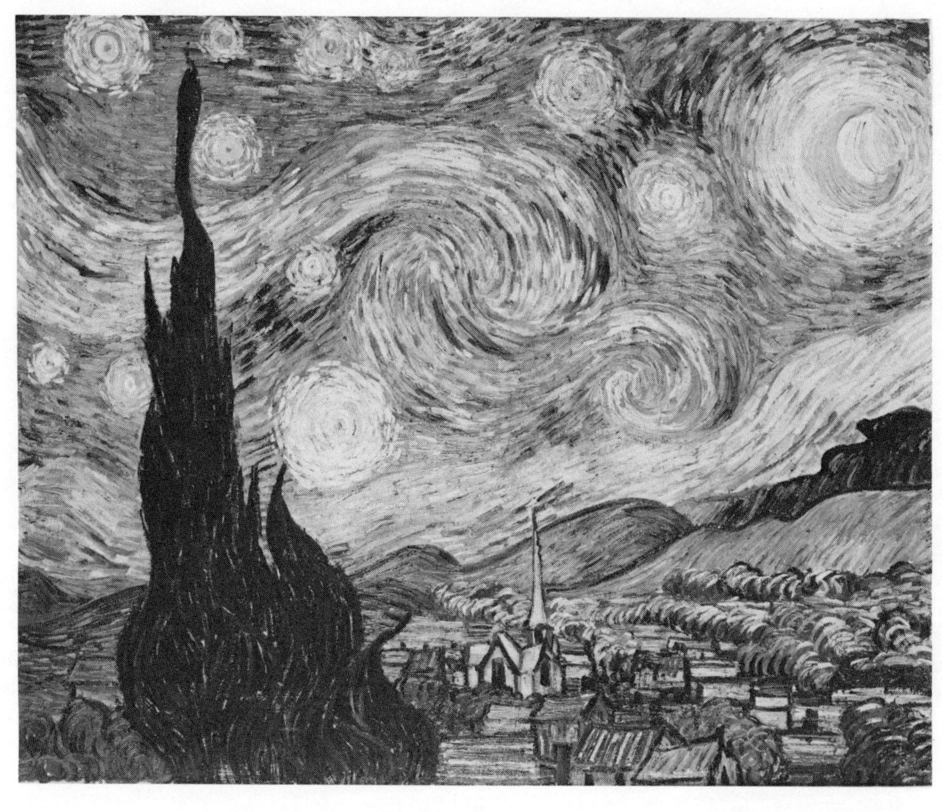

Fig. 12 Vincent van Gogh: *The Starry Night*, Saint-Rémy (1889). Museum of Modern Art, New York.

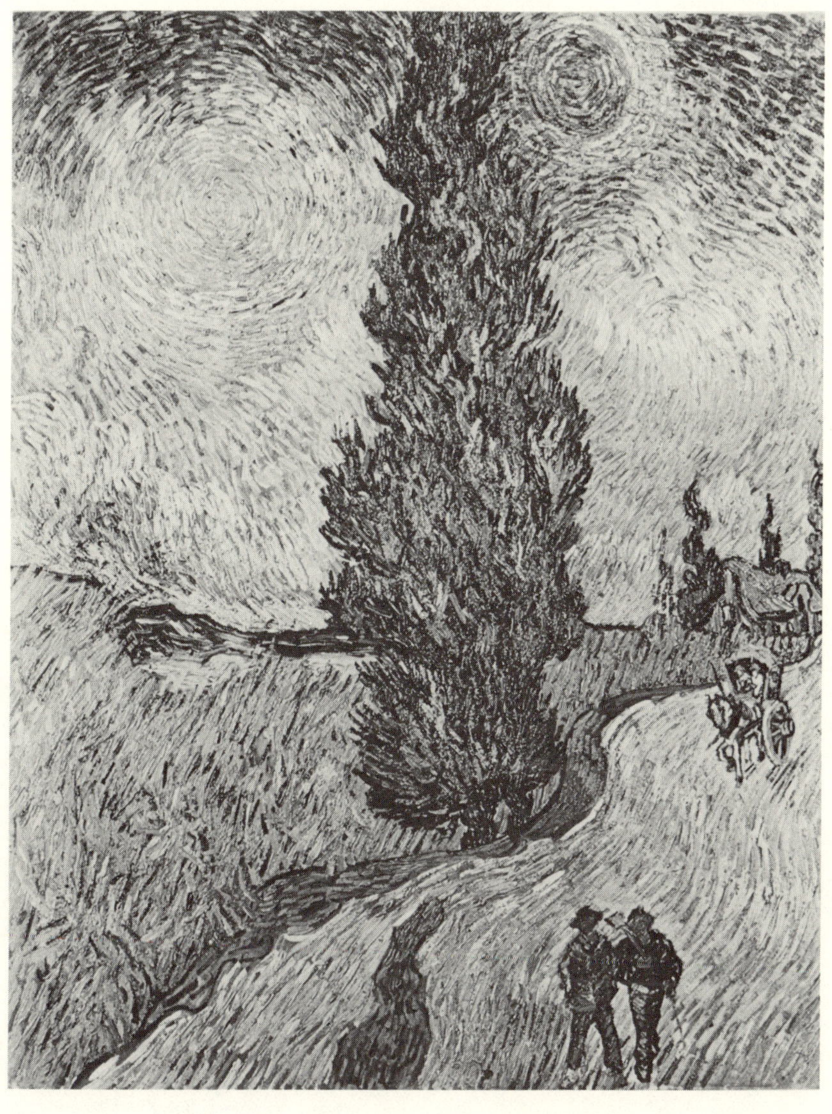

Fig. 13 Vincent van Gogh: *Road with Cypress and Star*, Saint-Rémy (1890). Rijksmuseum Kröller-Müller, Otterlo.

BELOW

Fig. 14 Vincent van Gogh: *The Skull*, Paris (1887).
Rijksmuseum Vincent van Gogh, Amsterdam.

Fig. 15 Vincent van Gogh: *Death's Head Moth*, Saint-Rémy (1889).
Rijksmuseum Vincent van Gogh, Amsterdam.

OPPOSITE

Fig. 16 Hendrick Hondius: *Vanitas: The End Crowns the Work* (1626).
Rijksprentenkabinet, Amsterdam.

Fig. 17 Hercules Segers: *A Cranium*.
Private Collection, New England.

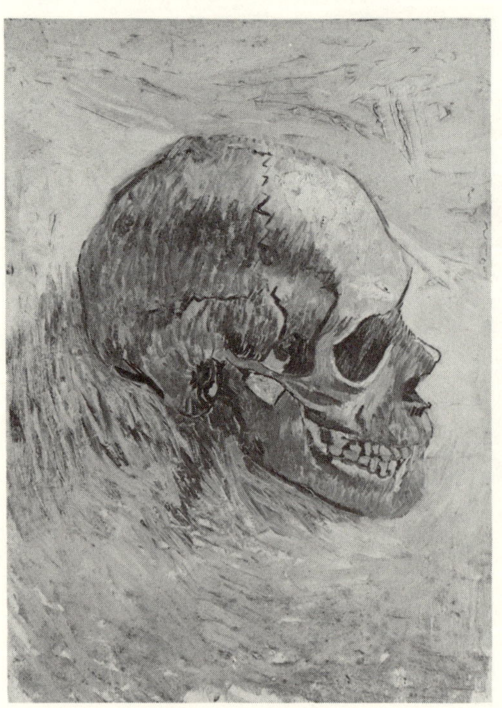

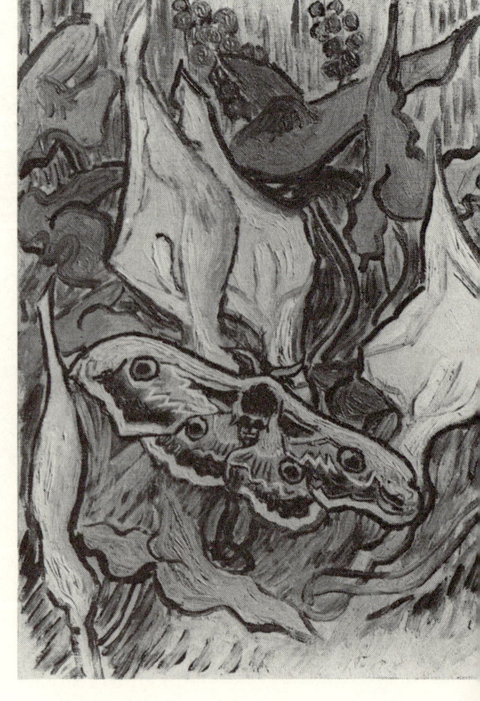

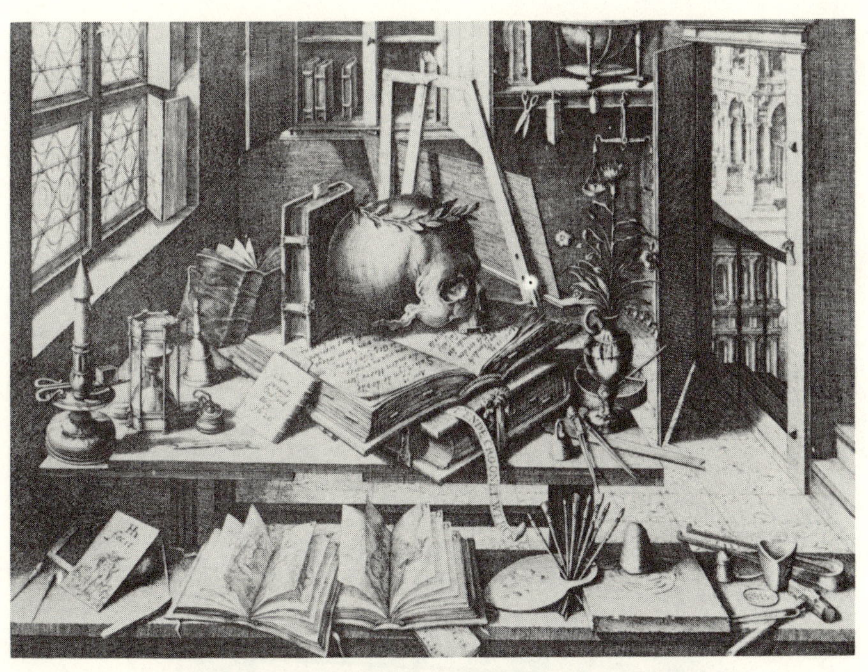

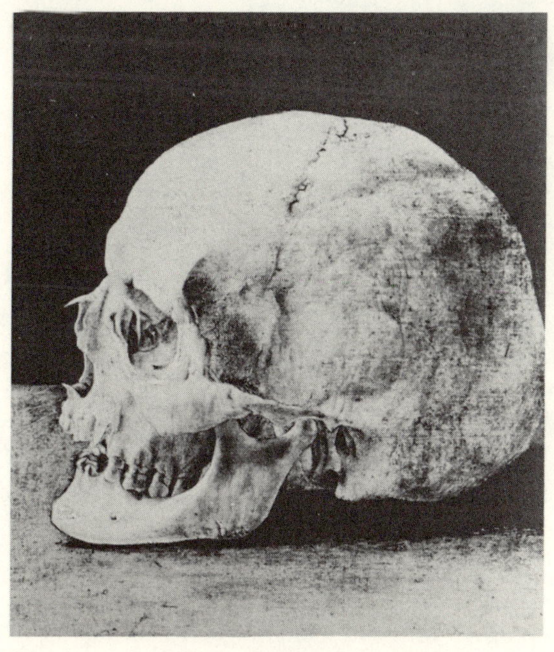

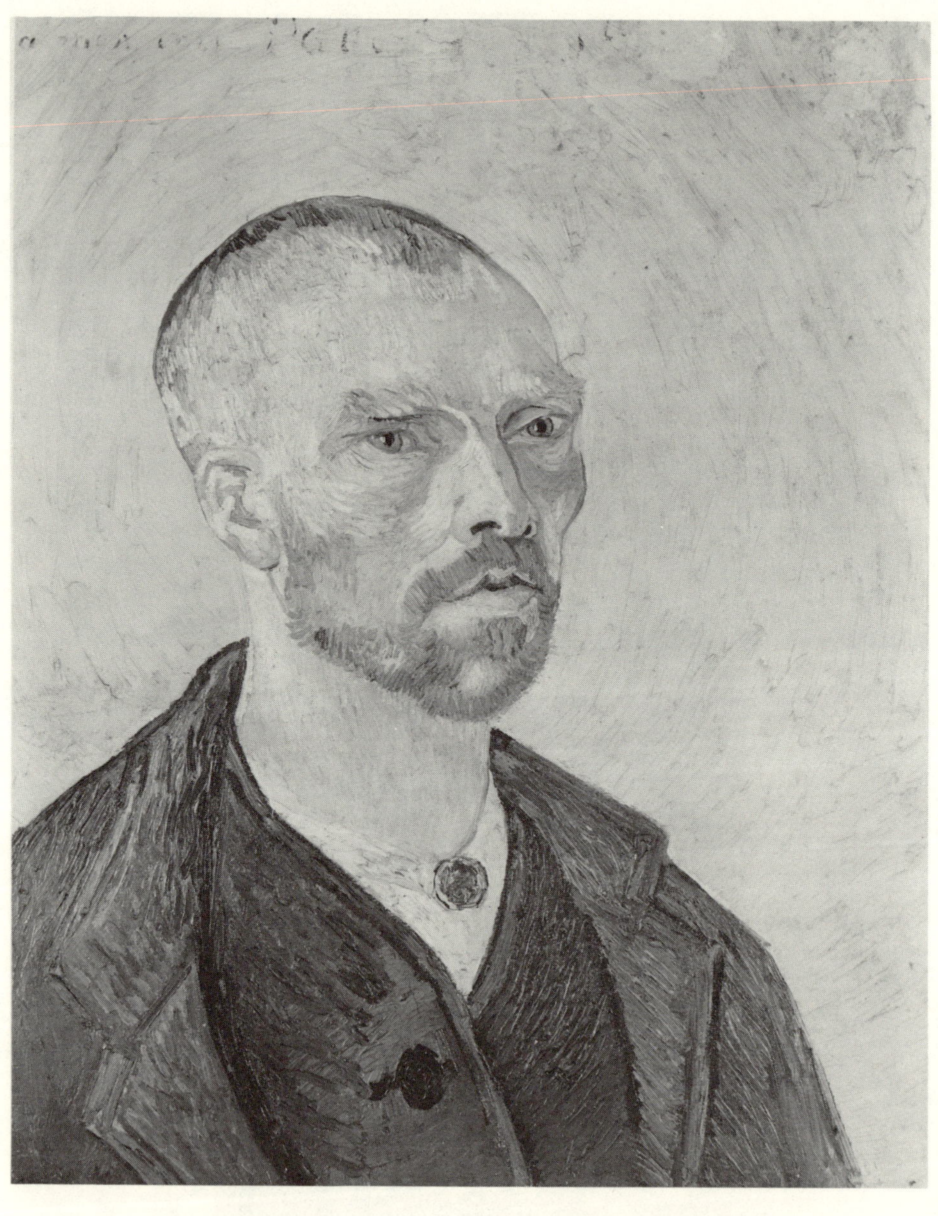

Fig. 18 Vincent van Gogh: *Self Portrait: Dedicated to Paul Gauguin*, Arles (1888). Fogg Art Museum, Cambridge, Massachusetts.

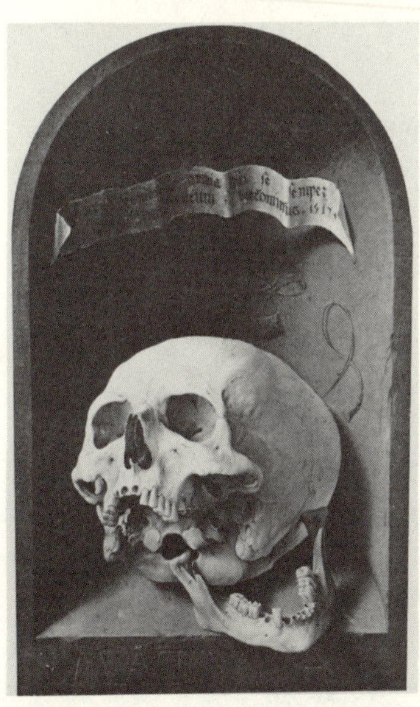

Fig. 19 Jan Gossaert: *Matura*, outside right panel from the *Diptych of Jean Carondelet* (1517).
Louvre, Paris.

Fig. 20 Vincent van Gogh: *Self Portrait before the Easel*, Paris (1888).
Rijksmuseum Vincent van Gogh, Amsterdam.

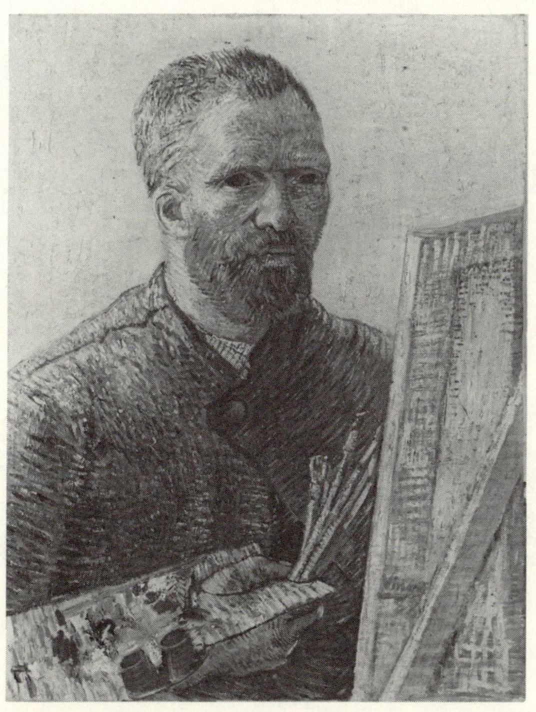

BELOW

Fig. 21 Paul Gauguin: *Van Gogh Painting Sunflowers*, Arles (1888). Rijksmuseum Vincent van Gogh, Amsterdam.

OPPOSITE

Fig. 22 Vincent van Gogh: *La Berceuse: Mme Augustine Roulin*, Arles (1889). The Art Institute of Chicago, Chicago, Illinois.

Fig. 23 Vincent van Gogh: *Still Life: Vase with Fourteen Sunflowers*, Arles (1889). Rijksmuseum Vincent Van Gogh, Amsterdam.

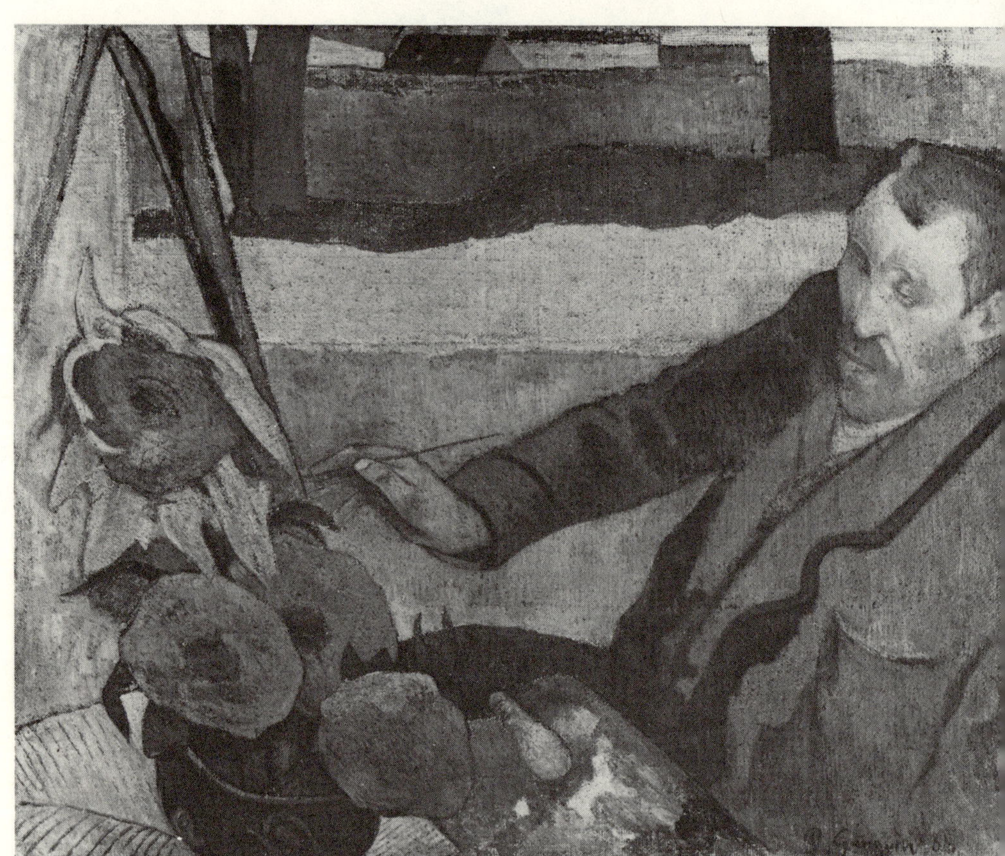

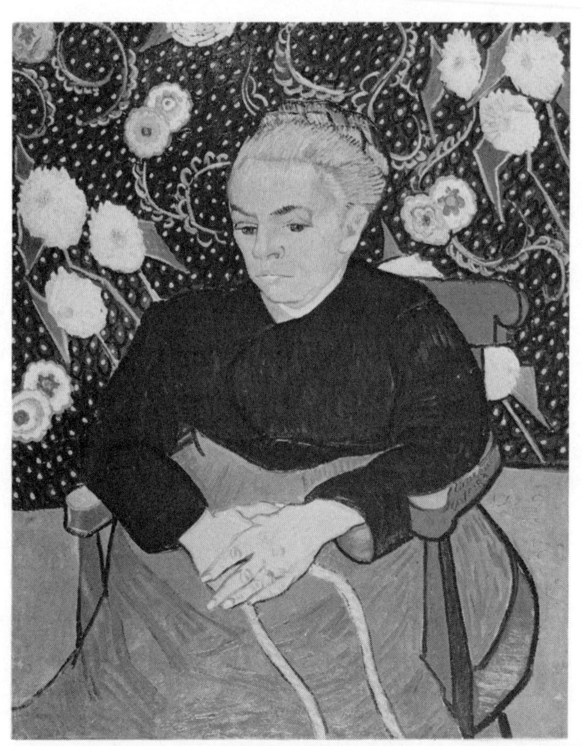

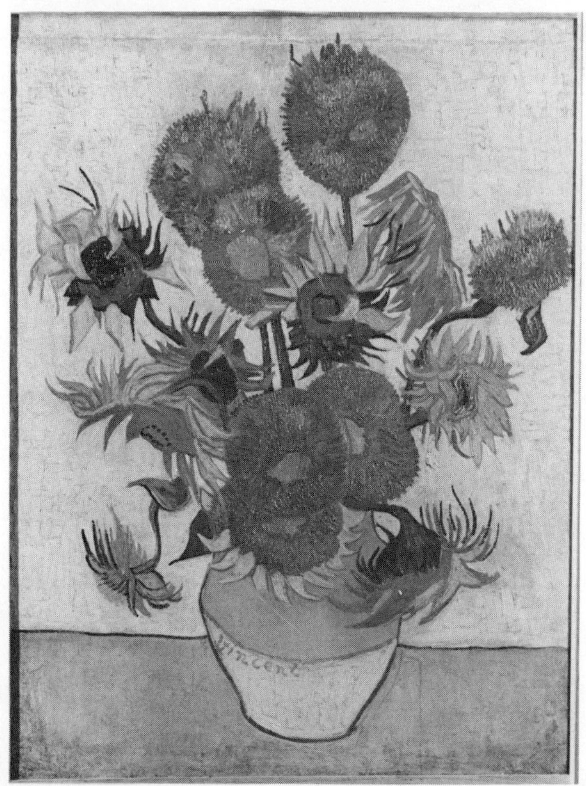
Vincent

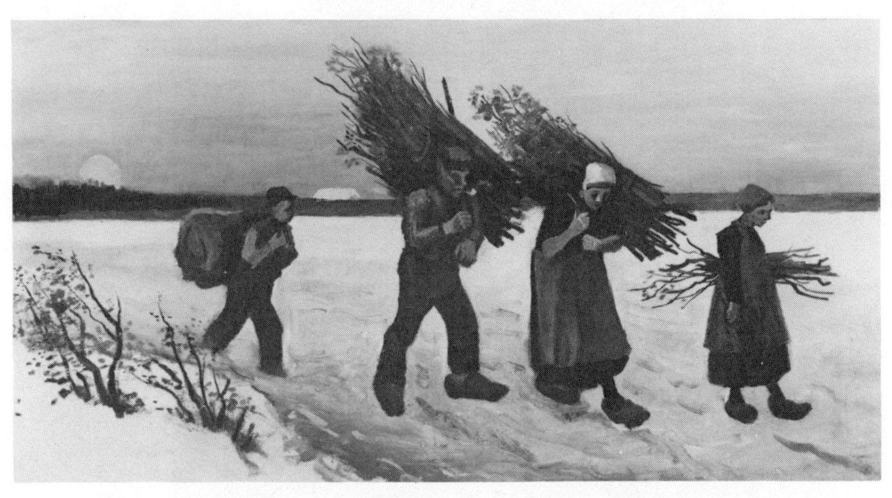

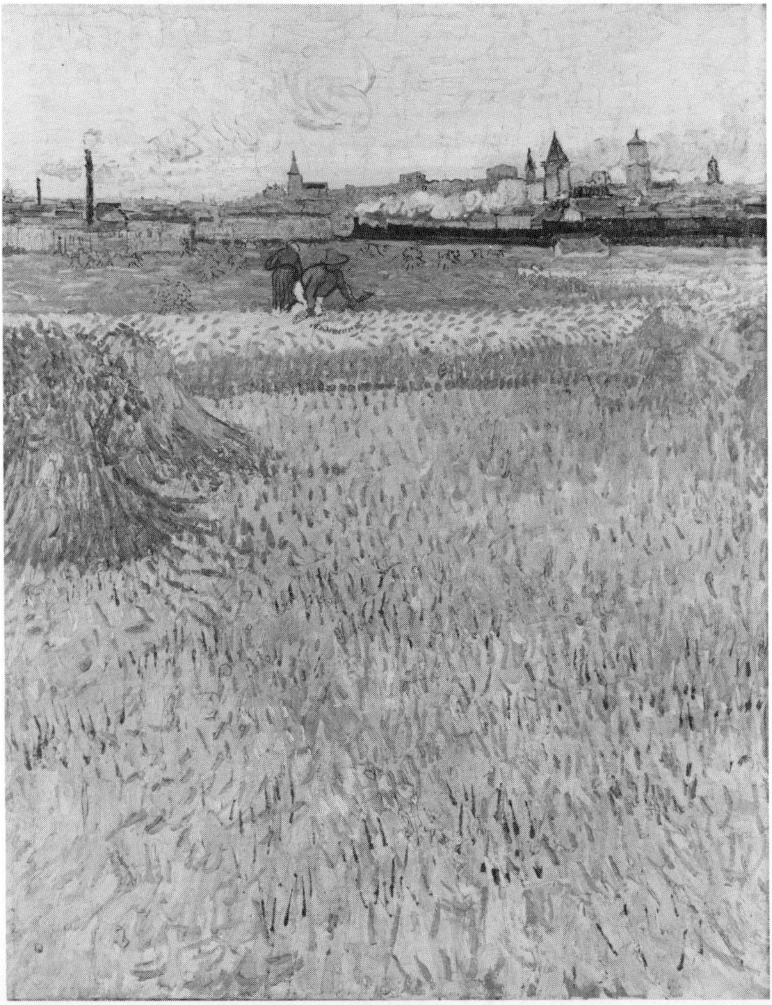

OPPOSITE

Fig. 24 Vincent van Gogh: *Woodgatherers in the Snow*, Nuenen (1884). Private Collection, on loan to the Art Gallery of Ontario.

Fig. 25 Vincent van Gogh: *The Mowers, Arles in the Background*, Arles (1888). Musée Rodin, Paris.

BELOW

Fig. 26 Pieter Breughel the Elder: *The Harvesters* (1565). The Metropolitan Museum of Art, New York.

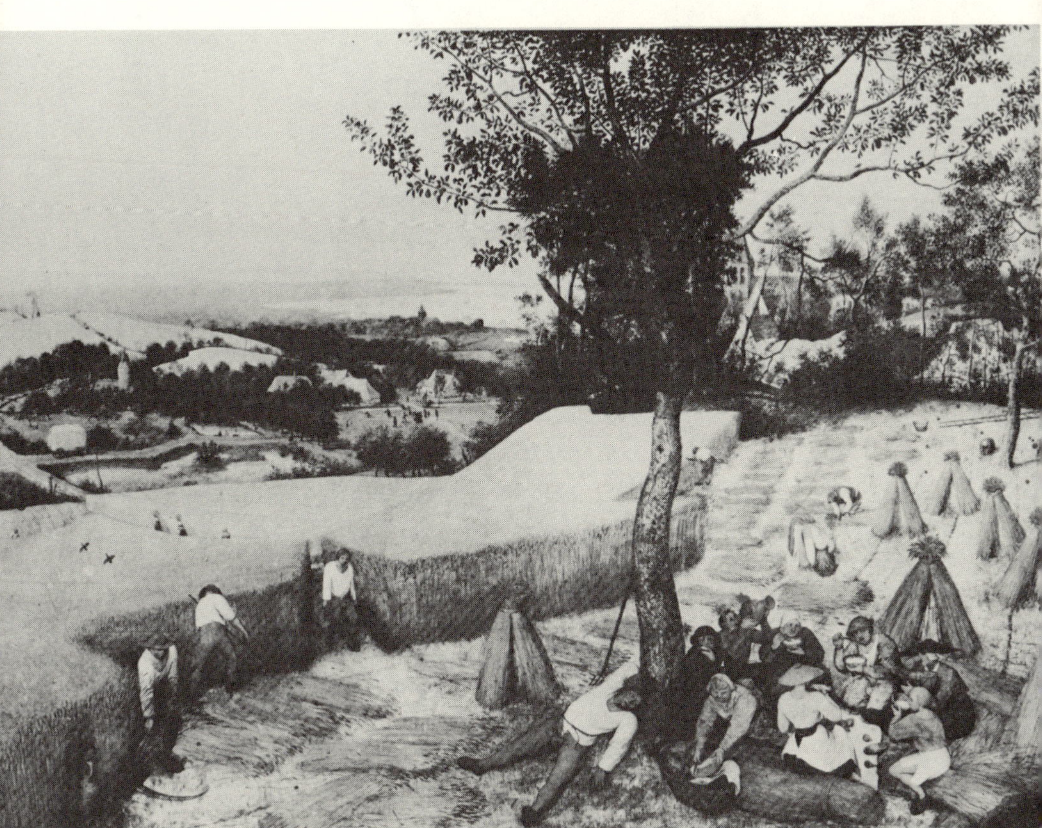

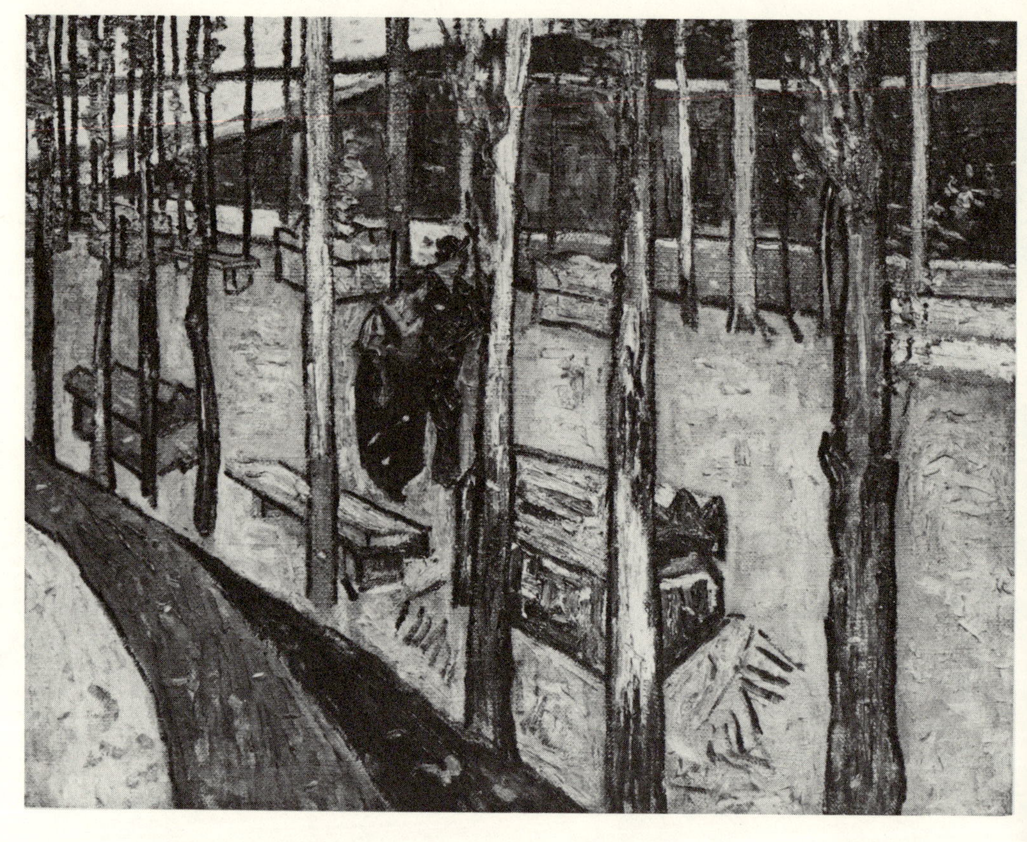

Fig. 27 Vincent van Gogh: *Les Alyscamps*, Arles (1888). Stavros S. Niarchos, Athens.

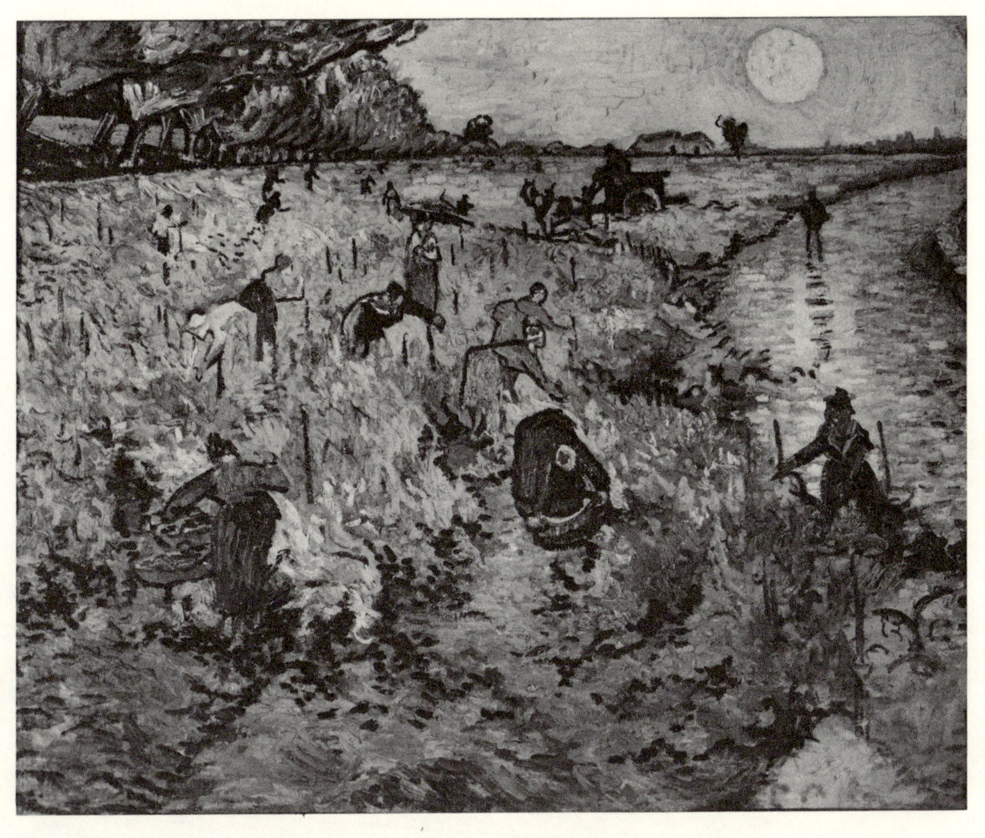

Fig. 28 Vincent van Gogh: *The Red Vineyard: Montmajour*, Arles (1888). Pushkin State Museum of Fine Art, Moscow.

Fig. 29 Paul Gauguin: *Grape Gathering–Human Misery*, Arles (1888). Ordrupgaard Museum, Denmark.

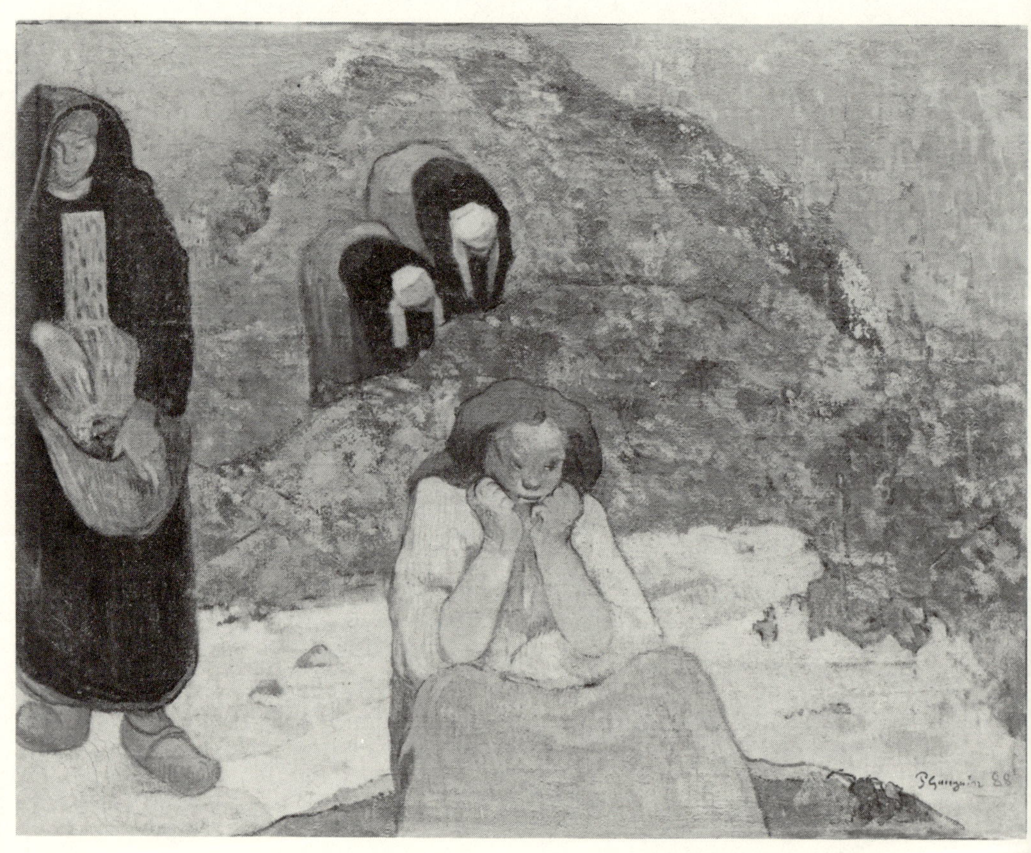

Fig. 30 *Peruvian Mummy*.
Musée de l'Homme, Paris.

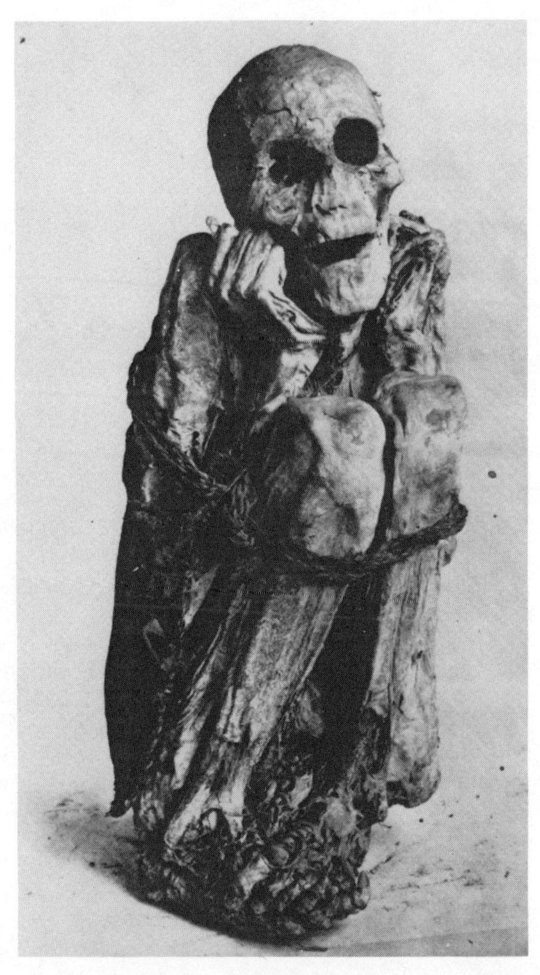

Fig. 31 Vincent van Gogh: *Sorrow: Sien*, The Hague (1882).
Garman-Ryan Collection, London.

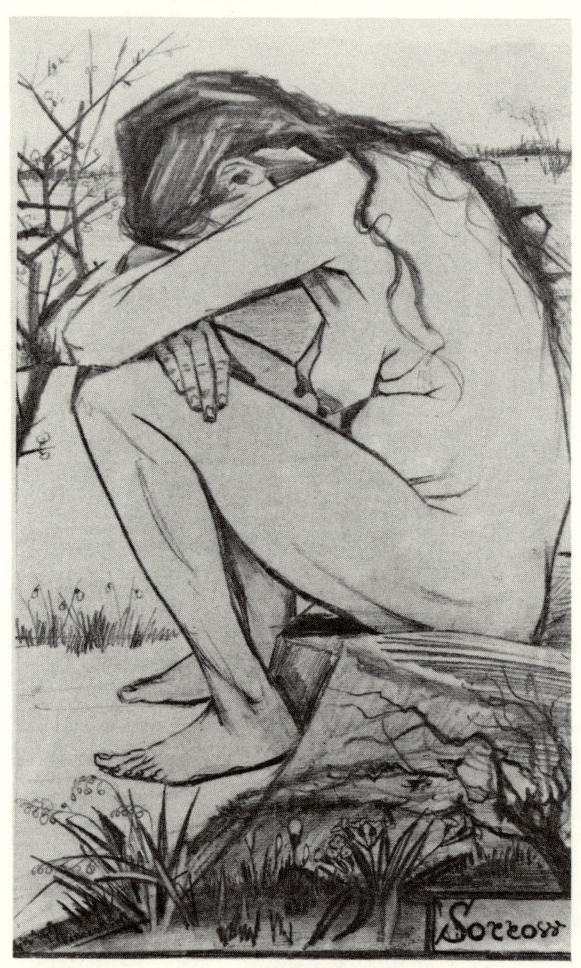

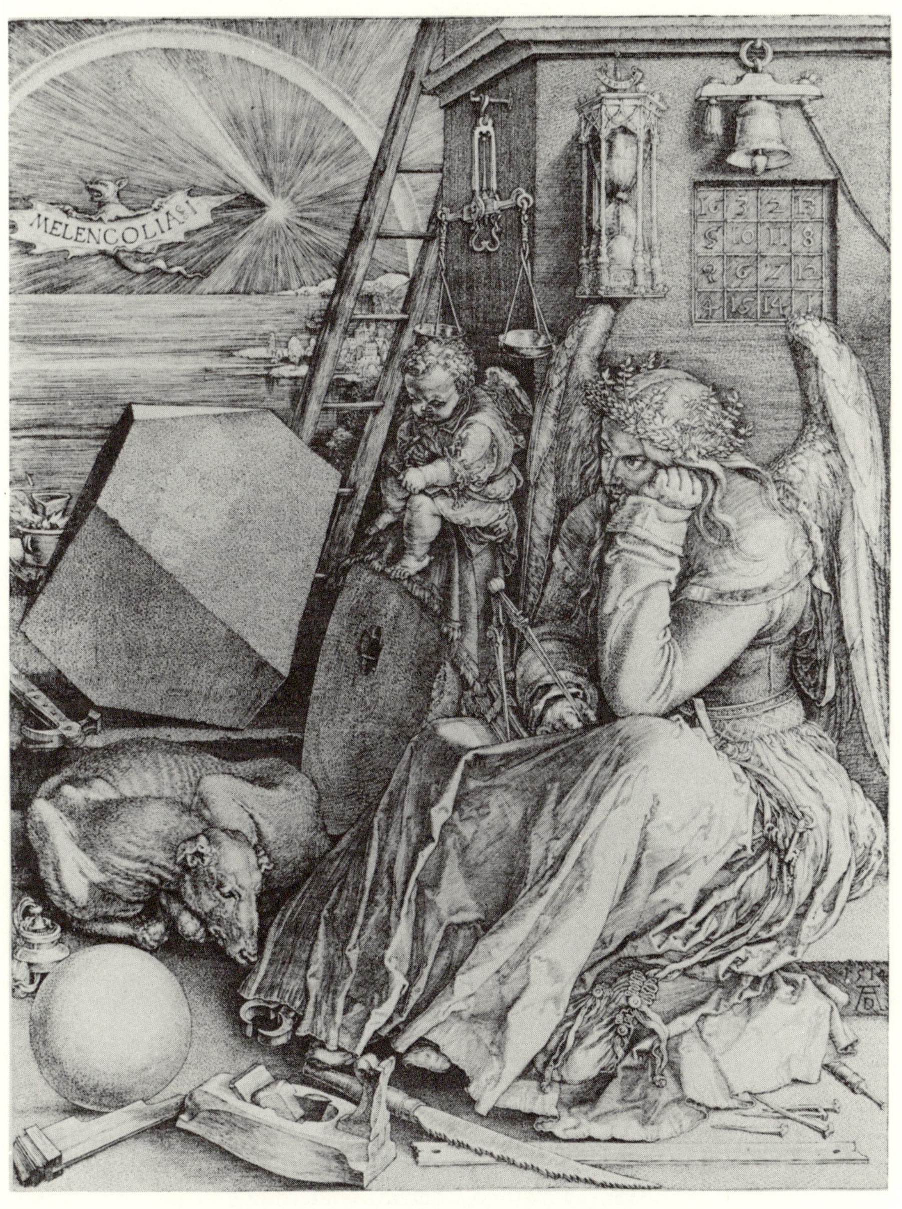

Fig. 32 Albrecht Dürer: *Melancolia I* (1514).
First State, Alverthrope Gallery, Jenkintown, Pennsylvania.

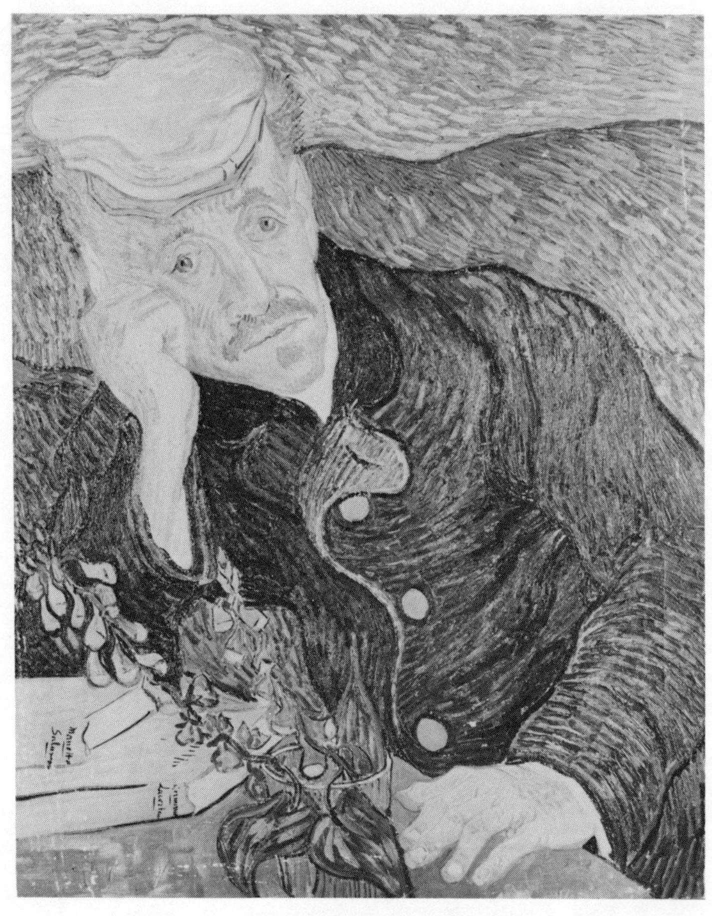

Fig. 33 Vincent van Gogh: *Portrait of Dr. Gachet*, Auvers (1890). S. Kramarsky Trust, New York.

OPPOSITE

Fig. 34 Eugène Delacroix: *Tasso in the Hospital of St. Anna Ferrara* (1839). Oskar Reinhart Foundation, Winterthur.

Fig. 35 Paul Gauguin: *Christ in the Garden of Olives* (1889). Norton Gallery and School of Art, West Palm Beach, Florida.

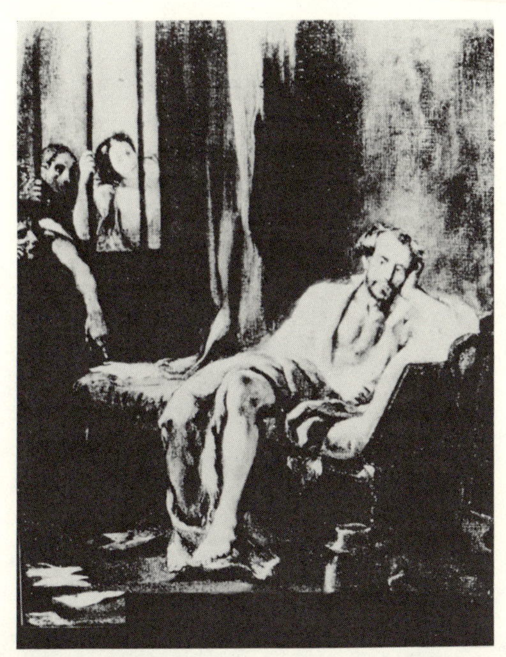

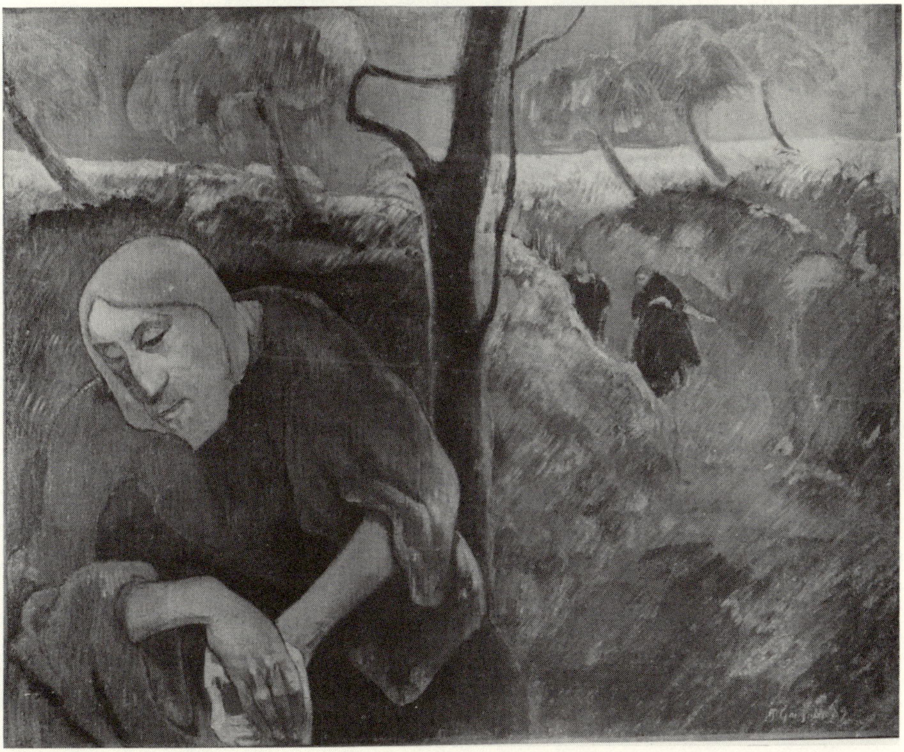

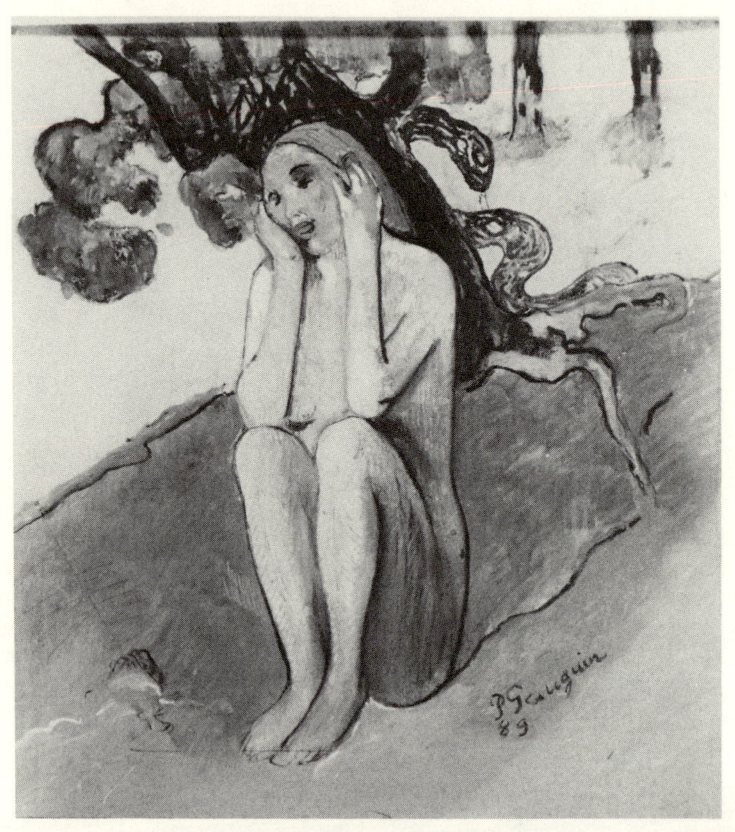
P Gauguin
89

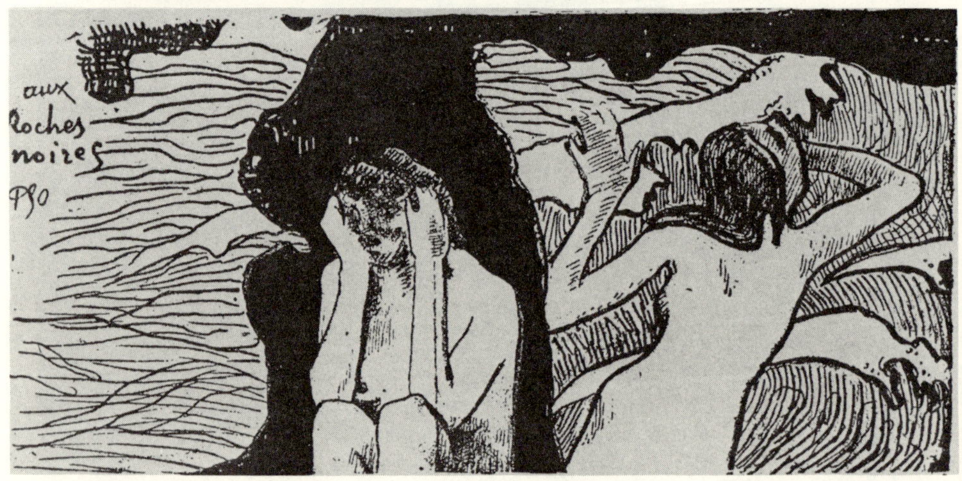
aux
Roches
noires

OPPOSITE

Fig. 36 Paul Gauguin: *Eve* (1889). Marion Koegler McNay Art Institute, San Antonio, Texas.

Fig. 37 Paul Gauguin: *Aux roches noires*, frontispiece of the Volpini exhibition catalogue (1889).

Fig. 38 Paul Gauguin: *Undine: In the Waves* (1889). The Cleveland Museum of Art, Cleveland.

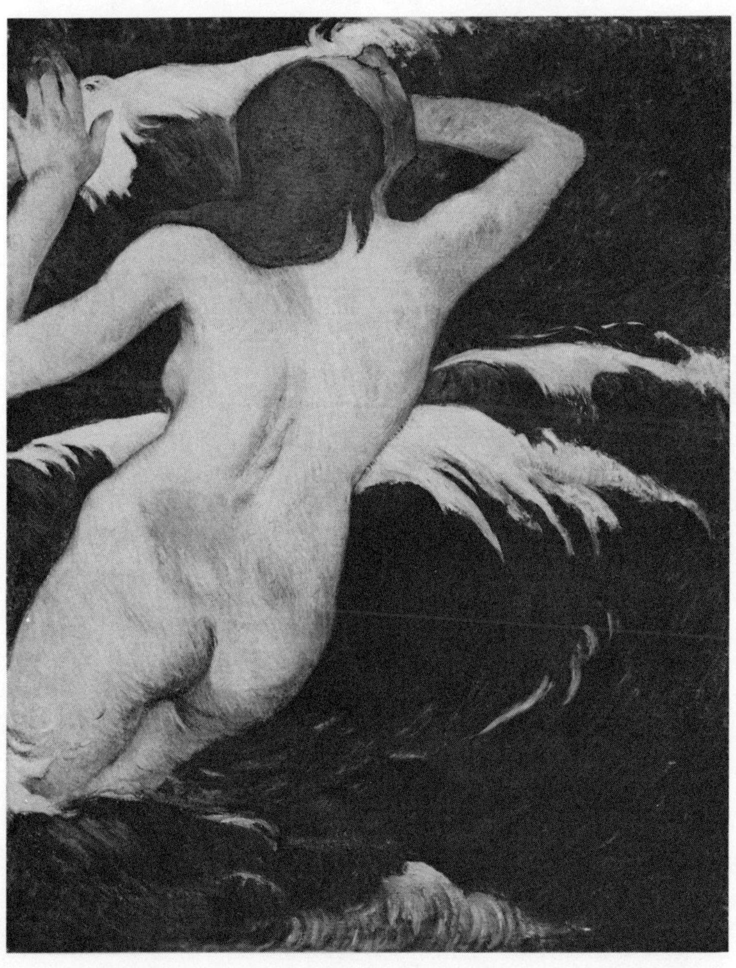

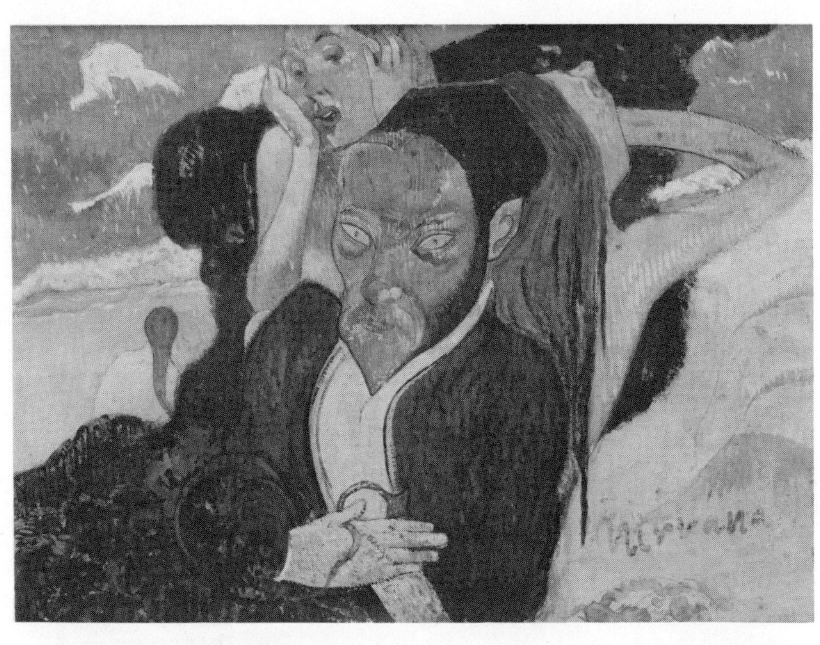

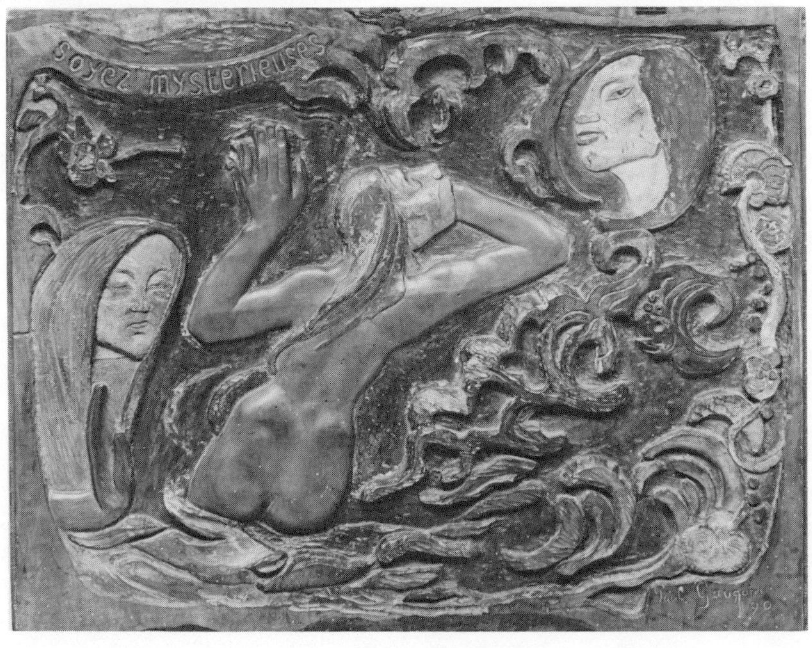
Soyez mystérieuses

OPPOSITE

Fig. 39 Paul Gauguin: *Portrait of Meyer de Haan: Nirvana*, 1889 (1890?).
Wadsworth Atheneum, Hartford, Connecticut.

Fig. 40 Paul Gauguin: *Be Mysterious* (1890).
Musée d'Orsay, Paris.

Fig. 41 Paul Gauguin: *Self Portrait* (1889).
Pushkin State Museum of Fine Arts, Moscow.

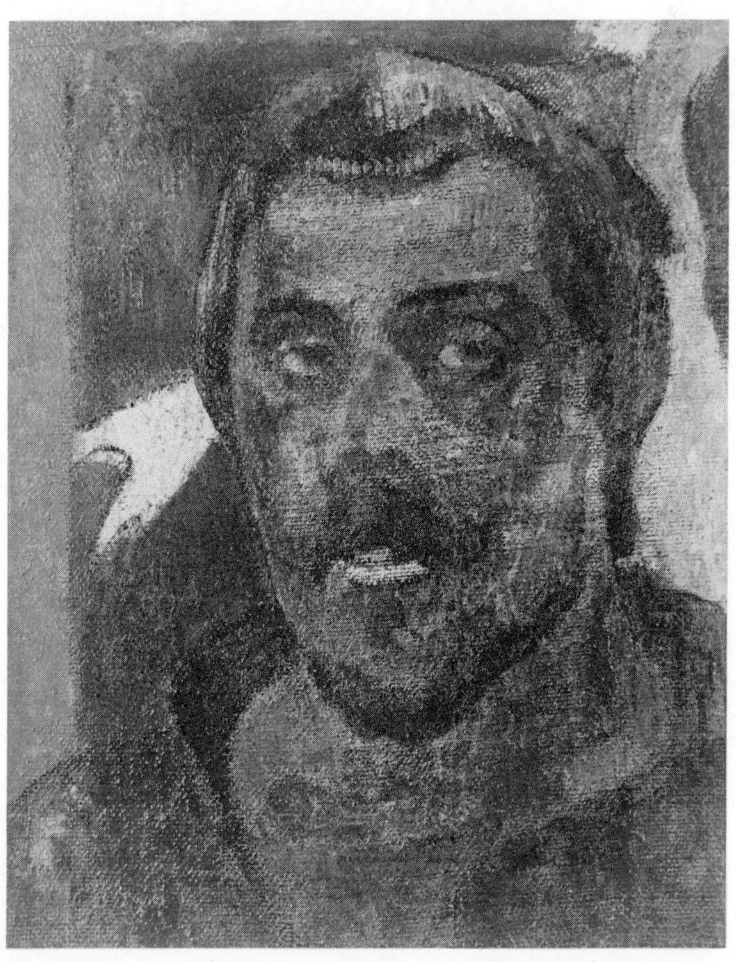

ABRAHAM A. MOLES
Université de Strasbourg

La Fonction des Mythes Dynamiques dans la Construction de l'Imaginaire Social

Au commencement était la *fable*
Et elle y restera toujours.
Valéry

Les "symboles" peuvent être considérés comme dérivés des *signes*, c'est-à-dire des assemblages d'éléments connaissables et répertoriables, mais qui, en même temps, se proposent comme des *fantômes du signifié*, qui retiennent une partie des critères de l'objet qu'ils désignent. De nombreux symboles sont de nature visuelle ou graphique et une grande part du mouvement de la recherche sur l'Imaginaire comme structure causale de l'explication sociale part des symboles graphiques, des monuments et des architectures comme un fait, pour y retrouver des "éléments symboliques," ceux des forces qu'ils contiennent. A cet égard, l'oeuvre de C. Jung sur les Mandalas, celle de Leith sur l'architecture révolutionnaire, fournissent des exemples convaincants.

Nous prendrons ici une attitude inverse à propos des *Mythes*, et nous chercherons plutôt comment les mythes s'insèrent dans le réel pour agir sur lui, pour former, pour "in-former" des effets sociaux. Ce texte voudrait suggérer une *méthode d'analyse des mythes* – en particulier des "mythes dynamiques" – dans leur contribution à l'imaginaire social et au *devenir* de la société technique.

Imaginaire social

Mythes et symboles — Création des mythes comme régularités élémentaires de la pensée

Réalité fonctionnelle Conformité d'une réalité sociale avec un champ de liberté

Action socio-technique

Notre champ de discussion sera ici essentiellement les *formes littéraires* sous tous leurs aspects, en particulier la notion de "texte de base" comme origine et conditionnement des comportements, en tant que générateur d'autres mythes plus précis, plus concrets, plus opérationnels, dans un *cycle mythogénétique* ici esquissé.

Place épistémologique du Mythe comme Contenant d'Imaginaire

Le propos des sciences sociales est donc *de rendre compte* de façon explicative, et si possible prédictive, du fonctionnement des ensembles humains de façon causale. On peut considérer la société comme un agrégat diversement structuré d'éléments: atomes sociaux, molécules, groupements, d'extensions et de niveaux divers, chacun caractérisé par un certain degré d'ordre exprimant la force de la forme à chacun de ces niveaux: rappelons qu'une *forme* est ce qui apparaît à l'esprit comme *n'étant pas* le résultat du hasard, et que toute régularité est une forme élémentaire dont l'existence est responsable d'un certain *degré de variance* dans le fonctionnement de l'assemblage proposé, en d'autres termes, elle fait un apport de causalité.

Jusqu'à présent, la plupart des sciences qui avaient à rendre compte du déterminisme social faisaient usage d'un certain mode de la rationalité: celle des "buts" poursuivis par les "êtres" ou groupements, cherchant à savoir comment les intérêts particuliers bien entendus se confondent dans l'intérêt général (la Main Invisible du Marché économique, la Volonté de Puissance, l'Intérêt des groupes à se concentrer ou à se disperser, etc.). Nous poursuivons en psychologie sociale l'analyse de ces formes dans les concepts de classes sociales, de pyramide de Pareto, d'organisation des entreprises et de l'Etat. Nous déduisons de chaque facteur (Trieb) qui s'attache à chacun des éléments de l'agrégat, des vecteurs d'attraction ou de répulsion, de conquête, d'acceptabilité, etc. dont l'ensemble veut rendre compte des formes sociales. Ainsi par exemple, pour étudier la Cité intellectuelle ou scientifique, nous discernons les motivations de ceux qui en font partie:

appétit de vérité
volonté de sécurité sociale

volonté de puissance
recherche de la conformité dans l'écart

comme les moteurs du mouvement de cet état intellectuel à des rationalités de stratégie croyance au progrès, d'invention, de créativité, d'organisation, etc.

En fait, il apparaît dans l'étude de ces sous-sociétés comme éléments de l'agrégat social que les précédentes séries de facteurs *ne suffisent pas* à rendre compte de la totalité des formes qui émergent sous nos yeux. Il y a ce que l'épistémologue appellerait un *résidu de variance* qu'ils n'expliquent pas. En d'autres termes, les facteurs de causalité sous-jacente dont:

le désir de vérité
la volonté de conformité
la volonté de puissance
la sécrétion d'ordres
etc.

ne rendent pas compte intégralement des variabilités constatées dans les comportements. Il y a d'autres formes régulières et observables qui prennent en compte la variance d'une société en plus des précédentes. Nous les appellerons l'"Imaginaire social" et nous essaierons ici d'en décrire quelques-unes. Ce sont donc des "régularités de la démarche de l'esprit" (Valéry) qui, elles aussi, régissent le devenir mais outrepassent, ou, quelquefois, sous-tendent, la raison "rationnelle" qui sert souvent de masque avouable à l'esprit "pur," c'est-à-dire rationnel. En fait, la rationalité comportementale s'applique au mieux à ce qu'on peut appeler l'ordre à courte distance du développement de la pensée, l'ordre proche n'est qu'une sub-structure d'un ordre lointain de comportement de l'esprit que nous voudrions élucider.

Résumons notre hypothèse: pour rendre compte de l'ordre social il faut certes d'abord prendre en compte le produit des intérêts diversifiés aux divers niveaux de groupement des individus, depuis l'atome social, la molécule du groupe de productivité créatrice, jusqu'aux grandes structures qu'on appelle les institutions, pourvues d'un but. Mais il faut aussi analyser des régularités plus profondes du mouvement de l'esprit, moins explicites et souvent déclarées a priori nulles et non avenues, par notre frénésie rationalisante, sous prétexte qu'elles sont trop labiles, trop fluctuantes, et trop vagues. Ce sont là des *phénomènes imprécis par nature* que l'explication scientifique du devenir social au sens plein du terme ne peut se permettre de rejeter. Nous avons à faire place non plus à une *mythologie* mais à une *mythogenèse.*

Mécanismes de l'Imaginaire comme facteur de la vie quotidienne: les Micromythes entre la micropsychologie et la psychanalyse

Ce fut certes le grand combat de la psychanalyse, il y a maintenant un demi-siècle d'essayer de prendre en compte l'irrationnel profond de l'esprit humain, soit dans son aspect des tendances *individuelles* profondes, comme l'on fait les psychologues freudiens, soit dans son aspect de *systèmes collectifs* comme l'a amorcé Carl Jung. Les combats véhéments contre les "behavioristes," voulant ramener à une "arithmétique des plaisirs et des peines" l'ensemble des comportements économiques et sociaux en classant dans l'écume de l'irrationnel provisoire tous les résidus de tendances qui, colorés par des religions parsemaient le comportement humain, sont désormais bien passés. Par leurs analyses soignées de l'image de l'univers et des tables de valeurs et des facteurs de comportement (tendances) incorporés à l'être, des psychosociologues comme Kurt Lewin et Maslow ont contribué très substantiellement à élargir une pensée behavioriste de la causalité comportementale, à enrichir de subtilités le conditionnement, à jeter le pont entre ces deux "pôles d'explication" de l'être: celui de *l'opérateur humain*, tel que nous le propose une systémique, et celui des *motivations subtiles* et profondément *irrationnelles* (en apparence) que la micropsychologie cherche à délabyrinther.

Sous cet angle la tâche du chercheur reste dans le domaine de la rationalité, elle veut, encore, ramener à des causes connaissables et prédictives les avatars comportementaux de l'être, mais pour cela elle prend désormais en compte les *pulsions irrationnelles* comme des "causes," subjectives mais objectivables, tout autant que les conditions de l'environnement immédiatement observable, seul cadre de connaissance que se permettaient les pères fondateurs du comportementalisme.

Les Sciences Sociales contemporaines admettent donc désormais explicitement que l'"analyse rationnelle" des comportements qui consiste à construire une causalité explicative basée sur des axiomes simples du type:

	"Stimulus	+ individu : réaction,"
	"bénéfices	> coûts,
ou, si l'on veut:	"avantages	> inconvénients,"

ne *suffit pas à rendre compte de la variété* des comportements sociaux et individuels observés dans la vie quotidienne.

La fonction du psychologue apparaît alors être celle d'étudier rationnellement l'irrationalité de l'homme, irrationalité qui, pour le micro-psychologue, est beaucoup plus une apparence de "l'observation lointaine" qui se résoud de près dans un faisceau de micro-motivations personnalisées, connaissables sinon connues. Comme le remarque Kenneth Boulding: "On ne peut taxer d'irrationalité celui qui agit en fonction de causes qu'il croit être vraies" – même si l'observateur scientifique extérieur les voit, lui, comme fausses. Toute théorie des actes reposera nécessairement sur l'Image du Monde dans la conscience, c'est peut-être l'absence de prise en charge de cette image qui fut la grande erreur méthodologique d'un behaviorisme trop extérieur à l'homme, c'est celle-ci que le micro-psychologue peut corriger.

Pour rendre compte donc de façon aussi prédictive que possible des actions humaines, nous avons à faire la part, d'un côté, certes de facteurs environnementaux, mais, de l'autre, aussi bien d'une *fonction de l'imaginaire* à contenu très largement social qui se combine d'une manière qui n'est pas toujours rigoureusement élucidée, avec les stimuli de l'environnement, l'idée de profit ou l'idée de bien-être, l'idée d'homéostasie et toute la "pyramide des valeurs" élucidée par Maslow.

Ce fut l'intuition de Kurt Lewin que le champ de notre conscience se présente comme un champ de valeurs, diversement attractives ou colorées, dont les unes sont des objets concrets et immédiatement désirables, les autres, des objets vagues, des respects, des amours ou des craintes, des forces de tradition qui se traduisent dans des habitudes ou des rites, et qui sont bel et bien là, présents, d'une subjectivité parfaitement objectivable, comme outils d'explication du comportement. Des mouvements variés des sciences humaines (psycho- ou socio-analyse) cherchent désormais à expliciter, à rendre compte, à cataloguer, tous ces aspects de l'imaginaire social aux contours quelquefois flous, ce qui ne nuit pas à leur *prégnance*, disons, plus simplement, à leur impact sur la causalité. Anthropologues et ethnologues, devant l'évanouissement de ces populations primitives et lointaines dont ils faisaient leur nourriture, se reconvertissent en spécialistes de l'imaginaire social; tout en restant de très lointains successeurs des idées de Carl Jung, d'Eric Fromm, ils se situent désormais dans la ligne d'une *anthropologie de la vie quotidienne*, d'une ethnologie de la société où nous vivons: le Centre de Recherche de l'Imaginaire de notre docte Sorbonne ou le Centre de Civilisation du xxe Siècle en seraient des exemples.

Ce qui caractérise épistémologiquement tout l'univers de l'Imaginaire, et qui a freiné son étude au siècle positiviste, c'est la texture même de ce qu'on peut bien appeler la pensée imaginaire, dont les processus, les chaînes de raisonnement, ce qu'on peut appeler les mécanismes déductifs n'ont en aucune façon cette rigueur de la logique formelle et se rattachent bien plus à l'infralogique sous-jacente au langage, aux régularités du logos, à des *concepts imprécis* et mal définis (Moles et Zadeh), à une causalité mentale floue, qui étaient assez peu du goût d'une science imprégnée par la Mystique de la Raison Absolue.

Il n'y a pas de "raison" absolue, il y a "des raisons" relatives, et il y a bien des façons de *lier* un item de discours à un autre: publicitaires, propagandistes et politiques nous le démontrent à loisir et à satiété. Ce sont bien pourtant parmi les grands motivateurs, tout autant que les "préposés aux choses vagues" (Valéry): les artistes ès-religion, les fabricants de morale, en tout cas d'éthiques, de coutumes et d'habitudes, que se concrétise le rôle de l'Imaginaire dans la conduite de la société.

La prégnance de l'imaginaire n'est pas liée à ce que la Science appelle son caractère déductif: *ce qui est fort n'est pas ce qui se démontre, mais ce qui se suggère, ce qui se sent*, ce qui se voit. C'est bien précisément la difficulté d'une anthropologie de la société dans laquelle nous vivons: trop familière, trop proche, la dissociation de l'observateur et de l'observé y est difficile, car l'une des méthodes optimales de la créativité en ce domaine est ce que nous avons appelé ailleurs "l'oeil neuf," le facteur d'étrangeté, la première impression, la récupération difficile de la naïveté, dont Lévi-Strauss dans un texte de "Tristes Tropiques" avait marqué au passage l'importance. Le changement d'environnement, le dépaysement du voyageur, la remise en marche de la machine d'action de l'être dans des conditions, des réglementations, des champs de valeurs différents, le contraint à prendre ceux-ci en compte, à les *faire venir* à la conscience explicite: "Die Sache zu Wort kommen lassen" comme le dit Heidegger. L'un des outils de cette intelligibilité, ce sont ces formes de l'inconscient appelées Mythes, et plus particulièrement "Mythes Dynamiques."

Définition des mythes dynamiques

Rappelons une remarque de Paul Valéry: "Un mythe, c'est le nom de tout ce qui n'existe et ne subsiste qu'ayant *la parole* pour cause. Il n'est de discours si obscur, de racontars si bizarres, de propos si incohérents, à quoi nous ne puissions donner un sens. Il y a toujours une supposition qui donne un sens au langage le plus étrange."

Pour définir les *mythes dynamiques* à proprement parler, nous dirons que ce sont ceux des mythes dont le ressort, est de *briser une loi naturelle classique*, en commençant bien sûr par les lois de la "Physis," de la Nature, les plus connues, telles qu'elles sont perçues dans l'environnement plus ou moins *quotidien* de l'homme et de la cité.

Reprenons encore Paul Valéry: "L'homme est incessamment et nécessairement opposé à ce qui est, par le souci de ce qui n'est pas, et il enfante, laborieusement ou bien par génie, ce qu'il faut pour donner à ses rêves la puissance et la précision même de la réalité et, d'autre part, pour imposer à cette réalité des altérations croissantes qui la rapproche de ses rêves."

Les autres êtres vivants ne sont mus et transformés que par des variations extérieures. Ils s'adaptent, c'est-à-dire qu'ils se déforment afin de conserver les caractères essentiels de leur existence, et ils se mettent ainsi en équilibre avec l'état de leur milieu. Ils n'ont point coutume de rompre spontanément cet équilibre, de quitter par exemple sans motif, sans une pression ou sans une nécessité extérieure, le climat auquel ils se sont accommodés. Ils recherchent leur bien aveuglément mais ne sentent pas *l'aiguillon de ce mieux, qui est l'ennemi du bien et qui nous engage à affronter le pire*. L'homme contient en soi-même de quoi rompre l'équilibre qu'il soutenait avec son milieu. Il contient ce qu'il faut pour *se mécontenter de ce qui le contentait*.

Quels rêves a fait l'homme et parmi ces rêves quels sont ceux qui sont rentrés dans le réel? Il y a chez les Grecs des héros qui se construisent des appareils volants, d'autres savent apprivoiser les fauves. Leur parole miraculeuse déplace les montagnes, fait se mouvoir les blocs, opère des constructions de temples par une sorte de télé-mécanique merveilleuse. Agir à distance, faire de l'or, transmuter les métaux, vaincre la mort, prédire l'avenir, se déplacer dans les milieux interdits à notre espèce, parler, voir, entendre d'un bout du monde à l'autre, aller visiter les astres, réaliser le mouvement perpétuel, *nous avons fait tant de rêves que la liste en serait infinie*. Mais l'ensemble de ces rêves forme *un étrange programme*, dont la poursuite est liée à l'histoire même de l'humanité.

Telle est donc la définition des mythes dynamiques: facteurs des résidus de variance expliquant le mouvement de la recherche scientifique dans son ensemble, par une socio-analyse du ghetto scientifique comme étant le témoin d'une humanité plus générale à laquelle il est lié et il participe, mythes caractérisés par le fait qu'ils basent leur action sur la *transgression d'une Loi* de la Nature. Ils représentent d'autre part cette idée d'une *volonté d'opposition, volonté du "contre,"* traduite de façon obscure, vague mais prégnante, comme un *mouvement permanent de l'Imaginaire Social.*

Vers un dictionnaire de mythes dynamiques

Suggérons tout d'abord une liste de mythes dynamiques pour éclaircir quelques aspects de la définition ouverte que nous en avons donnés:

- Le *mythe d'Icare*: échapper à la pesanteur, l'aviation, le vol hors de la Terre.
- Le *mythe de Prométhée*, de l'énergie artificielle et de la thermo-fusion.
- Le *mythe du voyeur invisible*, de Gygès, un mythe de la photographie.
- Le *mythe de l'homme ubiquitaire*, qui perce sous la notion de mass media et de bureau éclaté.
- Le *mythe de Babel*, de la traduction universelle (ils n'avaient qu'une seule langue ...), la machine à traduire.
- Le *mythe de la télé-présence*: recréer son image et son action de façon indépendante de la distance. Il est différent du mythe de l'ubiquité-genèse.
- Le *mythe de la pierre philosophale*: le pouvoir de changer les espèces de la matière (la chimie nucléaire et l'alchimie relèvent largement de celui-ci).
- Le *mythe de l'élixir de longue vie*, de la jeunesse éternelle dans la plénitude de la vie, qui est très largement illustré dans le Faust.
- Le *mythe de la quête du Graal*: parvenir au secret mystique, au terme d'une *péripétie*, et par conséquent au secret de l'univers (pensée due à la théorie du champ unitaire d'Einstein).
- Le *mythe de Tristan et Yseult*: mythe de l'aphrodisiaque personnalisé.
- Le *mythe de l'androgyne*, de l'unisexe et de ses possibilités.
- Le *mythe de la recréation à l'identique*: la conformité au modèle, la fabrication de séries, la haute fidélité sonore, la photographie en couleur et en relief qui alimente le *Musée imaginaire* proposé par Malraux.
- Le *mythe de la cristallisation* du monde: fixer matériellement un instant du devenir, la mise en boîte généralisée du monde (Kodak), the freezing machine de Milgram.
- Le *mythe du Golem*, sur la synthèse de l'être artificiel, l'esclave mécanique, le robot, Frankenstein, l'automate. Nous le commenterons plus loin au titre d'exemple.
- Le *mythe du pays perdu, de l'Atlantide*. (The lost world.)
- Le *mythe de la génération artificielle*.
- Le *mythe du labyrinthe*: un secret ouvert établi dans l'espace.
- Le *mythe faustien* et prométhéen de l'homme qui en réalisant change le monde, celui des grands travaux.
- Le *mythe du magasin universel*.

- Le *mythe de l'usine sans ouvriers*: affranchir la production des sujétions humaines de l'être humain comme espèce inférieure et provisoire de la production.
- Le *mythe du désert*: la quête d'un espace illimité, soustrait au contrôle social.
- Le *mythe de Don Quichotte*, le chevalier social qui transpose la mise au service d'un idéal quand celui-ci a perdu sa force sociale.
- Le *mythe de Don Juan*: l'amour éternellement renouvelé dans son objet.
- Le *mythe de Rockefeller*: passer par ses efforts de l'état de cireur de bottes à celui de Maître du monde.
- Le *mythe du produit pur*: qui cherche à atteindre un absolu de pureté et qui a régné sur une grande part de la chimie.

On pourrait faire de ce vaste répertoire une description statistique et noter la contribution des différents âges de la civilisation et des différents creux de celle-ci. On y remarquera le faible apport de l'occident. Devant cette multiplicité des aspects mythiques de la réalité, se pose immédiatement un problème méthodologique: comment construire un *répertoire* et comment le classer d'une façon exploitable pour y faire apparaître d'une part une mythographie des *mythèmes* (éléments d'impossibles supposés possibles) ou *mythogenèse*.

Les bases d'une mythographie; un exemple: le Golem

Une *mythographie* (Brockhaus) se traduira dans une série de fiches caractéristiques qui mentionnera le problème du *lieu d'enracinement* du mythe sous sa forme achevée, au sens d'explosion de celui-ci, la *langue préférentielle*; ainsi pour saisir le mythe de l'être artificiel exprimé dans "Golem," il faut savoir l'Allemand, le Yiddish, et un peu d'Hébreu, ne serait-ce que pour se familiariser avec un certain type de connotations, d'environnement historique et culturel. Chaque fiche conduit à établir la *forme canonique* d'un récit qui veut rendre compte de *l'essentiel* des aspects d'un mythe donné et les accompagner ensuite de leurs variantes.

Développons ceci sur un exemple que nous avons eu à approfondir, le Mythe du Golem.

A quatre heures du matin, le deuxième jour du mois d'Adar 1580, le Maharal et ses deux assistants vinrent sur les rives de la Moldau et modelèrent avec l'argile de la berge la forme d'un homme. L'un des deux assistants encercla la figure sept fois, de gauche à droite, le Maharal fit alors une incantation, et le Golem se mit à briller comme du feu. Alors l'autre assistant encercla sept fois la figure de droite à gauche, en prononçant d'autres incantations. Le feu du Golem s'éteignit et une vapeur s'éleva de son corps. Ils virent alors que des cheveux avaient poussé sur sa tête et que des ongles étaient apparus à ses doigts. Le Maharal lui-même encercla alors le Golem sept fois, et ils récitèrent ensemble le passage de la Genèse II-7: "et il souffla dans ses narines le souffle de la vie et l'homme devint un être vivant." Le Golem ouvrit alors les yeux et regarda les trois hommes. Puis il se dressa, ils le vêtirent comme un aide du Rabbi. [Remarquons que les quatre éléments des présocratiques: Terre, Eau, Feu, Air, sont ici présents.]

Ce Golem ne pouvait parler car seul Dieu peut donner le pouvoir de la parole. Le Golem servit pendant trente ans le Rabbi pour l'administration de la communauté juive de Prague, lui épargnant les travaux matériels et lui laissant plus de temps pour l'étude. Ce Golem avait un faciès vaguement mongolique, d'une force prodigieuse, il circulait dans le Ghetto et ses environs aux heures où les Juifs devaient en sortir, inspirant le respect et l'effroi à la population de la cité hostile qui l'environnait.

Au bout de trente ans, la paix s'était rétablie dans la communauté juive de Prague, et le Maharal jugea que le Golem était devenu inutile. Il monta avec deux assistants dans le grenier de l'Altneuschul qui existe encore et il fit venir le Golem, le fit s'étendre sur le sol, et le Maharal prononça sept incantations pour l'endormir, puis reprit en sens inverse l'ensemble des manoeuvres qu'il avait fait pour animer le Golem. Au bout de l'ensemble des opérations, ce Golem était redevenu une glaise, dont la forme était conservée: on la recouvrit d'un châle de prières. Le Golem est encore dans le grenier, dont le Maharal fit sceller la porte: il n'existe qu'une fenêtre grillagée, et pas d'accès.

Tel est l'essentiel de cette histoire, très connue dans le monde juif, qui a eu beaucoup de *variantes et compléments*: citons-en un, qui entre dans le propos de fournir un exemple pour une *mythoanalyse*.

Le Golem était sous les ordres précis du Rabbi, qui lui donnait des instructions, en ne manquant jamais de lui indiquer exactement comment il devait commencer ses actes et les terminer dans les moindres détails, en particulier à quel moment il devait arrêter son action. Un jour le Rabbi était absent; sa femme ordonna au Golem, en utilisant les indications qu'elle connaissait, le langage qui lui avait été expliqué par le Rabbi, d'aller puiser de l'eau au puits pour remplir le réservoir. Mais elle *oublia* de lui donner l'instruction de *'fin'* [les informaticiens voient ici une allusion], et le Golem continua à puiser de l'eau, indéfiniment, jusqu'au retour du Rabbi.

C'est cette légende qui a été recopiée par Goethe, puis par Paul Dukas, ensuite par Walt Disney (l'apprenti sorcier dans "Fantasia"). Cet exemple de variante fait bien partie du type d'analyse qui nous concerne: la variante est un attribut du Mythe qui enrichit ce dernier.

Un exemple de mythe dynamique spatial: le Far West

Suggérons encore l'esquisse d'un *mythe dynamique spatial*: le *mythe du Far West*. L'ouvrage "Going West" (Bib) est tout à fait typique d'une analyse contemporaine de ce genre qui entrera aisément dans une "Bibliothèque de l'Imaginaire." ... Le mythe du Far West (pour le Brésil c'est "Far North," pour la Russie c'est "Far East") est lié à un problème de *psychologie de l'espace*, celui de franchir des frontières, d'aller au-delà (to trespass, to go beyond ...), c'est l'idée d'errance, de recherche d'affranchissement de la pression sociale. Un foyer culturel s'étant constitué, sur la côte Est des U.S.A. s'impose en ce lieu une culture institutionalisée et les gens cherchent à s'en libérer. Que faire sur place? En Hollande, en Tchécoslovaquie, quand on se sent victime du Pouvoir social, seul reste *l'exil intérieur*. Dans ce pays neuf, ces vastes Etats-Unis, on s'en ira vers l'Ouest ... On y trouvera un endroit désert, où l'on s'installe après une certaine errance et on crée un "settlement" qui va à son tour *sécréter* des institutions et, par là, des contraintes sociales (les Mormons en sont un exemple). Quand on a bien institutionalisé, arrive un moment où, pour des raisons diverses, la pression locale s'établit et dépasse ce que certains individus sont capables de supporter. Souffrir ou partir? Partir où? De nouveau vers l'Ouest ... L'individu erre jusqu'à trouver un endoit ... et on recommence. Naturellement à un moment il a fallu s'arrêter. Les poètes américains ont, vers 1920, chanté la "clôture de la Frontière."

Quel est le contenu du mythe du Far West? C'est certes d'abord le mythe de l'Ouest, mais surtout le mythe du "far away," enfin force de l'errance. Le livre que nous avons cité est constitué de courts extraits tirés de sources variées: affiches, cinéma, romans, récits de voyages, à partir desquels s'est *construit le mythe* du Far West – les historiens diront que ce à quoi il se réfère n'a jamais véritablement existé – ce mythe qui pourtant a été un *moteur social* rendant compte, en la démythifiant, d'une part de l'histoire des U.S.A.

Une étude très soignée sur la poésie, la littérature, et l'iconographie de la construction du grand chemin de fer qui a traversé le continent américain au Nord: la Canadian Pacific, faite par Jones (Université de Sherbrooke) révèle dans un contexte différent des éléments très voisins de l'étude de l'Ouest. Plus précisément, elle révèle des attitudes connotatives différentes vis-à-vis de l'espace et de l'axe longitudinal du Canada, la conquête de l'espace vide par les Anglo-saxons ("A good tree is a dead tree: it's already lumber") et par les Canadiens français (vers l'infini de l'espace).

La Fiche mythographique

Comment faire des *fiches mythographiques*? La fiche sur le Golem constitue une proposition que nous avons développée sur un certain nombre d'autres mythes. Elle ne cherche pas à faire d'analyse de "contenu" mais plutôt une *analyse thématique*, une *glose philosophique*, et un *commentaire*, qui permettent d'établir le concept de *NOYAU* (Kernmythos): la fiche inclut un certain nombre de variantes proposant des *constellations d'affinités*. Nous établirons, par exemple, que le Golem est *thématiquement corrélé* avec *"l'homunculus"* de Paracelse, repris par Goethe et beaucoup d'autres, avec le concept de *robot*, développé par Karel Capek dans un roman célèbre, avec le concept *d'usine automatique*: les robots qui trahissent et se révoltent, ceux *d'ordinateur* et de télématique, avec le mythe *de Pygmalion*, avec le mythe finlandais, tiré du Kalevala de fabrication d'un être artificiel en raccordant des pièces détachées, des mains, des bras, des artères, des os, des nerfs ...): nous en connaissons les débouchés dans la science fiction contemporaine.

Mary Shelley, lors de son séjour en Suisse germanique, a eu connaissance de la légende juive du Golem, s'en est enthousiasmée, et l'a retranscrite en y mettant son talent personnel: le *mythe de Frankenstein* est identique au fond du mythe du Golem. Mais un fait qui caractérise ce mythe dans la société contemporaine, est que l'on se serve du mot "Frankenstein" tantôt pour parler du monstre créé, tantôt pour parler du savant docteur qui l'avait réalisé, en confondant la créature et son créateur.

Nous donnons en annexe une variante espagnole du mythe du Golem: "El hombre de Palo," que nous avons recueillie en Espagne. Il y a d'autres voisinages: ceux qui connaissent l'"Eve future" de Villiers de l'Isle Adam penseront, par exemple, à "La poupée," un conte de Marco Ferreri, qui a donné lieu à un film remarquable (Grandeur Nature), tout plein de sens philosophique. On est conduit ainsi à un réseau d'affinités qui sera un élément important de l'analyse mythographique. Revenons alors sur l'idée de *mytho-genèse*. Une première proposition est l'analyse de la "grandeur relative" du mythe dans la *culture de départ*, ici la culture juive de la Renaissance. Ce mythe particulier était important: tous les Juifs en avaient entendu parler comme les Français de La Fontaine ou de Perrault, et il y a à considérer la place du mythe *dans les cultures d'arrivée*, liée à leur réceptivité. Le mythe du Golem est certes moins répandu que celui de "Frankenstein" qui en dérive, mais le monde actuel inclut ce mythe dans ses préoccupations. Son importance se situe dans le fait qu'il épuise l'Imaginaire social à un instant donné, c'est-à-dire qu'il en trouve la meilleure cristallisation: c'est un *mythe carrefour* où se recroisent des séries de variations issues d'une origine commune qui transcende chaque culture; on le retrouvera en filigrane dans le "Metropolis" de Fritz Lang. Toutes ces productions de l'art d'une époque à travers la littérature, la légende, le théâtre, la peinture, voire la musique, aident la société de cette époque à se penser elle-même, à réaliser une *introspection sociale*.

L'analyse du "taux de crédibilité." Un conte sous sa forme ancienne est peu crédible, sauf sur des populations scientifiquement peu cultivées où il pouvait l'être beaucoup plus. Le rôle de la fiction, (théâtre, cinéma, littérature populaire, science fiction, etc.) sera entre autres de "conditionner," d'empaqueter le noyau du mythe dans un emballage de vraisemblance, augmentant cette crédibilité par des artifices pseudo-scientifiques, des dates, et des notes (manuscrit trouvé dans une bouteille, appareillage de notes autocritiques – Borges, Jules Verne, références historiques, etc.) qui réinsèrent le mythe dans le cadre scientifique du temps des lecteurs et par là le redynamisent.

La *"force problématique"* – ce concept est un critère d'analyse relativement pertinent: c'est la capacité d'un mythe de *poser des problèmes* (prégnance sociale): combien peut-on ainsi accrocher de problèmes sociaux sur un mythe dynamique? Pensons par exemple à l'idée de robot et à la question de l'usine sans ouvriers à propos du Golem. Ceci suggérera un facteur de succès du mythe dans les medias en tant que *l'Univers des Variations* (copies, démarquages, adaptations, etc.).

Exemple de fiche d'analyse mythographique

1 NOM PRINCIPAL DU MYTHE: Golem

2 REFERENCE AUTEUR DE LA FICHE, COMMENTATEUR: Moles, Ausubel, Bloch ADRESSE etc.

BIBLIOGRAPHIE: Moles, *Tentations conscience juive* (PUF, 1969), 242–68.
Ausubel, *Treasury of Jewish Folklore* (New York: Crown, 1952)

3 NOMS ANNEXES DU MYTHE: Leminkainen, Frankenstein, Robot, Homunculus

4 AIRES CULTURELLES: Prag, Europe Centrale, Espagne
5 LANGUES DE BASE: Yiddish, Allemand, Hébreu
6 REFERENCES BIBLIOGRAPHIQUES DE (2) et (3): Moles, *Création Scientifique* (Genève: Kister, 1956)
7 REDUCTION A UN TEXTE CANONIQUE MINIMAL: voir fiche annexe
8 Trois exemples de versions références dans trois cultures (aussi lointaines que possible):

A: El hombre de Palo	Voir fiche annexe
B: Pygmalion	Edith Hamilton, *Mythology*
C: Leminkainen	Holmyard, *Alchemy*

9 LISTE DE VARIANTES: Golem de Chelm: Perez, Ausubel
Veau artificiel R. Chanina: Bloch
10 CONSTELLATION D'AFFINITES: Homunculus, Robot, Usine automatique, Informatique, Ordinateur
11 MYTHOGENESE OU GENEALOGIE DES MYTHES: cf. matrices de proximité et sémantogramme
12 APPLICATIONS POSSIBLES DU MYTHE DANS LA FONCTION D'IMAGINAIRE SOCIAL: Télématique, Computer science, Grèves, fonction ouvrière, sexualité, jouets.
13 GRANDEURS RELATIVES DU MYTHE:
Place dans la culture de départ (1–2–3)
Place dans les cultures d'arrivée (1–2–3)
14 ETAPE DE LA VIE DU MYTHE: oublié – abandonné – déformé – vivant – à la mode
15 CHAMP DE VARIATIONS: estimé à partir du nombre de variantes (2, 4, 8, 16, 32)
16 TAUX DE REALISABILITE OU DISTANCE AU REEL: lointain, proche, réalisations partielles. Thèmes journalistiques, thèmes de fiction catastrophe
17 CREDIBILITE: (Quantité d'enthymème, ou force de conviction) Originelle faible
18 FORCE PROBLEMATIQUE: capacité d'aiguillage des problèmes actuels. Très grande
19 GLOSE PHILOSOPHIQUE OU COMMENTAIRE:
Cf. publication: Moles, *Le Judaisme et les choses* (PUF);
G. Scholem: *Grands courants de la mystique juive* (Payot).

Nous rattacherons le mythe du Golem au Rabbi Löw de Prague, le Maharal: c'est un personnage tout à fait intéressant; redécouvert par André Neher, il a écrit quelques ouvrages fondamentaux de la mystique juive (ses oeuvres sont, par exemple, à la bibliothèque universitaire de Strasbourg) et il est remarquable qu'une légende aussi fantastique ait pu être attribuée à un personnage, lui, bien réel. Le Maharal a vécu entre 1520 et 1610, près d'un siècle; venant de Breslau, il a émergé à Prague, où, déjà très célèbre à son arrivée, il a pris la direction de la communauté juive pendant près de soixante ans. A l'époque, Prague était gouvernée par Rodolphe de Bohème qui avait comme astrologue Kepler: il a eu à discuter avec des gens comme Parmigianino, Atanasius Kircher, et d'autres; le maniérisme italien constituait alors à la cour de Rodolphe un milieu intellectuel particulier, riche et dense. Le Maharal a introduit la pensée de la Renaissance à l'intérieur de la culture juive.

Reprenons encore cet exemple qui, il y a une vingtaine d'années, n'était pas très connu, sauf dans les milieux juifs, on ne connaissait guère que le nom de Frankenstein. Pourtant un livre de Norbert Wiener est appelé *God and Golem, Incorporated* et cette évocation du créateur de la cybernétique revient à l'idée essentielle: toute grande réalisation scientifique surgit d'un mythe dynamique. Le Golem, comme mythe de l'automate, est le mythe de la cybernétique et de l'automation. Pourtant des gens comme Wiener – créateur en titre de la cybernétique – Rachevski, Rosenblueth, sans poursuivre certes le but précis de la création d'un Golem, y ont fait des allusions parfaitement explicites. Or ces mythes n'agissent pas au niveau du conscient mais du subconscient, ils sont latents et doivent être révélés à l'ensemble social. Il y a un lien entre le travail de synthèse de la machine à reconnaître telle que l'a condensé le mythe du Golem, ou d'une machine à lire pour les aveugles, et l'idée de la cybernétique. En bref, il reste, toujours, un parfum de mythologie sous la recherche scientifique: une tendance organisatrice, *l'aspect historique*.

Le sémantogramme mythogénétique: les opérateurs

Pour terminer nous proposerons une autre approche: l'idée de *mythogénétique*: généalogie des mythes, que nous exprimerons sous forme graphique par un "*sémantogramme*." Voici un organigramme du mythe principal du Golem qui exprime comment (Fig. 1), le Golem se rattache à d'autres éléments de la pensée mythique: il y a toute une glose juive sur le sujet, une bonne part est sur cet organigramme. Mais il y a aussi les influences annexes, telles que Pygmalion et Prométhée (ces derniers avaient aussi fait un être de pierre et de glaise, prototype de l'être humain). Tout ceci est placé dans ce que nous appellons un "*opérateur*," qui se trouve être l'endroit, un *micromilieu*, dans lequel des éléments microculturels sont enfournés à haute densité, ils y sont

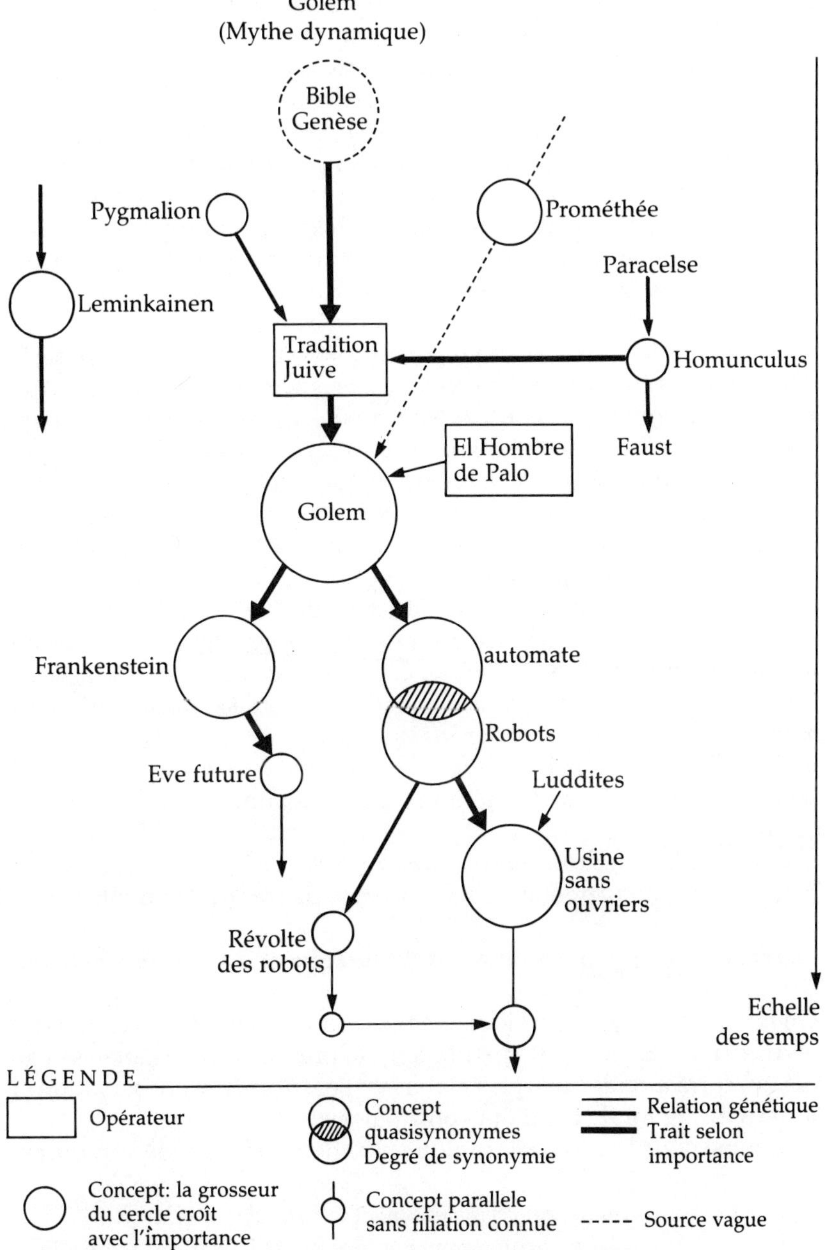

Fig. 1. Arbre mythogénétique (sémantogramme)

commentés, triturés avec un peu de génie, pour aboutir à des formes littéraires. C'est la genèse du mythe sous "forme canonique"; ce serait la tâche des "mythiciens," de retracer cette forme complète à partir du mythe initial après "l'explosion" culturelle qui se produit quand un mythe engendre une dynamique, c'est-à-dire une action: la poursuite des automates mécaniques du XVIIIe siècle est ici un bon exemple.

Il y a ensuite des filiations: sur l'organigramme la grosseur des cercles est en rapport avec la grosseur du mythe héritier par rapport au mythe originel (exemple: Frankenstein, l'Eve future, le mythe de l'automate, l'idée du robot, la révolte des robots que Kubrick suggère dans "2001, l'odyssée de l'espace," l'usine sans ouvriers, etc.).

Une méthode d'analyse (mythoanalyse sociale) émerge à partir de la remarque que la correspondance entre les mythes et les faits sociaux n'est pas biunivoque. A un même mythe correspondent plusieurs produits sociaux, et un même produit social est mis en réalisation par plusieurs mythes. Ainsi avons-nous dit que le mythe de Gygès, c'est le mythe de la photographie, mais le mythe de l'homme ubiquitaire est, aussi, sous un autre angle, un mythe de la photographie ou de la télévision: quelle est alors la différence? Nous avons aussi parlé du mythe de la cristallisation du monde dans des petites boîtes appelées caméras-Kodak; c'est aussi un mythe dynamique: mettre le monde en boîte est un grand désir mythique. C'est dire que *nous parlons plusieurs fois d'un même item de la société contemporaine en le reliant à plusieurs mythes*. De même, nous parlerons du *même mythe à propos de plusieurs items différents*. Il y a là un problème de *correspondance* à établir: il pourrait être traité par la méthode que nous appellerons de *mythogenèse*.

Pour ce faire, on construira un *tableau mythogénétique* à double entrée (Fig. 2), que nous appelons aussi "matrice de traduction mythique."

Les champs de prospection du Mythographe et du Mythogénéticien

Où trouverons-nous dans le monde social un champ d'expression des mythes dynamiques nous permettant de préciser par des analyses de cas, les correspondances qui s'établissent entre objets d'observation et formes de l'ignorance qui ont contribué à les déterminer.

Comme nous l'avons déjà indiqué plus haut, nous les découvrirons:

1. dans l'analyse critique du *développement de la recherche scientifique*.
   Exemples: les facteurs de détermination des fondations d'allocations de recherche, etc.

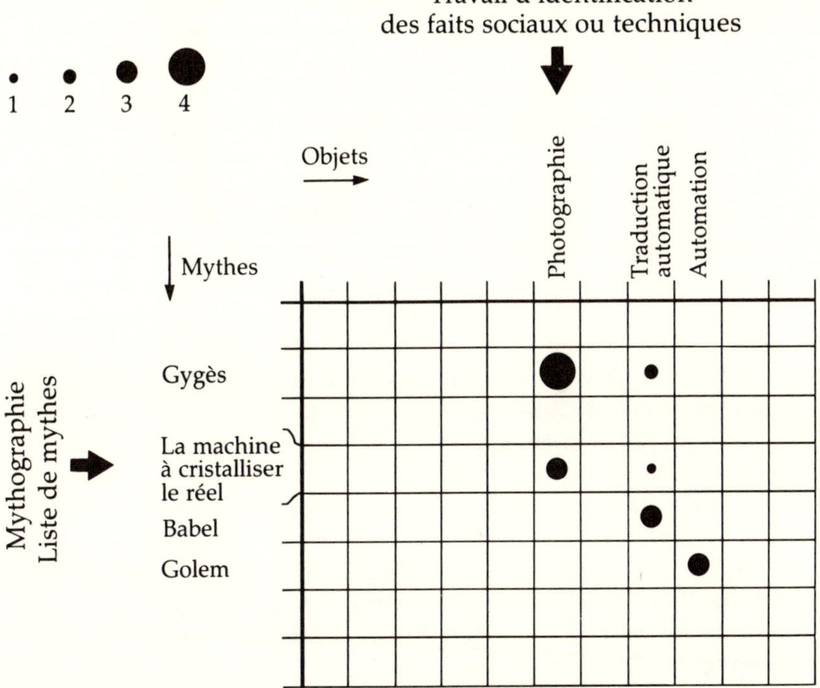

Fig. 2. La matrice de traduction mythique

2. dans la *publicité,* comme système d'exploitation conscient ou inconscient des mythes dynamiques pour donner à l'image publicitaire une résonnance, un impact qui dépasse le niveau rationnel – ou pseudo-rationnel – des besoins "fomentés" en touchant à l'imaginaire de l'être: songeons, par exemple, au mythe de l'ubiquité et à la publicité des compagnies de téléphone.
3. dans la *prospection futurologique* dont l'analyse micro-pyschologique va révéler des systèmes valorisant et l'orientation dans la réalisation des problèmes des mythes dynamiques.
   Exemples: thermofusion, voyage interstellaire, transformation des sexes, automatisation des télécommunications, copie multiple, etc. Ainsi le Centre de Recherche de l'Imaginaire étudie les relations entre le *Mythe Prométhéen* et le concept sociopolitique de *grands travaux.*
4. dans *cet univers littéraire* riche et sous-utilisé par la critique sociohistorique de la *science fiction,* une immense production de rêves à caractère dynamique et scientifique, créatrice de vocation, projection de la volonté de puissance,

dont la *mauvaise qualité globale* (avec des exceptions) a la vertu de ne masquer que faiblement les vecteurs sous-jacents qui excitent l'esprit de leurs auteurs comme catalyseurs de la culture et *l'image de l'Utopie*. On y décèlera entre autres le concept *d'antiutopie* dans la fiction dite sociopolitique (Huxley, Orwell) etc. "Die Zukunft hat ein Zeitplan" (Bloch).

Résumons les principales thèses et méthodes dégagées dans ce texte:

1. Symboles et mythes sont des formes décelables de l'Imaginaire individuel qui se retrouvent dans la "conscience" de la société, généralement au niveau d'un subconscient. Ils sont porteurs d'une part de la *variance* explicative du devenir social.
2. Les Mythes Dynamiques sont une catégorie particulière de mythes qui mettent en jeu l'opposition de l'homme aux lois de la Nature et les conséquences possibles de leur transgression. Universels, variables, subconscients poétiques, ils obéissent aux caractéristiques énoncées par Jung. Leur action vient s'ajouter, ou interférer, avec la raison déductive et claire pour composer le comportement de la société dans son appel vers le futur.
3. Les Mythes Dynamiques peuvent être répertoriés par une analyse de l'inconscient collectif tel qu'il se traduit dans les légendes, la publicité, la prise de décisions, la fiction, la recherche scientifique. On peut en montrer l'universalité (Mythographie).
4. Les Mythes Dynamiques comportent un axe d'*évolution* temporelle, peu à peu repris et développé et un axe de *variations* (variantes) dont chacun peut revêtir une signification culturelle, donnant naissance à un nouveau mythe, etc. La tâche d'une *mythogenèse* est d'élucider leurs interconnexions en se servant des mythogrammes ou cartes caractéristiques des mythes préparatoires à un traitement analytique.
5. Les Mythes Dynamiques sont liés de façon complexe et souvent obscure aux faits et objets sociaux dégagés par le sociologue (exemples: grands travaux, conquête de la lune, etc.). Ce sont des phénomènes imprécis (fuzzy concepts) dont les correspondances avec les objets *ne sont pas biunivoques*, on peut les élucider en dressant une matrice de traduction mythique ou tableau de correspondance qu'on analysera ensuite. Ce tableau est réalisé par l'analyse individuelle du chercheur (mythicien) et la discussion de groupe.
6. Les champs d'analyse des mythes sont ceux des symboles de la futurologie, de la science fiction, de l'utopie et de l'antiutopie, de la publicité, et de la décision socio-économique dans la mesure où celle-ci outrepasse la rationalité explicitable.

7. Les Mythes Dynamiques sont une part importante de l'Imaginaire social en fonctionnement, ils sont produits au niveau du rêve et de la volonté de puissance, ils se transforment selon des lois connaissables et génèrent d'autres mythes à travers les réalisations techniques et sociales. Ils sont des éléments d'un cycle socioculturel.
8. La méthode de base d'étude des mythes dynamiques repose sur:
   a) la collection et la mise *en forme canonique* des mythes comme "récits" ou "fait objectivable";
   b) la recherche de *mythes noyaux* (Kernmythos) construisant l'unité entre plusieurs variantes;
   c) la constitution d'une *"fiche mythographique"* énonçant quelques propriétés opérationnelles d'un mythe (grandeur, crédibilité, interpretabilité, mythèmes, force problématique ou prégnance sociale, actualité, champ de variations, etc.);
   d) l'établissement d'une *carte mythogénétique* ou d'un organigramme de filiation, dont l'ensemble devrait constituer un mythogramme plus ou moins complet;
   e) *l'identification,* ou glose, des mythes *avec les faits sociaux* auxquels ils apparaissent causalement reliés, identification non biunivoque construite par une matrice de correspondance ou de traduction mythique;
   f) l'examen de quelques conséquences sociales complété par une collection iconographique (exemples: publicité, monuments, symboles, etc.);
   g) la recherche de la "force génétique" d'un mythe pour en créer, soit par variations, soit par antinomie, d'autres plus élaborés ou plus spécifiques qui se trouvent entretenir la "vie des mythes à l'intérieur de la société" interne inspiré de Saussure.

Epigraphe de conclusion

Le commentaire est un réseau infini de boules de cristal reliées les unes aux autres par des fils de verre, que s'étend jusqu'aux extrémités du monde de la *connaissance.* Les noeuds du réseau sont les pièces du commentaire, les fils qui les tiennent sont la force de raisonnement du commentateur. Le texte est, lui aussi, un réseau de boules, plus grosses, articulées entre elles, mais ce réseau a une extension limitée, et les boules qui le réalisent doivent s'insérer dans le réseau des commentaires, chacune des boules imposant ainsi une distorsion au réseau primitif, distorsion qui s'en va jusqu'à l'infini. L'Art du commentateur, c'est de saisir aussi loin qu'il lui est possible, les perturbations d'un réseau qui lui est, de toute éternité, *préexistant.*

Annexe: El hombre de Palo

L'empereur Charles Quint n'aimait pas les horloges: elles lui rappelaient la fuite du temps et sa dissipation comme la substance même de la vie. Dans le vaste palais où il vivait à Tolède, il fit détruire les horloges et clouer, sur les cadrans, les aiguilles elles-mêmes.

Pourtant l'empereur du territoire sur lequel le soleil ne se couchait jamais avait horreur de l'inexactitude: il exigeait de ses ministres et de ses serviteurs la plus grande ponctualité dans leurs devoirs et leurs entrevues avec lui, il ne voulait pas attendre et les menaçait de destitution ou de renvoi au moindre manquement ou retard dans l'accomplissement de leurs tâches. Chacun devait être présent au moment qu'il avait choisi; courtisans, ministres, et servants rivalisaient d'ingéniosité pour réaliser leurs obligations à l'instant qui plaisait au souverain sans disposer d'aucun moyen matériel qui leur permit d'organiser leur temps, ils s'imposaient de longues attentes inutiles ou essayaient de connaître le moment de la journée d'après la position du soleil souvent peu visible dans les sombres couloirs. Tous étaient terrorisés à l'idée d'une erreur, par la contrainte que Charles Quint faisait ainsi régner sur son entourage.

Avec les années, l'humeur du souverain devenait plus sombre, et il décréta que seraient bannis tous les habitants de la ville qui seraient coupables "d'avoir divisé le temps en intervalles égaux par un artifice quelconque." Il fit arrêter à midi la grande horloge de la cathédrale et fit détruire tous les carillons de la ville. Quelques-uns de ses familiers avaient essayé de lui représenter les difficultés qu'il y avait à maintenir l'exactitude qu'il souhaitait dans ses relations, dans un monde sans horloges, mais il coupait net et les renvoyait chaque fois.

Il avait un ministre dans lequel il avait toute confiance, un marrane nommé Torrès Sola Camarero, qui s'avisa un jour d'un stratagème. Il savait que Charles Quint était très intéressé par les automates dont il avait fait faire à Nuremberg toute une collection. Or, il entendit parler d'un artisan de Crémone en Italie, qui disait-on, était le meilleur réalisateur d'automates du temps, un nommé Juanello. Torrès Sola en parla à l'empereur, qui, interessé, lui demanda de faire venir Juanello à Tolède. Celui-ci se présenta à la cour avec divers modèles, fort bien réalisés, d'automates écrivant et jouant de la musique. L'empereur lui demanda alors de montrer son talent et de construire un automate qui pourrait servir de domestique pour les habitants du palais.

Juanello se mit au travail, et un an après, il pouvait montrer à la cour un merveilleux automate: c'était un Homme de Bois qui était ainsi agencé, que chaque jour, il puisse aller chercher de l'eau dans un seau à la fontaine de la Grande Place de Tolède et la rapporter au palais. L'empereur fut ravi de la minutieuse perfection de cet automate dont tous les traits reproduisaient dans le détail un visage humain, et il décida de le garder en récompensant Juanello. L'automate fut installé dans la cour du palais et désormais, chaque jour, toujours au même moment de la journée, il se levait et traversait la ville d'un pas saccadé et régulier qui résonnait sur les pavés jusqu'au fond des ruelles, puis revenait avec des seaux d'eau qu'il versait dans le bassin du Palais sur la colline. On entendait dans les rues le choc des pas de l'homme de bois sur la chaussée et son passage était si régulier, si ponctuel, que les habitants de Tolède, les serviteurs et les ministres du souverain prirent l'habitude de se fixer sur lui pour établir l'horaire de leur journée. Charles Quint lui-même reconnaissait au loin le pas de l'homme de bois, qui devint ainsi le substitut de ces mécanismes de marque du temps que le souverain avait voulu abolir.

BIBLIOGRAPHIE

Ayrton, M. *The Maze Maker*. Stratford, 1974.

Bergon, F., and Z. Papanikolas. *Looking for West*. New York, 1978.

Bousquet, J. *Thèmes du rêve dans la littérature romantique*. Thèse lettres. Paris, 1964.

Braun, L. *Paracelse*. Strasbourg, 1981.

Corbin , H. *Paradoxes d'un monothéisme*. Paris, 1981.

Duport, J.-P. *Le fichier cristal*. Grenoble, 1979.

Durand, G. *L'imagination symbolique*. Paris, 1976.

Hamilton, E. *Mythology*. New York, 1953.

Hocke, F. *Die Welt als Labyrinth*. Rohwelt Deutsche Enzyklopädie, 1964.

Holmyard. H. *Alchemy*. Harmondsworth, 1953.

Holsti, Gerbner, and Krippendorf. *The Analysis of Communication Content*. New York, 1969.

Jung, C. *Psychologie und Alchemie*. Zürich, 1952.

Kafka, F. *Le château*. Paris, 1950.

Luckmann, T. *Phenomenology and Sociology*. London, 1978.

Maffesoli, M. *La conquête du présent*. Paris, 1979.

Moles, A. *La création scientifique*. Ed. Kister. Genève, 1957.

– *Sociodynamique de la culture*. La Haye, 1962–67.

– *Micropsychologie de la vie quotidienne*. Paris, 1973.

– "Du commentaire comme méthode de composition littéraire et philosophique," *Semiosis* (Stuttgart), No. 14 (1979), 5–12.

– "Un mito dinamico: il Golem," *Rassegna Mensile di Israel* (Milano), 33, No. 2–3 (1967), 67–72.
– "Le Golem, une attitude juive vis-à-vis des choses." In *Tentations et actions de la conscience juive*. Paris, 1968, 241–74.
Ranke, K. *Enzyklopädie des Märchens*. Berlin, 1975.
Tissier, J.-L. "La carte et le paysage." Colloque, Angers, mai 1981.
Tomas, A. *Atlantis from Legend to Discovery*. London, 1973.
– *Going West*. New York, 1982.
Valéry, P. *Oeuvres*. Paris, 1957–60.

WILFRED CANTWELL SMITH
Harvard University, Emeritus

Symbols in Religion

Human beings live their lives in an environment in which three sectors may reasonably be distinguished – provided that one not thereby infer that they are necessarily separate. Persons are involved with, participate in, three orders or levels or dimensions of reality. There is the realm of things: what we in the West often call the world of nature. There is the realm of people: the human order. And there is a less tangible realm – of values: aesthetic, intellectual, moral: beauty, truth, and justice, as the Greeks put it; a transcendant realm, to use another vocabulary; one having to do with hopes and aspirations and imaginative outreach and poetic sensibility. As my rather scattered attempt at characterizing it has already indicated, this third realm may be and indeed has been depicted or suggested in various ways, to put it mildly: the course of history has in fact evinced a strident diversity of accounts. Cultures have differed among themselves, and indeed within a given civilization centuries have differed among themselves, as have, often, social classes, in their portrayal of this third order. Yet no substantial group of human beings over any significant span of time has failed to report an awareness, however incomplete or tentative – and some reports have not been tentative at all! – of an order of reality different from the mundane and the everyday: one that at least supplements this latter, if it does not indeed undergird or in principle override it.

Cultures, centuries, classes, individuals, have differed too in their degree of apprehension, or proclaimed apprehension, of the transcendent dimension to human existence. Some – as, for instance, Dante or certain Buddhist sutras illustrate – are quite detailed; while in other cases one finds only a sense, dim or vivid, of what ought to be in contrast to what is, a vision or a vague feeling of how things might be alongside the awareness of the concrete *status quo*. I am simply reporting that there is a virtually universal human propensity to recognize that there is more to the universe, to ourselves, to each other, than meets the eye.

Human awareness of all three levels of reality has differed from place to place and from time to time, let alone group modes of interpreting that awareness to oneself, individually or corporately. The fraction of the physical universe that a given society has known, as well as the way that it has understood that particular fraction, has ever been culture-specific and age-specific. Similarly for the sample of human society and the limited span of human history available to any interpreting group. Most conspicuously, and for our purposes here most engagingly, the range of intangibles, and especially the form in which a culture has presented to itself the order of reality in which those intangibles are to be envisaged, have been particular.

Modern Western culture has been in the process of widening and deepening and universalizing its grasp, certainly, of the physical world, directly and brilliantly; and, directly or indirectly, of the human and the transcendent. By "indirectly" I mean – as is my job as a comparative historian of religion, for instance – that, if we do not know better than did our ancestors or than do other cultures beauty or God, at least we have a vastly wider awareness than anyone previously, by far, of what human beings over the centuries and across the globe have thought and done and felt in these realms: of what it has meant to be human in these regards.

My presentation here seeks to establish that from that enlarged awareness of varied perceptions we can indeed learn something signifiant about the matter. Our enhanced, albeit second-hand, knowledge of what has been the case empirically can lead, however indirectly, to a deeper understanding of what is the case ontologically, I contend – if we can develop the requisite accuracy of discernment and appreciation, and the requisite constructive intelligence.

The first thing that we incontrovertibly learn, of course, is multifarious diversity. The variegated panorama, if we sensitively let it, humbles and illuminates.

The variety is not only among the divergent symbolic patterns that various cultures have found helpful for talking about and relating to what I am here calling the third realm of human invovement. Of that, more presently. Variety is manifest also in the divergently understood relations among the three realms. Some have seen the three as continuous with each other; some, as discrete; some, as overlapping yet otherwise almost unrelated; some, as virtually identical though diversely perceived. If boundaries be discerned between any two or among all three, they have been diversely located. (India, for instance, has usually drawn a less sharp line between animals and humans than between plants and these two; our "animate" and "inanimate" have for Hindus been, as it were, literally "with soul" and without. Hindus have also regularly seen their gods as on this side of the ultimate mystery of the universe.) Of preliminary significance for us is the variety of rank-ordering of the three levels. Most cultures throughout history have seen and felt the natural, the human, and the ... what shall we call it? *das Geistliche*, as in that ascending order, with the third as not only the most important, and patently the most valuable, but also as the most primary, the most powerful, the most enduring. Some have held that the world of nature derives its significance and value from its relation to the other two; many that the first and second are mutually interdependent; almost all, that the human world, at least, or both it and the first, derive significance and value, even existence, from a relation to the third. Important for us is to recognize that the recent secular West has reversed this, seeing the human as derivative from the natural, and the realm of poetry, aspiration, justice, value, and such as in turn derivative from the human.

We have developed our concept of "symbol" and related categories to characterize human representation of what is transcendent, as we here are exploring.

An example that has engaged my interest is the word "heart," and its counterpart in other languages. Manifestly, this term has been used to denote both the physical organ that thumps away within the chest, and a less tangible quality of human beings which finds expression in such attitudes as sympathy, affection, generosity, and the like. To say that so-and-so is a heartless person would normally communicate the idea that he or she is inhumane, is unfeeling, is lacking in that minimal sense of solidarity with one's fellows that we regard as a normal part of being human. It would not be heard as signifying that that heartless person is poised in some split-second interval at a crucial point in a heart-transplant operation. Yet so adamant have we in recent Western culture been in insisting that the material is what is real, that quality is less cosmic than quantity, that virtue is ontologically derivative at best, and perhaps even imaginary, that almost without exception any modern Westerner would opine that to call our anatomical entity "heart" is a literal use of words, while to call by that name something in the realm of human affection, or our capacity for transcending our isolated individualism in caring for each other, is a metaphor. It has seemed obvious to most among us nowadays, if the point be once raised, that the material reference for such a word is the primary or basic one, the moral reference is secondary, metaphorical, derivative.

Now in addition to English there is a certain number of other languages as well (including some outside Western culture, and a few even outside the Indo-European linguistic group) where a single term has been used both for the moral quality and for this particular bit of anatomy. Indeed, it has been fairly common practice in human history to correlate human emotions and one or another part of the body – though different cultures and languages have contrived the pairing diversely. Our question here is: when that happens, in which direction has the "metaphorical" impulse (if we are to use that particular hierarchic concept) been working. Historically, the answer is not obvious, though I think that I have come to know what the correct answer probably is. I myself have not followed through a preliminary investigation – I should be interested to have someone check this by a more conclusive count than I have yet managed – but I have some reason to believe that in actual human discourse the word "heart" and its counterparts have in fact been used more often in reference to the intangible than to the tangible reality; and that the further back one goes in history or afield culturally the more true this is found to become. In other words, the recent West's interpretation here, that the one use is metaphorical, is not representative of the concrete situation, so much as it is illustrative of a particular *Weltanschauung*. Because we have deemed the material world primary, we have bent our understanding of language to conform to this; just as we have assumed that poetry comes less close to the truth than does physics, brings us less directly into touch with what is really real.

The same point can be seen on a larger scale, by comparing *Weltanschauungen* more generally. To illustrate how a notion such as "symbol" does and might serve us, we may note a fairly dominant Indian outlook, the *advaita*, as systematized and articulated by, for instance, the prodigiously intelligent early mediaeval philosopher Sankara, "the Hindu Aristotle." The orientation is often called Indian monism; and in the West is sometimes said to take the view that the mundane world is an illusion. This is a misrepresentation. A closer approximation, I may suggest, though of course Sankara did not use this phrasing of ours, would be to say that in the *advaita* system the natural world, and indeed the human world, are seen as symbolic: of Brahman, the ultimate formless reality. For that matter, in this and related Hindu perceptions, the world of the gods is seen so also.

Difficult though it be for a modern Westerner to get the feel of this, so relentless has been our resolve to start with the material universe as foundational and self-subsistent, yet in fact a careful study of Sankara's thought makes clear that it is in the end as logically arbitrary to choose the view that the concept of Brahman, for instance, is a symbolic representation of something empirical, as vice versa.

Although both views are logically sound, yet since I personally come out of a Western background, and am an historian committed to basing any theories that I may hold on empirical data drawn from the course of human history, I myself have tended to perceive this Hindu and other sorts of metaphysical and religious outlook as symbolic. Since most of you in this audience are also Western and all of us are modern, I allow myself to trust that my presentation, developing this thesis, may indeed suggest how helpful, even effective, our concept "symbol" can become for interpreting the religious history of humankind, and for enabling us to understand this major aspect of human affairs. I shall close, however, by moving on from there to pointing out certain difficulties that emerge, problems that next need attention. It will then be apparent, also, why I have started as I have done here.

First, however, the positive value of our concept "symbol." It has been developed in the study of religion to interpret the human propensity, evinced especially in religion, to deal with that "more" in human life than meets the eye. It is by the use of symbols, we say, that one points to what one does not visually see, talks and thinks about what transcends words, feels about what one does not touch. The symbols have over the centuries proven sometimes more, sometimes less, adequate to such a task, but in any case indispensable and ubiquitous: their use so is a characteristic and inherent human capacity. Moreover these symbols, it turns out, have the power not merely to express man's otherwise inchoate awareness of the richness of what lies under the surface, but also to nurture and to communicate and to elicit it. They have an activating as well as a representational quality; and an ability to organize the emotions, and the unconscious as well as the conscious mind, so that into them people have poured the deepest ranges of their humanity, and from them derived an enhancement of the personality.

As remarked, quite diverse types of thing have served the purpose: a beaver, the sky, a ceremonial procedure, silence; erotic love, or austere ascetisicm; the Qur'an; an historical figure; reason. Whatever the variety, one way or another peoples have been able to designate some item from within the visible world (the rest of us would say) and to sacralize it in such a way that it becomes then for them the symbol or locus of the intangible, the transcendent. In Japan, a simple open gateway (*torii*) marks off the shrine precincts: one passes through it, leaving behind psychologically, "symbolically," the humdrum ordinary world to enter the sacred space of the temple; and, after worship, one again moves through the gate in the other direction, to re-enter now the realm of everyday life, but as a renewed person. Virtually all peoples have set aside some portion of what outsiders would regard as ordinary terrain to serve for them as sacred space, erecting in it temple, church, or shrine whereby is then represented for them, often with great force, quite another dimension of reality.

Similarly with time: the Jew, for instance, sets apart one day in seven, whereby the other six days symbolize the mundane world with its bitter imperfections, perhaps its devastating pain, and at best its transient successes, while the Sabbath creatively represents the inviolate splendour of transcendence – with which therefore the other six days, however bleak, cannot keep him or her out of touch. Every people has its festivals, weekly or seasonal or occasional, its sacred times when life in its empirical and work-a-day aspects is transcended, and life in its timeless dimension is reaffirmed and reactivated: moments when truth, significance, and worth are recognized and cultivated – and carried back then into the ordinary world.

Human beings have sensed that the *status quo* (nowadays, the *fluxus quo*) is not the final truth about man or the world. They have felt, to take one example, that social justice and concord, personal righteousness, health, and joy stand over against the current observable condition of strife, loneliness, wickedness, poverty, and sorrow not as fancy against truth, wishful and irrational dreaming against reality, but in some fashion *vice versa* – as a norm by which the present imperfect world is judged; in some sense a truth in relation to which empirical actuality is in some sense an error. This too has been affirmed symbolically. One rather common way of doing so has been by representing a more perfect world elsewhere. Some have located their utopias chronologically in the past ("Once upon a time"; or Golden Age theories, as in Greece and India); or in the future (millennialisms, a coming just ruler, secular ideas of progress, a life after death); or geographically somewhere else (the medieval Irish "Isle of the Blessed" in the then inaccessible Western Sea); or high above the sky (heaven, the heaven of heavens); or in a domain beyond time (Paradise); or in another realm than this universe (a metaphysical order, idealist realities).

However it be symbolized and articulated, a moral dimension to human life has been perceived and affirmed. Man has been aware not only of the profitable and the disadvantageous but also of the better and the worse, and has been inspired by some power to pursue the better; he and she have known that some actions are right, some wrong, and that it matters. At most times and most places, morality has been an integral part of the religious complex (although situations have on occasion arisen when the two have become historically dislocated – when a given form of religion has seemed not good; or to put it another way, when persons' sense of what is worthwhile, and the inherited symbols by which worth used to be formulated, have no longer converged).

If the panorama of human religious life is, in its outward form, selected mundane data symbolizing the more than mundane, then the task of the student of religion is to know those data but to consider them not in themselves but in their role in human lives. Our concern is not primarily the doctrines and scriptures and prayers and rites and institutions, but rather what these do to a person. Not the tribal dance, so much as what happens to the African dancing; not the caste system, so much as what kind of person the Hindu becomes within it, or without it; not the events at Sinai, so much as what role the recounting of these events has played in both Jewish and Christian life over the centuries since; not the Qur'an, so much as what the Qur'an means to a Muslim.

In illustration, let us consider as an example a statue of the Buddha, and take note specifically of one small part of it, the pose of the right hand. Among several such stylized poses used throughout the Buddhist world, we may choose just one, the *abhaya mudra* ("fearlessness pose"), in which the right arm is somewhat raised, that hand held straight up, palm facing out. Over and above the more universal significance of such a gesture (power, authority, benediction), itself worth exploring, in the Buddhist case this represents also an incident from the life of the Buddha, in which reputedly a wild elephant charging him and his group was stopped in its tracks when the teacher raised his hand so, and became tame. The gesture gives artistic expression, then, to the Buddha's fearlessness in the face of the threat, and also to his conferring of fearlessness, and of grounds for fearlessness, on his disciples: his serene triumph over danger.

To say that this particular feature of sculpture symbolizes for Buddhists the overcoming of fear is to indicate not merely that it depicts an event in someone else's life, but also that it effects a change in one's own – since, to repeat, symbols not only represent but activate. The animal in its fury in the remembered anecdote may itself be taken as symbolic, representative of the pressures and assaults of life, which faith in the Buddha gives one the inner resources to withstand: the passions, for instance, to which such faith bestows on one the power quietly to say "no." To understand this particular item in the religious life of Buddhists, accordingly, is to know the history of how a Japanese emperor or a Thai merchant or a Chinese peasant through contemplating it in some nearby temple has had his life transformed, her fear removed, the personality healed. A parallel may be observed of the role in the lives of Christians, over the centuries, of the story of Christ's stilling of the tempest. His words, "Peace! be still!" read in the Lesson, and the portrayal of the scene in stained-glass windows or in hymns, have served to symbolize, for persons of faith, on the one hand Christ's power over the elements in his own life, and on the other hand the power that their faith in Him has in their lives, they have then found, to confer peace, to quell storms.

"In order, then, to understand Buddhists," as I have repeatedly observed, "one must look not at something called Buddhism, but at the universe, so far as possible, through Buddhist eyes." It is not the symbols themselves that one must grasp, so much as the orientation that they induce; how the whole complex of symbols enables those who live in terms of it to see a sunset, a broken marriage, prosperity, the onset of cancer, one's election to public office.

Of course, religious symbols and sets of symbols have been used also for mean and destructive purposes. Man's wickedness, not just his or her capacity for virtue, has been expressed and even encouraged by the symbol system at times. Through it persons have found their freedom, their transcendence of the immediately given, their ability to move beyond being merely an organism reacting to the environment; but sometimes they have used it destructively, or have become victims of its inherent ambiguities. Nothing has turned a society into a community so effectively as has religious faith: to share common symbols is about the most powerful of social cohesions. And yet few gulfs have been greater than those that separate differing religious communities, few hostilities so fierce as those between groups whose symbols differ.

Religious symbols do not raise men and women above the human level; only to it.

The preceding handful of paragraphs, giving the case for what I called earlier "the positive value of the concept 'symbol,'" paraphrase a presentation that I did ten years ago when I was asked to write the Introduction to the sector on Religion in the New Encyclopaedia Britannica. I have allowed myself to reuse this material here, partly because I imagined that some among you, not being religionists, may not have seen it; and partly because for those who have, it provides a base in relation to which to note new developments over the intervening decade.

My first new point in this connection has to do with a recognizing of involution within the symbolization process. This leads to what may seem a more humanist interpretation: a converging of the second and third realms. Involved here, in the subtle interaction between these two, is the question as to which side symbolizes which, raised as a new issue in my earlier section.

Gothic cathedrals are works of art so patterned at times as to represent symbolically the New Jerusalem. This symbolism was deliberate and explicit. The New Jerusalem, on the other hand, we may to advantage characterize as an idea symbolizing in turn, at the imaginative and conceptual level, a perfecting and hypostasizing of part of the experience that the worshippers had on a Sunday morning as they attended the service. The New Jerusalem notion was important to mediaeval Christians – as comparable yet quite different notions and forms have been important and meaningful to Buddhists, Muslims, and others – because it postulated and crystallized for them, in a form intellectually and emotionally efficacious, their sense, otherwise inchoate and elusive, that human beings are inherently (rather than instrumentally) valuable; that life is worth living; that other people are worth loving; that integrity is worth preserving, beauty and truth worth pursuing. These are facts about the human condition – at least, I see them as facts; I do not know whether you agree. Yet they would not have been effective in human life, and perhaps hardly even apparent, were it not for their having been almost constantly affirmed and reiterated throughout history in symbolic modes. At almost all times and places the overwhelming majority of human beings have reported that they have seen such facts, and they have expressed them in what we call their symbols; have reported that those symbols have enabled them to see them, and to order their lives in terms of them.

Certain moments have arisen when the capacity has waned of people to recognize and to feel these facts, and to act upon them; and/or the power of inherited or newly proffered symbols to enable people to recognize and to feel them and so to act. Such moments have in the past not been widespread nor long-lived; but while they last they are dispiriting and disruptive for those involved and for their fellows. Important, then, is to ask not only how far the symbols have been effective, but also how far or even whether what was symbolized be true.

Many another example too might illustrate how the experience of a reality that is in fact present both in space and in time yet is otherwise intangible, has been rendered intelligible, visible, audible, palpable, in symbolic forms and empirically operative then in human lives – while purportedly relating those lives to an alleged reality elsewhere or elsewhen. The Jewish Passover, for instance, celebrates symbolically an alleged Near Eastern event of the second millennium BC whereby the distant ancestors of those currently observing the Passover were reportedly liberated from sore oppression, and were constituted into a cohesive, independent, and joyous community. I do not know what happened 3500 years ago on the Nile or at the Red Sea or Mt. Sinai; but I do know that each year, in a great range of places largely in Europe and now in America, mediaeval and modern Jews have through the observance of this symbolic rite in fact found liberation from the oppression under which they, more than most of us, have regularly suffered and that would otherwise long ere now have crushed them; and have in fact been lifted out of the isolated individualism to which all human beings appear to be otherwise dismally vulnerable, to find solidarity and joy in community; and have in fact been made an independent group active in history and not merely passive.

Again, it is my contention that these qualities are part of the truth of the human condition; and I use the word "truth" here responsibly and with deliberation. As an historian I recognize that other groups have symbolized comparable truths in quite other fashions. The Crucifixion and Resurrection as celebrated in Christian life are formally divergent from, substantially convergent with, the Exodus in Jewish. Hindus, Taoists, Muslims, may have other emphases; certainly they have other symbols. Yet the historical situation would seem to be that unless a group symbolize these truths in some fashion, it tends to lose hold of them. One might say, to be lost hold of by them. The truth lies always in the here and now that lends itself to being symbolized in what are apparently distant, and to outsiders usually imaginary, sometimes grotesque, forms. Yet that truth seems in danger of becoming inoperative if it is not symbolically set forth. A simple statement, about human worth and dignity and freedom and corporate loyalty and integrity and transforming renewal and the rest, would seem not to suffice. Symbols are more powerful than are bare affirmations; poetry more cogent than prose. Yet – to make a bare affirmation – what they symbolize is here all the time, surrounding and infusing us.

(Note, in passing, that in talking here of bare affirmations and of symbols, I am still operating within the Western pattern that regards bare affirmations in prose about the here and now as more solid than the poetry of symbols, even in the course of arguing that the two are more closely and dynamically intertwined than that Western outlook traditionally concedes.)

Empirically, the historian notes two matters: (a) that religious symbols work; (b) that often – some would say, usually – they do not work very well. What is represented in Passover or Easter or Christmas, or the Muslim Laylat al-Qadr ("Night of Power," celebrating the revealing of the Qur'an), and other such, is an ideal that has been fallen short of, in practice, by Jews, Christians, Muslims, and the rest, over the centuries, in the more or less standard fashion in which human beings do in sorry fact fall short of ideals, sometimes egregiously. (I am using Greek terminology here, in speaking of ideals. Metaphysics, too, may be seen as symbolic.) Since religious ideals symbolize normally the highest that a given culture can apprehend (with the recent West as a partial exception), they are the ones most drastically unattained, one might say. In addition, the observer must note that religious symbols seem somehow to lend themselves exceptionally readily to distortion, perversion, and as an excuse for sheer wickedness. Sensitive participants are often aware of this, yet feel that the symbols and the ideals must nonetheless be maintained and, if possible, purified.

On the one hand, he or she would be an obtuse historian who failed to recognize the historical import of the various annual or weekly or daily symbolic religious representations by human beings of those ancient-history cosmic accounts, each itself symbolized in turn in scripture, in painting, in music, in theological conceptualities, in architecture, vestments, and all. Yet would not he or she further be an unduly cynical or gullible historian who imagined that those Jews, Christians, Muslims, and all maintained these practices and thoughts and feelings and forms all these centuries without something in their on-going contemporary lives and immediate experience of which that fourteenth-century BC or first-century AD or AH tale was in turn the symbolic expression?

My hasty verbalizations here of course do not begin to exhaust the symbolic significance of such matters, and many may feel that I have grossly underportrayed what has been at stake. I am attempting simply to suggest that always contemporary symbols throughout human history have in fact symbolized a metaphysical or transcendent order that in turn has symbolized, no doubt in purified and isolated form, a dimension of actual human life that is both real and authentic, that has been empirically present in history and is empirically evinced. Religious symbols are the empirical evidence that my third realm is indeed there, is a reality; and I am suggesting that it overlaps or converges with at least the second, the human. What theists call the divine and what Westerners call the human, meet. The relation between the two has been diversely conceptualized, interpreted in terms of various world-views; those of us who are Western and modern and who employ the concept "symbol" have to articulate an interpretation of that relation that will be coherent and will do justice to our modern awareness of the empirical historical data. It will not do justice if it underestimates either the human or the divine. Helpful for doing this, I am suggesting – to summarize this part of my paper – would be our recognizing the involuted nature of the symbolic process, its double dynamics, in its correlating our participation in the two.

May we not say that the historical significance, and the historical validity, of the symbols lie always in the present, rather than in a distant past or the remote reaches of the universe; and not only the historical, but indeed also the transcendent significance and the transcendent validity; adding, as one must, that this is because the symbols enlarge our appreciation of that present?

Less prosaically, might one perhaps say, not yet that samsara *is* nirvana, perhaps a limit affirmation beyond the feel of most of us, in this vale of tears; but that religious symbols have enabled persons and groups to touch the hem of that garment; and, more dynamically, enabled them to live in such a way as to make that become (to enable that to become) less starkly untrue than it would otherwise be – or than it has been (or, than it has otherwise been seen to be)?

My final point is again historical; but in this case more existential.

In the interpretation of other people's religious life, it has proven a decisive step forward to adopt the concept "symbol" for understanding the ideas, the practices, the art, the involvements of cultures whose forms and whose conceptual frameworks have differed, often drastically, from one's own. The West's first attempt (from the eighteenth century) to interpret to itself the variegated religious life of the world was in terms of "believing": that religious groups believe this and that. That category is now known to have been generated at that point more or less *ad hoc*, perpetrating the idea that religious forms and activities all rest on theoretical beliefs. This view has now been seen as quite untenable; but for the West it was quite convenient, even comforting, at the time, enabling both secularists and Christians to perceive others' positions as wrong. We can now recognize this understanding as untenable not just because it lent itself far too readily to outsiders' deprecation. It not only underestimates human beings outside one's own culture, but also grossly overestimates the carrying power of unsubstantiated theories. To see symbolizing rather than believing as a basic religious category has allowed a major, indeed a momentous, advance.

Yet it is not clear but that even this idea needs further refinement, if it is to serve for adequate understanding. That refining is an important current task. And it has to do with self-involvement. The notion of symbol seems admirable for interpreting other people's affairs, but to limp badly with regard to one's own. It is a good maxim that one should not call people names behind their back: I distrust any explanation of human behaviour that does not apply to oneself. It has helped immeasurably to recognize others' patterns as symbolic; but we – especially we in the West – have yet to learn to live in full consciousness of our own symbolizations. Most Westerners have not yet learned to recognize our own conceptual frameworks as contingent. Christians have resisted seeing the Christian form of faith as one among the others, one with much to learn both from those others individually and from the variety itself. Secularists still resist – or have not yet sensed that this is a challenge – recognizing secularism as one ideology among many others, one whose basic categories are by no means final and that is by no means in a position to interpret in its own insular and precarious terms other ideologies, such as what it has come disparagingly to call religious ones.

To return, however, to symbols; and to the concept's greater serviceability in interpreting others' life than one's own. A Roman Catholic may happily agree that a rosary or a crucifix is symbolic; and the rest of us do well to recognize them so too, rather than dubbing their use superstitious, as both Protestants and secularists used to do. On the other hand, Catholics resist saying that the Virgin Mary or the Crucifixion itself is symbolic: "merely symbolic," they would interpret the outsider's view as averring; and their Church has devoted much energy over the centuries to explaining that, and how the Eucharist is substantially more than that. The doctrine of the Real Presence is precisely a thesis that it is not "merely" a symbolic presence; and it is up to us as scholars to understand what is going on here, in that asseveration, and to render it intelligible. Similarly, Muslims may recognize a mosque as symbolic, or Jews a synagogue, while neither has usually been traditionally willing to say that the injunctions of the Law are so. (Mystics have been an exception, and have been strongly criticized.) Those of us who are parents and who take seriously our caring for our children give an absolute status to the hold on us of that sort of involvement, to which we should feel the concept "symbol" quite inadequate. Nor would most of us affirm as symbolic of something else contingently, the moral imperative not to rape nor to murder.

The symbolizing interpretation takes more seriously than do earlier alternatives the concerns of others, but does not rise to what we take seriously ourselves.

It is not only religious people who find themselves in this dilemma. Few secularists have recognized their view that religion is an illusion as not literally true, but as one symbolic perception and representation of a higher reality – even though considered in a world-history perspective this is obviously the case. To regard "religious " world-views as illusory is a symbolic way of affirming the cosmic validity of the secular world-view. Myth might be thought of as a symbolic tale or symbolic ideology, and many Westerners can perceive not only the Ojibwa world-view but Marxism or Christian thought as a great mythic construct; whereas a recognition is coming only slowly that science too is a myth – and that seeing anything as a myth is itself mythic. Surely philosophy is that. I look forward to a really good book some day, serious and convincing, and highly illuminating, by an historian of religion on the grandiose Western myth of secularism. Now that it is waning, and in any case now that we know what we do of world history and of human thought, we are beginning to be able to see it historically as both noble and tragic – as having been both noble and tragic, and as now waning. It will be alarming, however, if the liberals among us are unable to contrive that it be superseded with something more promising than the religious right, Muslim or Christian, or than nihilism.

Confronted with the emerging problem of self-involvement in symbolism conceptuality, I recently proffered the notion of second-level symbols, first-level, and zero-level. A fundamental characteristic of symbolism is that nothing that serves as a symbol is a symbol in and of itself: a given thing is symbolic to some persons, not to others; or even is symbolic to others of something quite else, even contradictory. A second-level symbol for me, then, is when I recognize it as symbolic for so-and-so though not for me. X has been symbolic of P for Hindus, I may ascertain; Y, for Buddhists, of Q; Z, for Muslims, of R. (At a more sophisticated level, one must say, "for certain Hindus," "some Buddhists," "these Muslims.") Or X may be symbolic of A for these people, of B for those. These then are first-level symbols for the groups or persons concerned, second-level for me. The term "zero-level symbol," on the other hand, is a way of designating matters such as the Real Presence, or the person of Christ, or the Qur'an, that to those involved are cosmic absolutes, yet to the scholarly observer are human and contingent symbols.

Significant here is the dynamics that turns out to be operative. When first we meet an alien matter that to us seems grotesque or irrational but to others is of transcendent significance, it becomes understood when we recognize it as symbolic, when it becomes for us a second-level symbol. Gradually, however, as we become familiar with it, and especially more familiar and friendly with those for whom it is translucent, and if we are sensitive, we begin to be able to see it, even begin actually to feel it, as they do. Gradually then our appreciation of the human scene widens and deepens, and the world's second-level symbols approach or become first-level. Moreover, the more sensitive one is to others' sensitivities, and especially as one becomes more familiar and more friendly with a wider range of outsiders to one's own group, and appreciates how one's own first-level symbols are second-level for them, and even one's zero-level are second- or first- for them, gradually one begins to converge one's zero- and first-level ones, too.

Differences among the three levels have historically been of momentous consequence; but historically are today in process of becoming, or can be made to become, outgrown.

Christian theologians are beginning in our century, especially as we approach the century's end, to recognize for the first time the figure of Christ as symbolic, and indeed to recognize theology as such as symbolic.

Indeed, some of us are coming to feel that all human perception of the universe is symbolic, though recognizing also that our understanding of the concept "symbol" is not yet developed to the point where this will serve. We see it as helpful for other people's religious life, not for our own; or for religious matters generally, not for our perception of the material world (to return to my talk's opening points). This has to do in part, perhaps, with Westerners' – and Muslims' – inveterately dichotomizing tendencies. Jews, Christians, Western secularists, and Muslims have all worked with a strong either/or outlook, with conflict dualism, whereby we have tended to feel that if we are right then anyone who disagrees is wrong. A or not A. This orientation has at times achieved marvels and at times wrought untold mischief. Even for science, certainly for religion, we must outgrow this – and move beyond also its concomitant: a debilitating relativism that opines that anything goes, that nothing is firm, nothing is true.

This is right, that wrong, or else everything is equally valid – and in the end equally invalid: this is a dismal pair of alternatives to have fallen into. It is so certainly religiously, probably between the secular and the religious, and perhaps generally. At the religious level it is noteworthy that Hindus have for centuries been good at these matters. Strikingly to us, many of the sophisticated among them have for ages seen all religious forms and religious ideas, including their own, as symbolic, and have lived cheerily with this self-incriminating awareness. We in the West are perhaps now in a position to learn, from our wider and deeper knowledge than we have previously had of human history and of alternative world-views, and with the help of hints from sophisticated thinking among some of these, to outgrow narrowness without collapsing into nihilism, both of which have been threatening us of late.

This, then, I suggest, is where we currently are in this realm: having made much progress in understanding religious symbolism, yet having to make still more – and fairly quickly, lest our world be torn apart by misunderstanding and strife. I personally have a number of considerations for discussion with the various theological worlds as to how theology may best proceed; but this is not a gathering focusing on the study of religion as such, and I desist. Nor is there time to pursue implications for secular thought, though I am persuaded that these are many. I should like to hear a discussion, for instance, on my notion that to call a spade a spade, for example, is a metaphor.

Such matters, however, will have to wait for some other occasion. In the meantime, I trust that the little that has been put forward may prove suggestive.

JAMES A. LEITH
Queen's University

Symbols in the French Revolution: The Strange Metamorphoses of the Triangle

Since Durkheim many anthropologists have shown that in primitive societies different cosmologies not only reflect but reinforce various social structures. Using rituals and symbols, such cosmologies mask, legitimate, and sanctify power.[1] Other social scientists have extended this analysis to certain modern societies as well. Usually these scholars have emphasized the need for a symbolic centre around which the members of society can unite.[2] One could argue that there was such a cosmology in Old Regime France that helped to uphold the monarchical, aristocratic, hierarchical social structure. Aristocrats had dress, swords, and coats of arms that distinguished them from the common people. At the centre was the person of the king, ruler by the grace of God. Although the king's likeness appeared in statues, low reliefs, and coins, in the vignettes that formed the headings of laws his authority was usually represented by symbols: the coat-of-arms of the Bourbons with its three *fleurs-de-lys*, the crown, the sceptre, and the hand of Justice (Fig. 1). The three lilies, which had appeared in the later Middle Ages when the monarchy was expanding its claims, were intended to associate the crown with the Trinity.

During the eighteenth century the *philosophes* had helped to undermine this cosmology, contrasting it with the state of nature, but because they feared social upheaval and were often themselves beneficiaries of the existing system, they had hesitated to carry their theories to a radical conclusion. Meanwhile the growing wealth and number of non-noble proprietors made the hierarchical social structure increasingly anachronistic. In 1789 a series of revolts by different groups led to a new view of society: the idea of a kingdom of subjects divided by privileges inherited from history was replaced by that of a nation of citizens united by rights derived from nature. Such a change required a revised cosmology with new rituals, symbols, sacred laws, and sanctuaries. Since the monarchy was to survive three more years, some of the old monarchical and religious symbols coexisted for a time with new ones. Then with the overthrow of the monarchy in August of 1792, and the Dechristianization movement fifteen months later, a number of revolutionary symbols that had been evolving were called on to fill the void – statues of Liberty, Phrygian bonnets, Liberty trees, tricolour cockades, carpenter's levels, and fasces. During the Terror of 1793–4 these were joined by sacred Mountains.

In order to win the support of the new order, revolutionaries usually engage in propaganda. Social scientists have distinguished two main sorts of propaganda, agitational and integrational, in both of which symbols play a key role.[3] Agitational propaganda is essentially negative. Its purpose is to arouse hatred and contempt for the old order. This involves a process of delegitimatization and desacralization of the institutions and symbols previously viewed with reverence.[4] In the early stages of the French Revolution feudal symbols were not only removed from public view, but were often destroyed ritualistically to impress on the people the end of the old order, as in the burning of coats-of-arms on the Champ de Mars on 14 July 1792. At the time of the overthrow of the monarchy the statues of the King in public places were toppled. During the Festival of Unity and Indivisibility on 10 August 1793, that is, on the first anniversary of the end of the monarchy, royal coats-of-arms and other emblems were burned in front of the statue of Liberty, the goddess whose likeness had been raised on the pedestal of the former statue of Louis XV on the square which had borne his name, but which had been rechristened "Place de la Révolution." Then, as Dechristianization broke out a few months later, Christian symbols were destroyed, and traditional processions parodied on the streets. Desacralization reached its crescendo.

Since revolutionaries must not only discredit the old regime, but also rally the masses to the new order, they customarily turn to integrational propaganada. It is essentially positive. Its aim is to legitimatize and sacralize the new ideas and institutions. Above all it attempts to create a new centre around which the masses can rally. Although the monarchy still survived during the first three years of the French Revolution, the figure of Liberty and the *autel de la patrie* were emerging as alternative centres of allegiance for the citizenry. In 1791 the Jacobin Club of Montpellier erected a "Colonne de la Liberté" on which the revolutionary goddess replaced the King, even though he was still on the throne.[5] By the time of the first anniversary of the overthrow of the monarchy all of the elements of a civic cult were available that could sanctify the republican regime. There were dogmas – the Rights of Man and the republican Constitution; there were rituals – processions through the streets, civic oaths, and communal feasts; there were sacred architectural structures – civic altars, allegorical statues, and commemorative shrines; there were republican martyrs – usually Lepelletier, Marat, and Chalier; and there were the symbols already mentioned, including a holy Mountain. The attempt to create an aura of sanctity around republican institutions and ideals is clear in the Festival of Unity and Indivisibility in 1793, during which the procession through Paris stopped for special ceremonies at six "stations" reminiscent of the Stations of the Cross.

Since the symbols used by revolutionaries must serve to identify adherents to a mass movement and offer focal points around which they can rally, such symbols are usually simple visual entities. They seem, therefore, more easily recognized and deciphered than many literary symbols. One thinks of the Nazi swastika, eagle, and red-white-and-black flag. One things too of the Bolshevik hammer-and-sickle, red star, and red flag. Or one thinks of the *Maoist* little red book, red sun, sunflower, and once again the red flag. Perhaps the French revolutionaries had a somewhat more varied arsenal of figures and symbols, but most of them were fairly simple, although they could sometimes be combined into allegories just as rich as the Beasts of the Apocalypse on the tympanum of the central doorway of the façade of Chartres. The Phrygian bonnet, tricoloured cockade, fasces, carpenter's level, Liberty Tree, and sacred Mountain were all easily recognizable and suitable for use in a multitude of places – on clothing, banners, monuments, letterheads, bookbindings, frontispieces, calendars, furniture, dishes, membership cards, and jewellery. In fact the extent to which revolutionary symbols affected the little things of life is evidence of how deeply the upheaval penetrated the social fabric.

Not only are revolutionary symbols usually simple visual entities, but they are often familiar forms adapted to a new use. The Nazi swastika was an ancient geometric form, and of course the eagle dates back to Roman antiquity. The Bolshevik red star seems to have been a communist version of the star of Bethlehem that the wise men followed,[6] and the hammer and sickle were familiar emblems of workers and peasants. Even the Maoist little red book was a descendant of the traditional Confucian code, and the sunflower was certainly familiar. The French revolutionaries likewise modified ancient symbols for their purposes. Whereas Louis XIV had used the sun, the source of light and dominant over the earth, as his chief symbol, the revolutionaries used it to represent the dawn of a new era. On popular engravings it is often shown rising up in the background, bringing enlightenment to the world (Fig. 2). The architect Louis Combes, in his project for a grandiose National Assembly for the site of the Bastille (Fig. 3), proposed to decorate the inside of the dome with the sky exactly as it had appeared on the night of July 13–14, with the sun rising on the horizon, dispelling the clouds (Fig. 4). Later during the Terror we find the sun, bearing what appears to be the likeness of Robespierre, coming over the horizon, in an engraving with the inscription "Jaiclair tout l'univer [*sic*]" (Fig. 5).

The Phrygian bonnet, the most common symbol of the Revolution, had been inherited from Roman times, when it had been worn by emancipated slaves; it had been used as an emblem of liberty in previous rebellions in the western world. The fasces, the awesome bundle of rods, often enclosing an axe, which had been carried before Roman magistrates (the rods were used to beat the condemned man and the axe to execute him), had been used by monarchs as a sign of state authority. At the peak of the Revolution it became the symbol of the *République une et indivisible*. Even the tricolour was composed of old ingredients, the white of the royal standard plus the blue and red of the city of Paris. It appeared early in the Revolution as the sign of hoped-for unity between the people and the King, but it survived as the revolutionary colour combination. In the nineteenth century revolutionaries in other countries nearly always chose three-coloured bands, whether horizontal or vertical, to serve as their standards. The Italians simply changed the blue stripe on the French tricolour to green, the colour Masons used to signify rebirth.

Two other central symbols, the foci of revolutionary rituals, the Liberty Tree and the Mountain, were also deeply rooted in the past. The ancestry of the Liberty Tree, which proliferated after 1790, went back to ancient people, who viewed trees as symbols of life-force or the dwelling places of the gods, to the Judaic-Christian tradition of the Tree of the Knowledge of Good and Evil in the Garden of Eden, to the great tree in the centre of the heavenly kingdom described in Revelation, and to the popular celebration of fertility around the May tree or pole. The Mountain, of course, became a symbol during the Terror because it was the nickname of the radicals who sat in the high benches of the Convention and who won ascendancy in 1793. This name, however, evoked deep memories, both Christian and pagan: Moses brought the Ten Commandments down from Mount Sinai,

Christ preached a Sermon on the Mount, and Apollo and his nine daughters lived on Mount Parnassus, to cite only a few associations. During the Terror some artists showed the republican Constitution of Year II emerging from the Mountain amid thunder and lightning "semblable aux tables de Moyse" (Fig. 6). Mountains were constructed in former churches and were depicted on objects of everyday life. The most awesome symbolic Mountain was the one erected on the Champ de Mars for Robespierre's Festival of the Supreme Being. It was large enough to accommodate a choir of 2400 on its slopes, plus an orchestra and officials (Fig. 7).

The symbols of the French Revolution were often held by, or associated with, allegorical figures. Usually these figures were female, largely, I think, for a simple reason: most abstract entities in French are feminine in gender – *la France, la Nation, la Liberté, l'Egalité, la Nature, la Raison, la Justice,* and so on. Even the Fatherland and Brotherhood are feminine in French. In any case there was a long tradition of female allegorical figures representing virtues. There was, however, one conspicuous male, Hercules, an ancient figure in Western Civilization who took on a new role during the Revolution.[7] Before the Revolution Hercules had frequently been associated with French kings to suggest their power, but during the Revolution he became democratized. For example, he appeared on the certificate given in 1790 to the conquerors of the Bastille (Fig. 8). When the church Ste. Geneviève was transformed into the Pantheon, a shrine for Frenchmen who had served their country well, a figure of Hercules representing popular force was commissioned for the pericycle of the dome.

Under the radical Republic Hercules moved further onto the stage. The People was now theoretically sovereign, and *le Peuple* is masculine in French. In the Festival of Unity and Indivisibility, a huge statue representing the People, armed with a club and standing on a Mountain, was shown at the fourth station, crushing a hydra representing counter-revolutionary federalism (Fig. 9). He appeared again on the top of the column next to the Mountain constructed for the Festival of the Supreme Being (Fig. 10). Meanwhile David had proposed a colossal statue of the People, trampling on symbols of the Old Regime, for the promontory of the Ile de la Cité next to the Pont Neuf where a statue of Henry IV had once stood. A figure similar to this proposed colossus appeared on the stamp at the end of the *Bulletin des lois* near the end of the Terror (Fig. 11). Also we find a similar image of the People in some children's books of the period. In his proletarian guise, Hercules is another clear example of an old symbol put to a new use.

Now that we have an overview of the symbols of the Revolution and their roles, I would like to examine in greater detail the use of the equilateral triangle during the turbulent decade. Its strange mutations reveal much about the origin, use, and fate of a revolutionary symbol. Humans have always considered this figure as an ideal geometric form. A triangle is, of course, the simplest way of enclosing a space with straight lines; if the three sides are equal, the triangle takes on an aura of perfection. Pythagoras and his followers were also intrigued by the consequences of replacing the sides with four circles (Fig. 12).[8] In such a case, if one reads starting from any of the three corners, one gets the same sequence of numbers – one, two, three, and four – always adding up to ten. For the Pythagoreans four and ten were sacred, a key to the universe. Christians used the equilateral triangle made up of straight lines to represent the mysteries of the Trinity. One finds it often in churches over the altar, frequently with the Hebrew word for God in the centre, and usually set among clouds and radiating light, as we see in Saint-Louis-en-l'île in Paris (Fig. 13). Masons too used the equilateral triangle to represent the Divinity, but for them the three sides stood for Past, Present, and Future. One finds it used in this way on the Great Seal of the United States, with an all-seeing Eye in the centre (Fig. 14).

The French Revolutionaries continued to use the equilateral triangle as a symbol of the Divinity. Early in the Revolution, for example, the proponent of an educational system aimed at regenerating Frenchmen used it as the central symbol of a huge engraving accompanying his pamphlet. This complex poster attempted to relate some of the early achievements of the Revolution to an all-encompassing view of God and the universe, a clear example of the search for a unifying view of existence which one finds running through the decade (Fig. 15). As the Monarchy was turned into the Republic, and the Christian Trinity was converted into the Supreme Being, the equilateral triangle continued to be used to depict him. The admission ticket for those participating in the Festival of the Supreme Being featured a large equilateral triangle (Fig. 16), and posters of the period frequently featured a luminous one in the heavens, with or without the all-seeing Eye (Fig. 17).

Since the Divinity was considered the ultimate source of laws, the triangle was often used to give an air of holiness to republican legislation. On the membership card of one of the committees of a section or ward of Paris, for example, one finds the triangle framing the injunction "Respect à la Loi" (Fig. 18). A more complex engraving, entitled "Trinité Convent[ionnelle]," conveys several messages (Fig. 19). It features a triangle with the word "Loi" in the centre, again giving it an aura of sanctity. At the same time the apex supports a sans-culotte, the representative of the common people, while the base crushes a representative of the clergy on the left and Louis XVI on the right. Around the triangle an inscription declares "Nous voulons que les trois ne fassent qu'un." The previous power of the king and the church was now to be united in the single will of the citizens who, the central circle proclaims, are now all sovereigns, but who should be guided by the law. The triangle and the circle were set in a larger circle recording the dates of some of the principal achievements of the Revolution.

While the equilateral triangle continued to symbolize the Divinity and the sacred nature of the laws, it was employed in new ways from the very beginning of the Revolution. Just after the representatives of the three traditional Estates of France – Clergy, Nobility, and Commoners – had merged in a single National Assembly, the triangle was used frequently to signify this new unity. For example, an engraving labelled "Mieux vaut tard que jamais," shows representatives of the three orders united in the centre of a triangle (Fig. 20). The three points are decorated with objects associated with the three estates – religious regalia, a cannon, and a plough. Two other trinities appear on the engraving – three fleurs-de-lys, and the motto, "Liberté, Propriété, Constitution." The same idea was used in a project by a young architect from the provinces called Mouillefarine, one of several architects to propose a plan for the site of the Bastille. He proposed a "Place de la Liberté," from which a broad boulevard would lead to a semi-circular square on the banks of the Seine and a bridge across to the left bank. The bridge, to be called the "Pont de Réunion," was to remind the people of the new-found national unity. It was to be decorated with allegorical figures serving as lampposts, fasces on the piers, and an obelisk. Significantly, the obelisk was to be triangular, representing the recent equality of the three orders, and set on a circular pedestal, signifying hope for the eternal duration of their alliance (Fig. 21).

Under the constitutional monarchy which lasted until 1792 the equilateral triangle was used in other ways. Since many of the early revolutionaries still hoped that Louis XVI would become the law-abiding father of his people, they sometimes associated him with other good kings such as Louis XII and Henry IV, uniting them by an equilateral triangle (Fig. 22). There was a mysticism of numbers here: XII plus IV equals XVI. Much more common, however, was the use of the triangle to represent another trinity that appeared for a time – the King, the Nation, and the Law. The triangle was printed with these three names associated with it on letterheads, the flags of the new National

Guard, and on the new paper money, for instance the *assignat* worth 10 sous issued in 1792 (Fig. 23). This example shows how short-lived this trinity was. The triangle, labelled "La Nation, La Loi, Le Roi," appears even though the bill is dated Year I of the Republic. Events had moved faster than the engravers. Soon the triangle on *assignats* bore yet another trinity – "Liberté, Egalité, Sûreté." Later we find the trinity of republican Martyrs – Marat, Lepelletier, and Chalier – associated with the sacred triangle (Fig. 24).

In this last example the sacred triangle takes the form of a symbol familiar during the radical phase of the Revolution: the carpenter's level. In the eighteenth century the level in common use consisted of a plumb line hanging from the apex of a triangle. When the base rested on a level surface the plumb line came to rest in the centre. This level, which the Masons had used as one of their symbols, became the principal symbol of equality. My contention is that, since the level was the same shape as the equilateral triangle representing the Trinity or the Supreme Being, some of the aura of sanctity surrounding the latter was transferred to the former. For instance, at the top of an elaborate engraving of the Declaration of the Rights of Man of 1793, a more radical Declaration than the one in 1789, the equilateral triangle with an all-seeing eye in the centre appears in association with the level (Fig. 25). In a sketch by the architect Lequeu the level itself radiates light, just like the triangle in churches (Fig. 26). In a little engraving entitled "Musique Républicaine" the level, again radiating light, appears in the heavens in conjunction with the all-seeing eye (Fig. 27). Also we find the level, not only associated with the triangle as a symbol of the Divinity, but substituted for it as a luminous object of worship, as in the little engraving "Le Geova des Français" (Fig. 28).

Even more significant is the heading of the *Bulletin des lois*, which began publication during the Terror. On the left of Liberty in the centre is the familiar level, and on the right the symbol of the Divinity as the source of law (Fig. 29). Also intriguing is the modification of the image of Liberty that occurred a few weeks later. The angle of her head was changed, which is not very significant, but at the same time an axe was added to the fasces, and a triangle suggesting a level was placed in her hand. She was thus consciously radicalized (Fig. 30).[9] There were now three triangles in the heading. At this time one comes across levels of Equality in all sorts of places – on furniture, china, letterheads, statues, medallions, and jewellery. When the Convention abolished slavery, a popular song exclaimed that "la couleur tombe et l'homme reste," and engravings appeared of negroes and negresses wearing the level around their necks (Fig. 31).

The level of equality also appeared frequently in the architectural projects submitted to the great art contest launched by the Committee of Public Safety in the middle of Year II, that is, in the spring of 1794. The architectural projects were intended to republicanize space with monuments in the main squares of Paris and revolutionary temples, assembly halls, and other public buildings throughout France. The architect Delannoy proposed twin shrines for the Place du Carrousel near where the Arc de Triomphe de Napoléon now stands (Fig. 32). One monument, commemorating the capture of the Bastille on 14 July 1789, contained a statue of Liberty and was decorated with Phrygian bonnets around the entablature. Its twin, commemorating the overthrow of the monarchy on 10 August 1792, displayed a statue of Equality, and was embellished with levels (Fig. 33). The architect Jean-Jacques Lequeu submitted a plan for an assembly hall for local meetings of the people. It shows a tympanum over each doorway in the shape of a level, so that citizens entering the hall would be reminded of the new ideal (Fig. 34).

The plans for revolutionary temples were even more revealing. Lequeu submitted a plan for a Temple of Equality, a spherical edifice with a statue of Equality inside. She holds a level and stands on a globe which in turn is supported by levels (Fig. 35). The prize-winning project for such a temple was designed by the architects Jean-Nicolas-Louis Durand and Jean-Thomas Thibault. The original is lost, but there is a copy in the Staatliche Graphische Sammlung in Munich (Fig. 36). They proposed an unorthodox rectangular structure, each pillar of which stood for a civic virtue. A statue of Public Happiness can be glimpsed inside. For the pediment they proposed low reliefs of Liberty and Equality facing each other, the one holding a Phrygian bonnet, the other a level. In between was the declaration "Elles sont inséparables." An equilateral triangle was to hang from the peak, inscribed with the word LOI. When a version of this design was later published under Napoleon the civic virtues were changed, the allegorical figures on the pediment were given flowers to hold, the declaration that Liberty and Equality were inseparable was removed, and the triangle disappeared.

This proliferation of triangles coincided with the peak of the Terror, which ended following the overthrow of Robespierre and his colleagues in Thermidor Year II, July 1794 in our calendar. Soon what is now called the Thermidorian reaction set in, and in 1795 the Convention passed a new constitution to replace the radical one they had approved two years earlier. It called for a conservative republic with voting qualifications intended to enfranchise the propertied classes.

Legislative power was divided among a Council of Five Hundred and a Council of Elders, one to initiate laws, the other to approve them. Moreover, executive power was divided among five Directors, giving rise to "the Directory" as the name of the regime. The new moderation was revealed eventually in a new heading for the *Bulletin des lois* (Fig. 37). Beginning in June 1797 the heading became very complex in comparison with the one we saw earlier. The level is still there, but is reduced in size and almost lost among other emblems. At the same time Hercules, symbol of popular power, was replaced at the end of the *Bulletin* with a stamp displaying the Laws encompassed by a serpent. Law replaced insurrection.

Despite this diminution of the level of Equality, there were still some striking examples of the desire to use the equilateral triangle in a bold fashion during the Directory. In Paris, for instance, the architect Cointeraux advocated imposition of such a triangle on the city, giving the centre of government a sacred air. "Je dirai, d'abord," he wrote, "que tout doit prendre une nouvelle face dans un nouvel empire tel que celui de la République française." Cointeraux advocated leaving the Council of Five Hundred where it was in the Bourbon Palace, putting the Council of Elders in the uncompleted church of the Madeleine, and accommodating the Directors in the Tuileries Palace. When these three buildings were connected by straight lines, an equilateral triangle would result (Fig. 38). Appropriately, the two representative assemblies would form the base, while the executive branch would form the apex. The whole would point east toward the rising sun. The domed central part of the Tuileries Palace was to be called the "Dôme de l'Unité," the part next to the rue Honoré would be known as the "Pavillon de la Liberté," and that next to the Seine would be known as the "Pavillon de l'Egalité," creating another holy trinity. He proposed calling the centre of the triangle created by the three branches of government the "Centre Métrique," the point from which all distances in France would be measured in future, instead of from the traditional point, the cathedral of Notre Dame. On his plan he showed this focal point radiating light like a sacred centre. This shift of the centre of reverence from Notre Dame to the locus of secular government symbolized one result of the Revolution.

The sacred triangle in both its forms, however, lost prestige during this period. In 1796 a group of radicals led by Gracchus Babeuf conspired to overthrow the new Directory in order to establish a society of equals in which goods would be evenly distributed. This conspiracy was suppressed and the leaders were executed or imprisoned, but for many the ideal of equality was once again associated with violence. In an engraving recalling the Terror as a warning for the future, Robespierre and his colleagues were shown approaching Death, "La Dame du niveau, ou la soeur Egalité," who wears a triangle and a guillotine around her neck (Fig. 39). The artist seems to associate the triangle with the triangular shape of the blade of the guillotine. Death is being embraced by Marat and crowned with a Phrygian bonnet by Danton. All the Terrorists wear pendants in which levels, instead of skulls, combine with crossed bones as symbols of death. The level and the notion of the Trinity were both debased when they were used to glorify the Three Directors who staged a coup on 18 Fructidor Year v (4 September 1797), purging opponents who had been elected to the Council of Five Hundred. An engraving showed the three politicians under a giant Phrygian bonnet decorated with a level (Fig. 40). The caption hails them as saviours of the Fatherland, "la Trinité Républicaine," who had rescued the Constitution.

The case of the triangle in the French Revolution suggests that a sacred symbol can be used to legitimatize or sacralize a movement, but that the symbol itself can become discredited. Some of those who had been privileged under the the old regime rejected the level as a symbol of social equality because such equality was unacceptable to them, "the nightmare of aristocrats" as Lequeu described it. Others became bitterly disappointed as the various ideals expressed by the equilateral triangle proved illusory – harmony among the three orders; the trinity of three good kings; of the Nation, the Law, and the King; of Liberty, Law, and Unity; or the three republican martyrs. Both the level and the equilateral triangle were degraded by their association with terror and death. Moreover, when the idea of the trinity was used to glorify politicians who had staged a coup to save a shaky regime, it lost some of its sacred aura. Meanwhile faith in some of the other revolutionary symbols had declined. After the overthrow of Robespierre the Convention ordered the suppression of all symbolic Mountains, and one comes across engravings ridiculing the Phrygian bonnet as the "bonnet sans tête" and the Liberty Tree as the "arbre sans racine" (Fig. 41).

But if particular revolutionary symbols became discredited, the need for some symbolic underpinning of the government remained. As Frenchmen wearied of strife, instability, and economic dislocation, they became ready to accept the rule of a strong man. The fourth and final coup of the ill-fated Directory on 18 Brumaire Year VIII (9 November 1799) brought Napoleon to power. As Consulate gave way to life Consulate, and then Empire, the revolutionary symbols gradually disappeared. The change can be seen in the *Bulletin des lois*. The heading in which Liberty surrounded by triangles had appeared, and later a complex of more moderate emblems had been displayed, was now replaced by a mere number. At the same time the stamp at the end in which Hercules had once trampled symbols of the Old Regime, and where the tablets of the Laws had taken his place under the Directory, was replaced by one suitable for the Empire (Fig. 42). Napoleon's seal combined old monarchical symbols – the crown, the sceptre, and the hand of Justice – with the ancient Imperial Eagle. A figure of Charlemagne replaced the *fleur-de-lys* atop the sceptre. Not a triangle was to be seen.

NOTES

1 Emile Durkheim, *Elementary Forms of Religious Life*, trans. J.W. Swain (London, 1915).

2 Mary Douglas, *Natural Symbols: Explorations in Cosmology* (London, 1970). See too Edward Shils, *Center and Periphery: Essays in Macrosociology* (Chicago and London, 1975), and Clifford Geertz, "Centers, Kings, and Charisma: Reflections on the Symbolics of Power," in *Culture and Its Creators: Essays in Honour of Edward Shils*, ed. Joseph Ben-David and Terry Nichols Clark (Chicago, 1977), 150–71.

3 Jacques Ellul, *Propaganda: The Formation of Men's Attitudes*, 1st Amer. ed. (New York, 1965), esp. 70–9.

4 James A. Leith, "Desacralization, Resacralization and Architectural Planning during the French Revolution," *Eighteenth-Century Life*, 8, n.s. 3 (May 1982), 74–84.

5 Théophile Schmidt, *La Colonne de la Liberté de Montpellier élevée en 1791 et détruite en 1814* (Montpellier, 1925).

6 Evidence for this can be seen in a poster, the top half of which shows aristocrats and priests leading the people toward a white star suggesting that of Bethlehem, while the bottom half shows commissars, Soviet soldiers, peasants, and workers following the red star.

7 Lynn Hunt, "Hercules and the Radical Image in the French Revolution," *Representations*, 1:2 (Spring 1983), 95–117, rightly calls attention to the use of Hercules during the Terror, but she goes too far in arguing that there was an intention to diminish or push aside the "moderate" figure of Liberty. In the great art contest launched in the spring of 1794, there was a program for a colossal figure of the People in the guise of Hercules for the promontory of the Ile de la Cité, but there was another for a

huge bronze statue of Liberty for the largest square in Paris, the Place de la Révolution, now the Place de la Concorde. Also at the great Festival of the Supreme Being Liberty played a conspicuous role, and carried a club just like Hercules. Furthermore, a very militant Liberty–she is accompanied by cannon, lightning, and a volcanic eruption–continued on the letterhead of the Committee of Public Safety. Finally, Liberty survived throughout the whole period of the first Republic on the seal of the state used to authenticate laws.

8 Carl Jung, *Man and His Symbols* (1964; London, 1972), 40–2; illustration on 42.

9 The fact that Liberty appeared in the heading of the *Bulletin des lois*, and was made more radical at the peak of the Terror, while the People in the guise of Hercules appeared on the stamp at the end, shows that there was no intention to push Liberty aside, as Professor Hunt argues (see n. 7 above). Also Hercules holds Liberty and Equality on an orb, suggesting that they rule over the world with the support of the People. Professor Hunt argues that their small size shows that they had diminished in importance, whereas they are shown as large as possible without making them appear too heavy to support with one hand, even by Hercules.

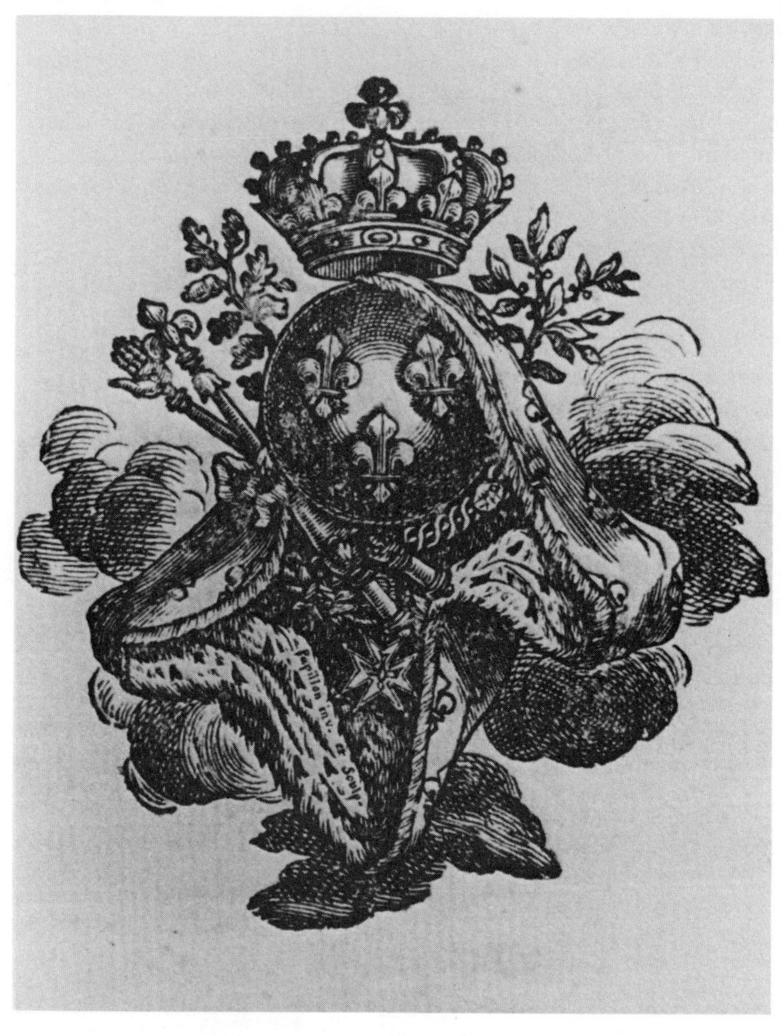

Fig. 1 Bourbon coat-of-arms in 1787.
Archives Nationales (Photo: Josse).

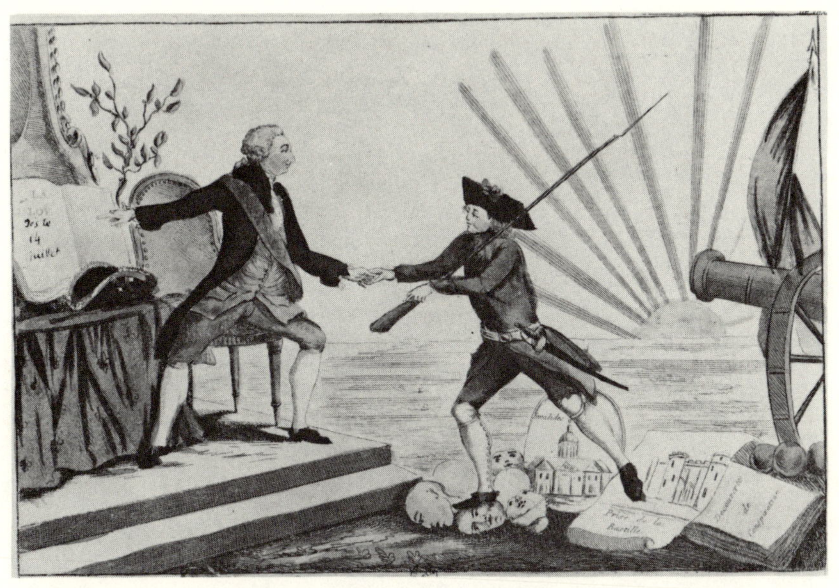

Fig. 2 "Le Grand Pas de fait, ou l'aurore d'un beau jour 1789." Bibliothèque Nationale, Estampes (Photo: B.N. Service Photographique).

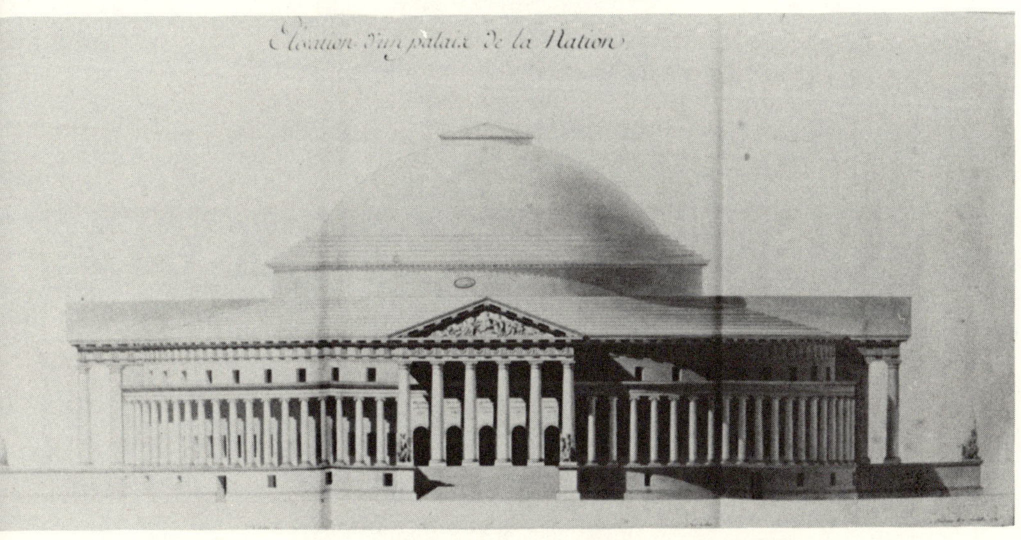

Fig. 3 Louis Combes, Project for a National Assembly. Elevation. Archives Nationales (Photo: Josse).

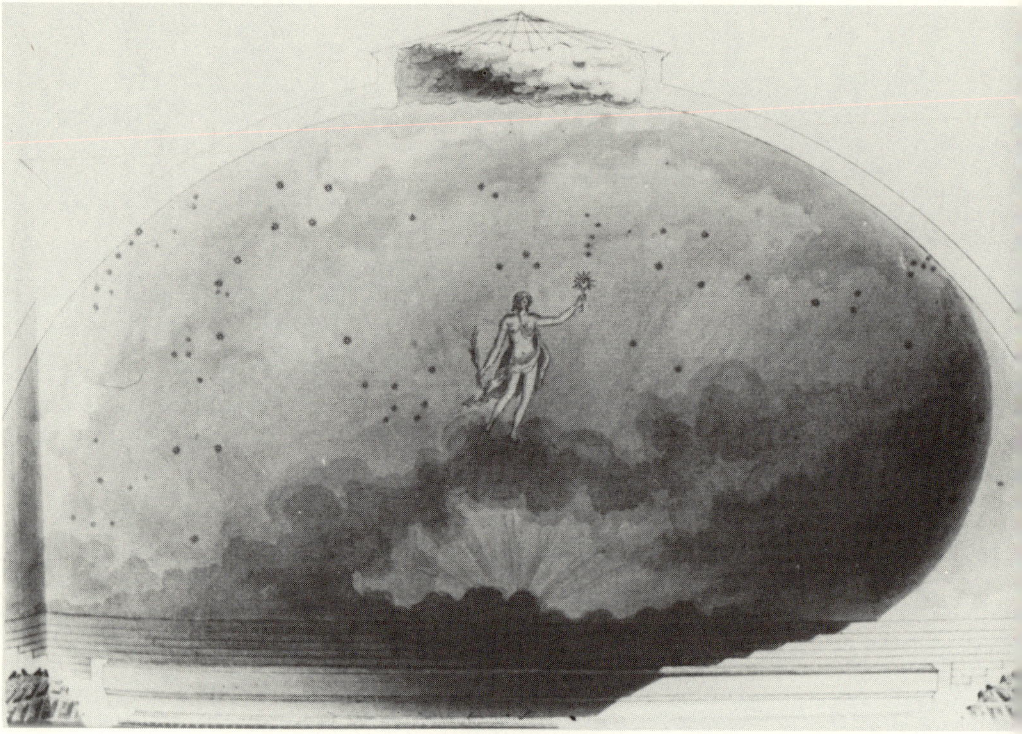

Fig. 4 Louis Combes, Project for a National Assembly. Detail of the cross-section.
Archives Nationales (Photo: Josse).

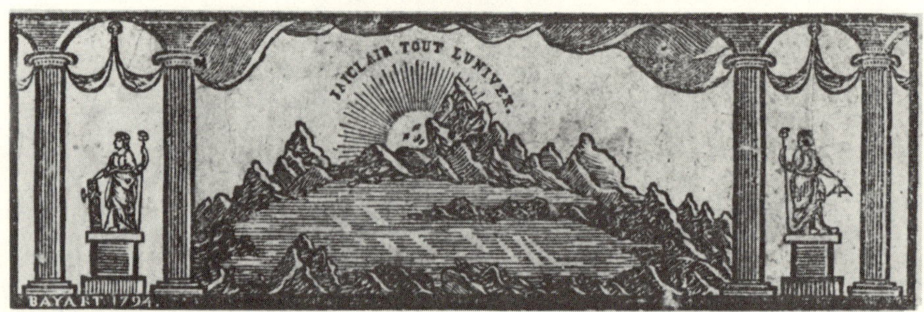

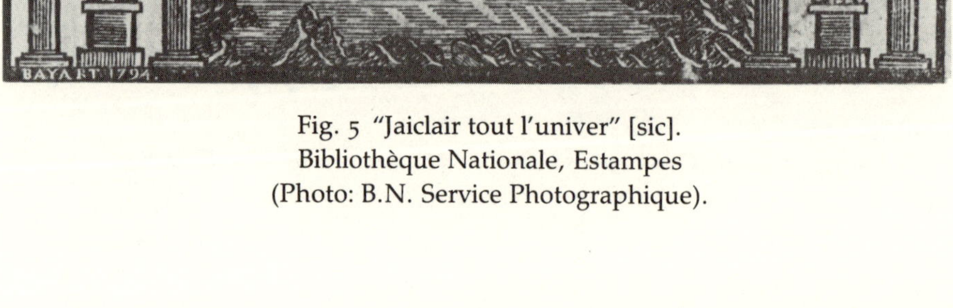

Fig. 5 "Jaiclair tout l'univer" [sic].
Bibliothèque Nationale, Estampes
(Photo: B.N. Service Photographique).

Fig. 6 "La Constitution Républicaine, semblable aux tables de Moyse, sort de la Montagne au milieu de la foudre."
Bibliothèque Nationale, Estampes
(Photo: B.N. Service Photographique).

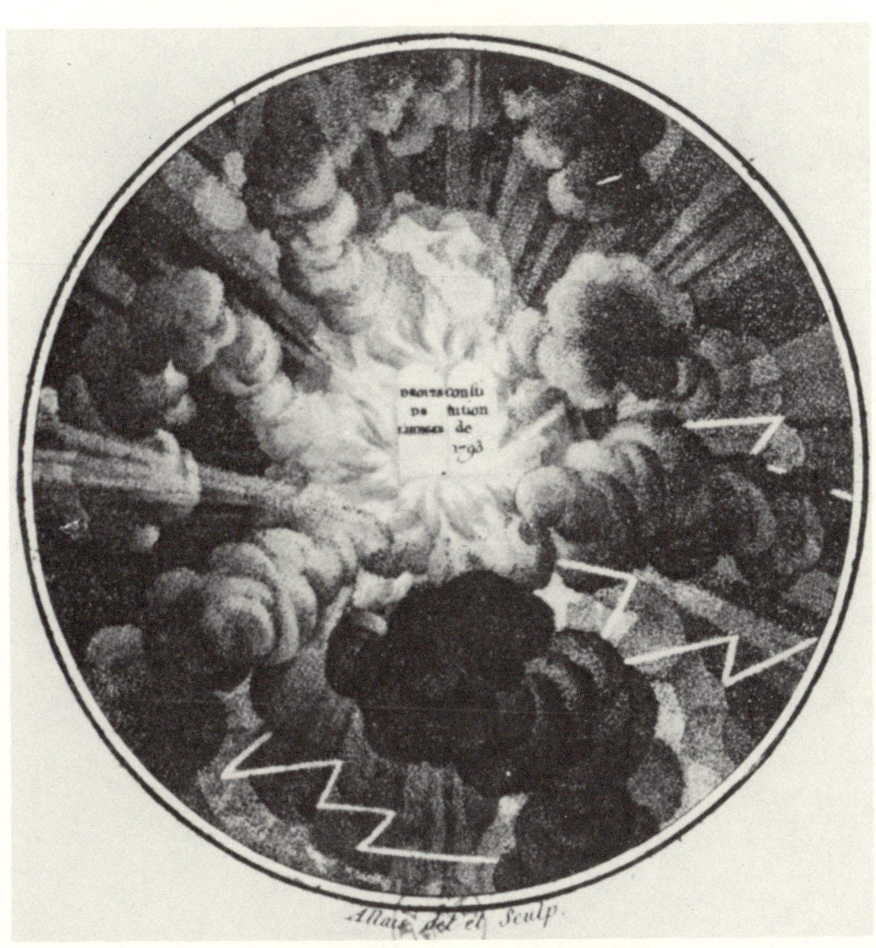

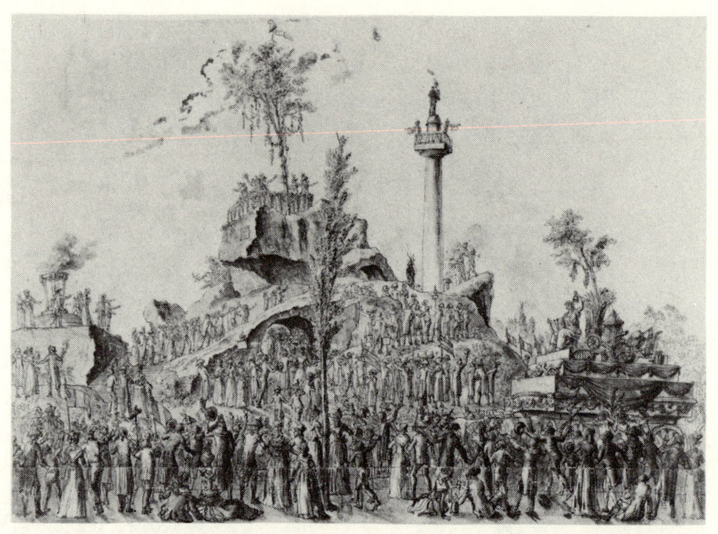

Fig. 7 Mountain on the Champ de Mars, 8 June 1794. Bibliothèque Nationale, Estampes (Photo: B.N. Service Photographique).

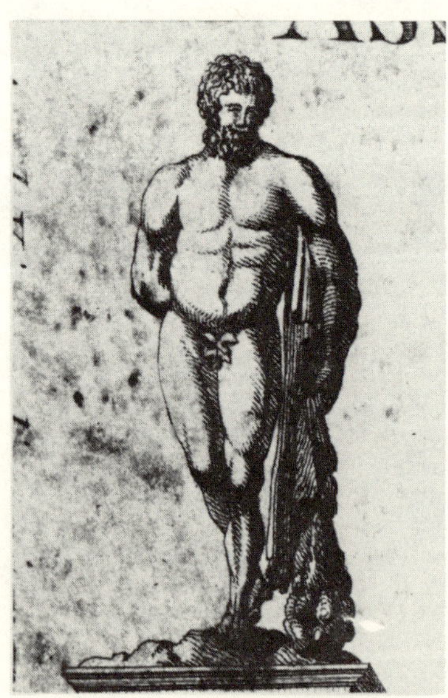

Fig. 8 Detail of the certificate given to the conquerors of the Bastille, 1790. Archives Nationales (Photo: Josse).

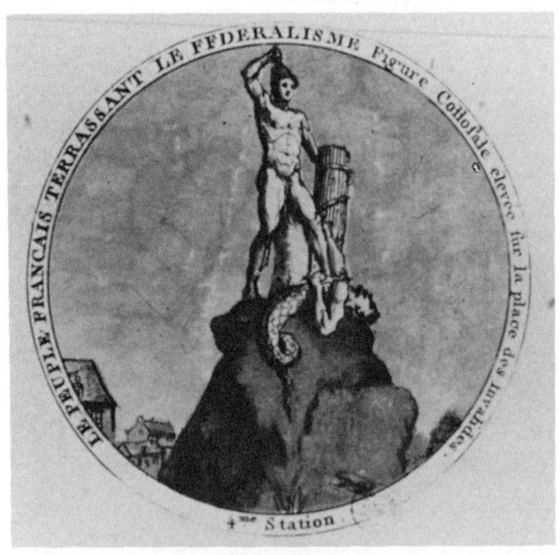

Fig. 9 Fourth station in the Festival of Unity and Indivisibility.
Bibliothèque Nationale, Estampes
(Photo: B.N. Service Photographique).

Fig. 10 Figure atop the column next to the Mountain on the Champ de Mars, 8 June 1794.
Bibliothèque Nationales, Estampes
(Photo: B.N. Service Photographique).

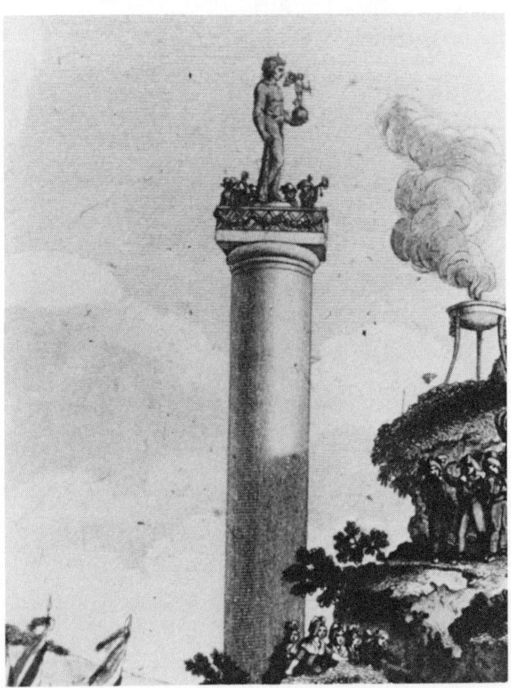

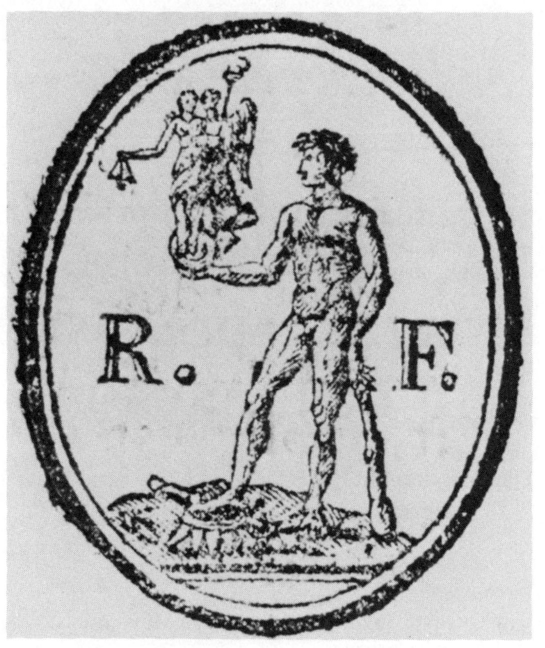

Fig. 11 Stamp at the end of the *Bulletin des lois* in Year II. Archives Nationales (Photo: Josse).

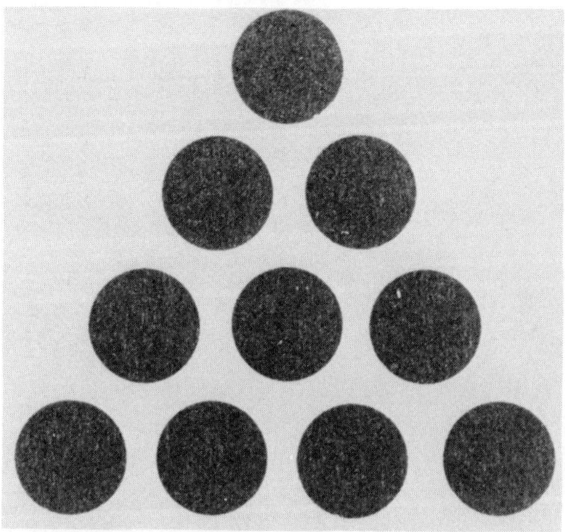

Fig. 12 Pythagorean equilateral triangle (Photo: Leith).

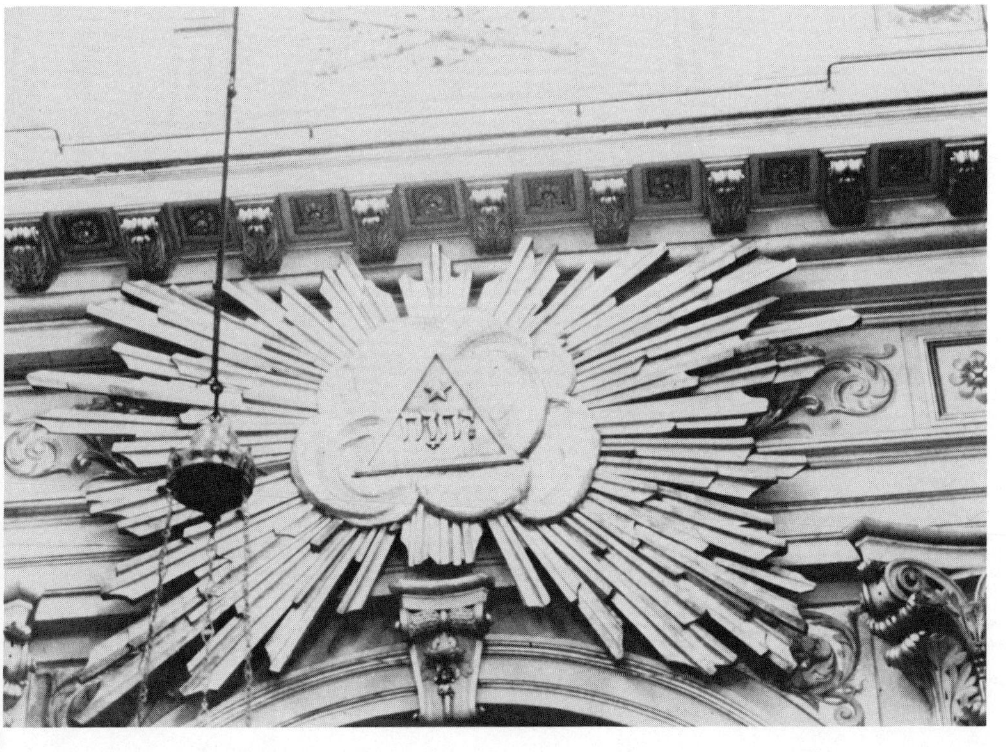

Fig. 13 Triangle representing the Trinity in Saint-Louis-en-l'Île in Paris (Photo: Josse).

Fig. 14 Detail from the back of an American one-dollar bill (Photo: Leith).

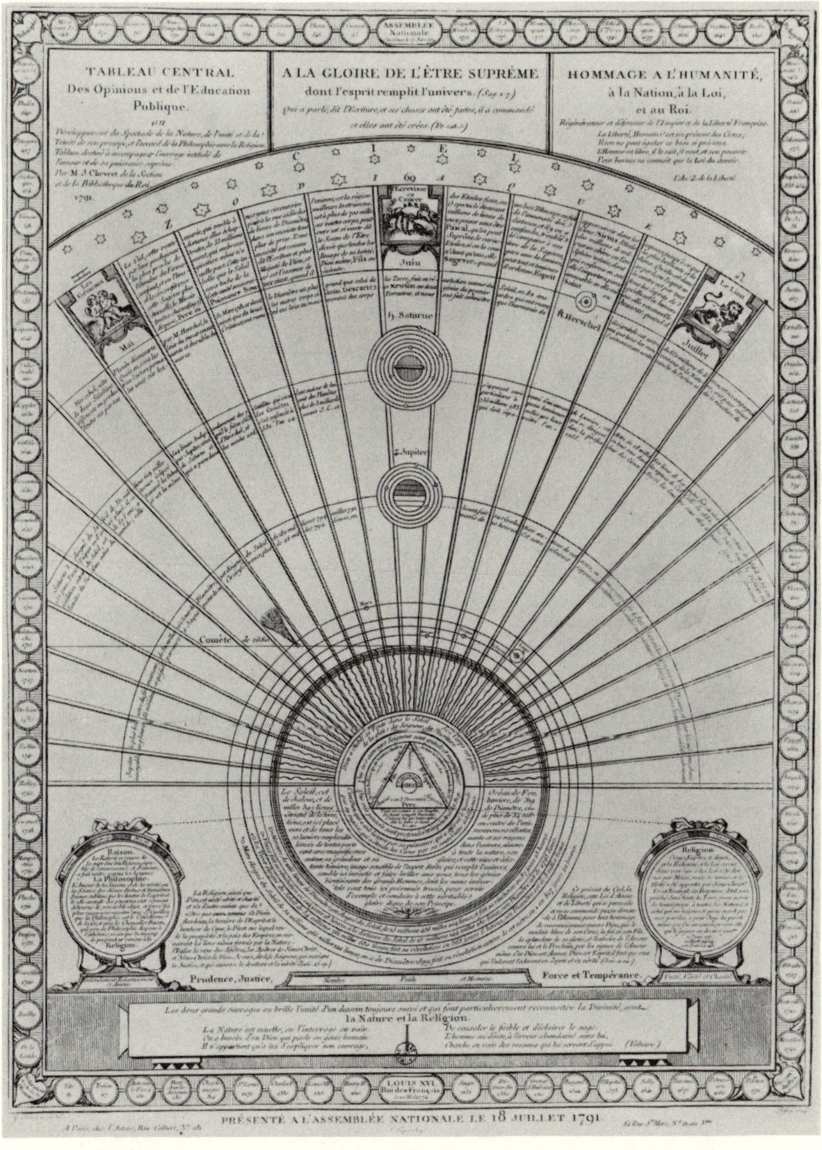

Fig. 15 "Tableau Central des Opinions et de l'Education Publique," 1791. Bibliothèque Nationale, Estampes (Photo: B.N. Service Photographique).

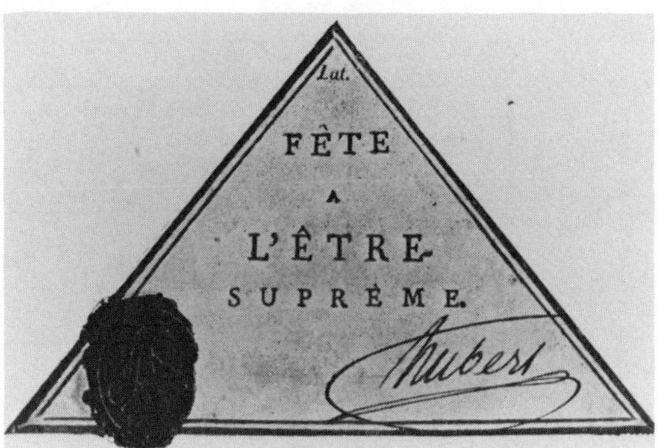

Fig. 16 Admission ticket to the Festival of the Supreme Being.
Bibliothèque Nationale, Estampes
(Photo: B.N. Service Photographique).

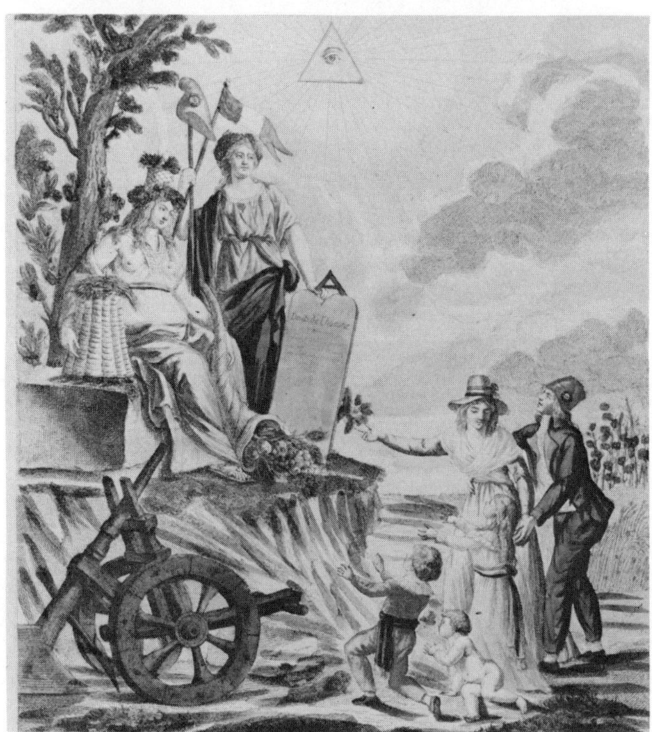

Fig. 17 "Fête célébrée en l'honneur de l'Etre Suprême ..."
Bibliothèque Nationale, Estampes
(Photo: B.N. Service Photographique).

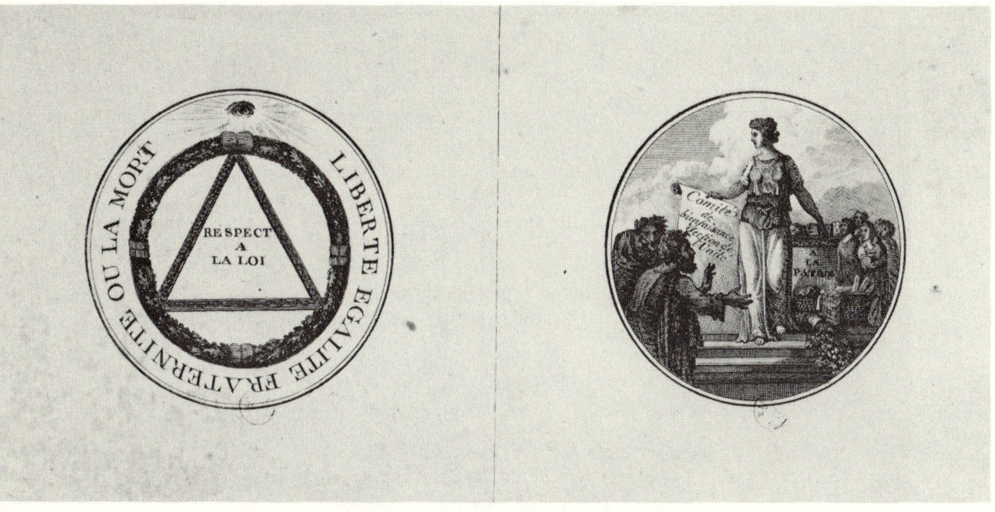

Fig. 18 Membership card of the Welfare Committee of the Section de l'Unité.
Bibliothèque Nationale, Estampes
(Photo: B.N. Service Photographique).

Fig. 19 "Trinité Convent[ionelle]." Bibliothèque Nationale, Estampes
(Photo: B.N. Service Photographique).

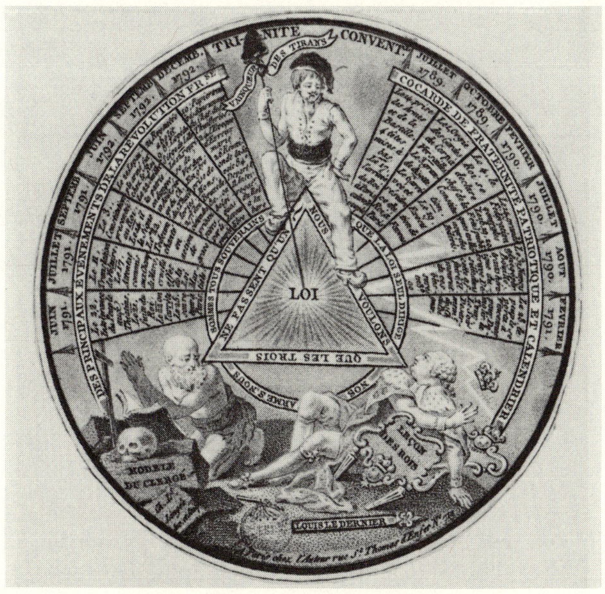

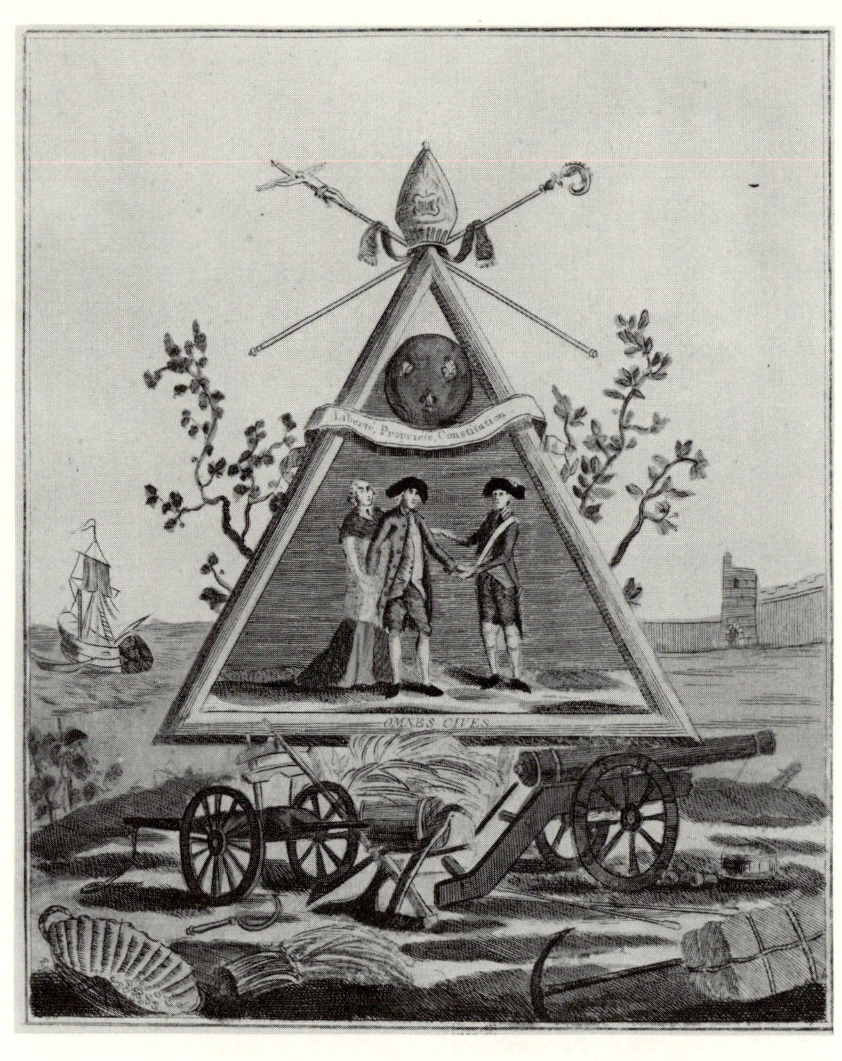

Fig. 20 "Mieux vaut tard que jamais." Bibliothèque Nationale, Estampes (Photo: B.N. Service Photographique).

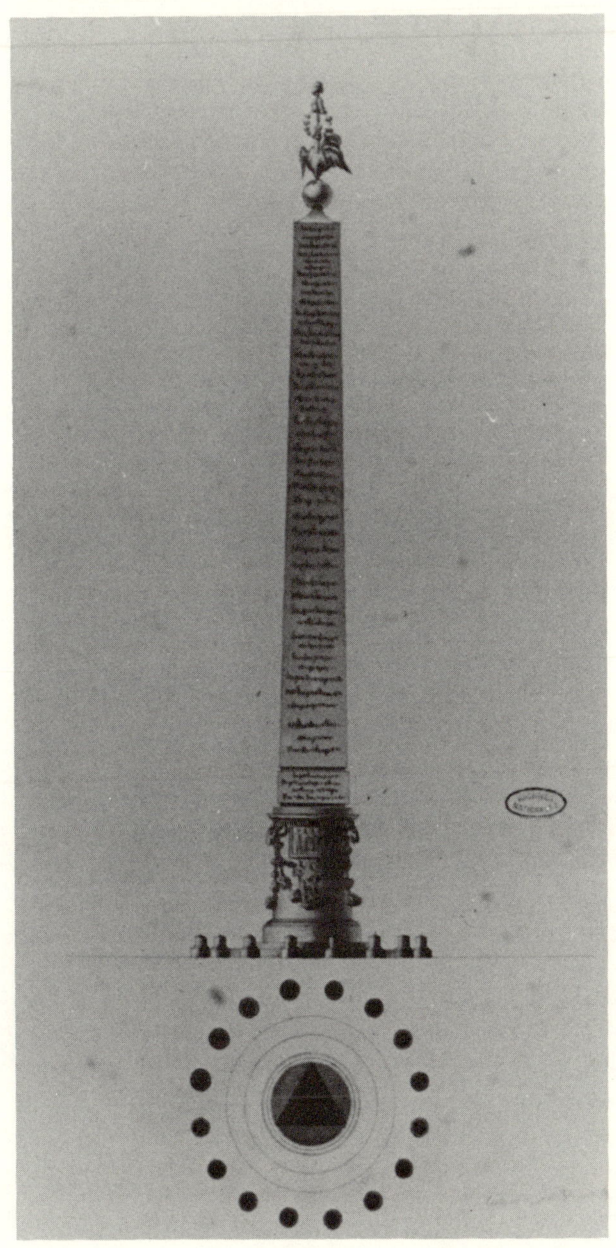

Fig. 21 Mouillefarine, Obelisk for the "Pont de Réunion."
Archives Nationales (Photo: Josse).

OFFRANDE DE LA PATRIE A LOUIS·XVI·

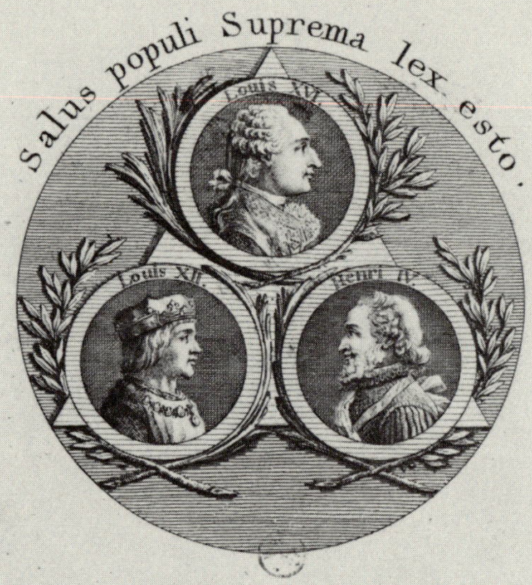

Amav·ere dici pater atque Princeps

La plus Souveraine des Loix, Cést la Felicité Publique. *Elle doit faire taire toutes les Loix, et les usages qui lui sont Contraires, elle doit dissiper ces restes d'Institutions gothiques qu'une horde de Barbares vint semer parmi les Bons et sages Gaulois nos ayeux. Ainsi toutes les Nations cherchant à perfectionner l'Ordre Social, il seroit honteux que les François fussent les Seuls qui aimassent à retrograder. mais l'Interet général de la Nation S'opposant aux abus de prejugés qui étéignent toute émulation et toute Industrie, tout Sentiment D'honneur et de Courage ne sçauroient subsister Sous un Prince. qui aime son peuple. qui en est aimé et qui ne Veut point le laisser avilir. Ventre Saint Gris* disoit Henri. quatre *s'en - pren dre a mon peuple Cest s'en prendre à moi.*

Fig. 22 "Offrande de la Patrie à Louis XVI."
Bibliothèque Nationale, Estampes
(Photo: B.N. Service Photographique).

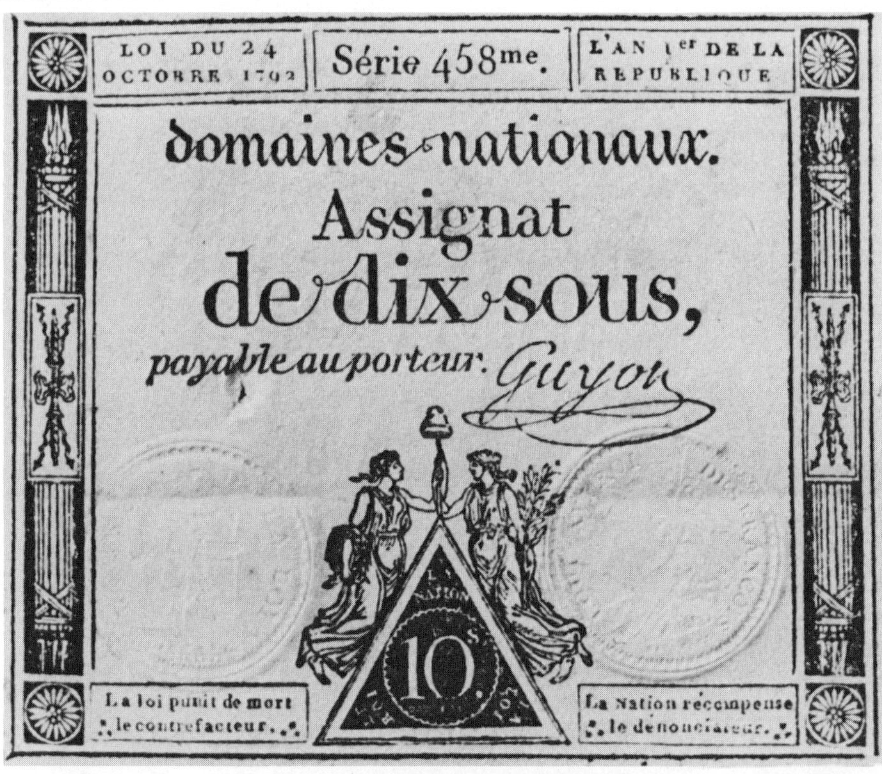

Fig. 23 Assignat worth 10 sous, 1792.
Archives Nationales (Photo: Josse).

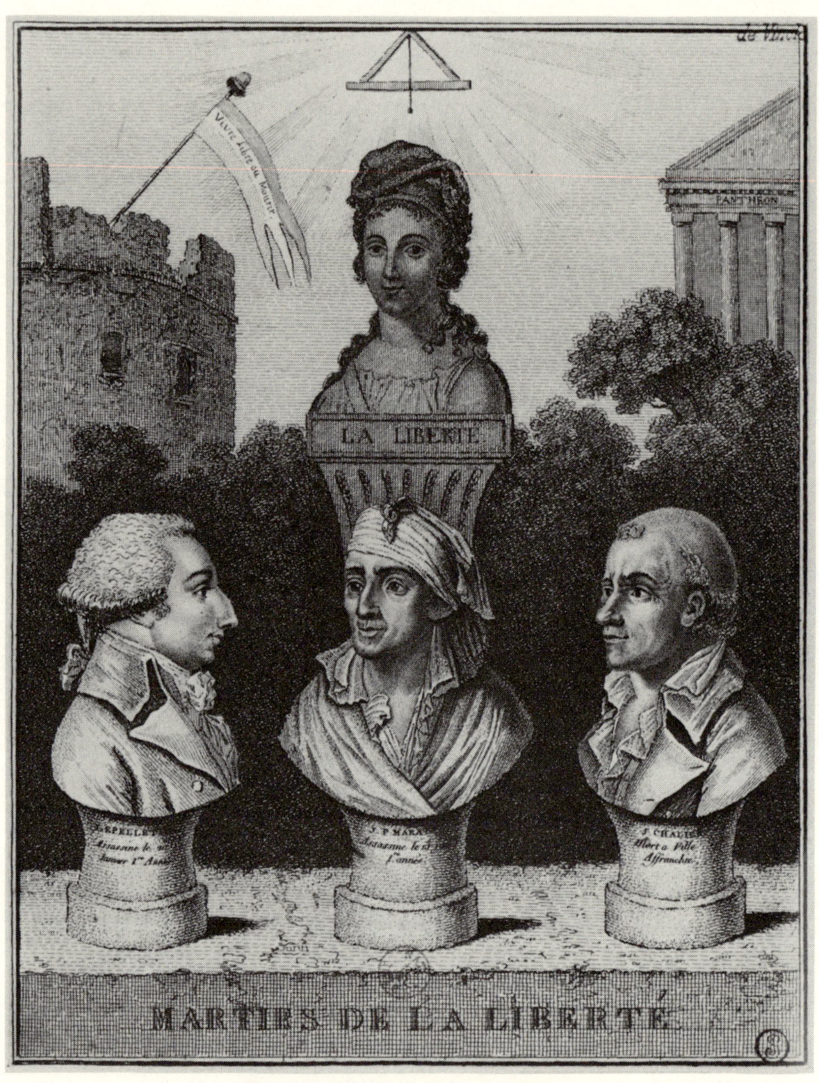

Fig. 24 "Martirs de la Liberté."
Bibliothèque Nationale, Estampes
(Photo: B.N. Service Photographique).

OPPOSITE

Fig. 25 Declaration of the Rights of Man, 1793.
Bibliothèque Nationale, Estampes
(Photo: B.N. Service Photographique).

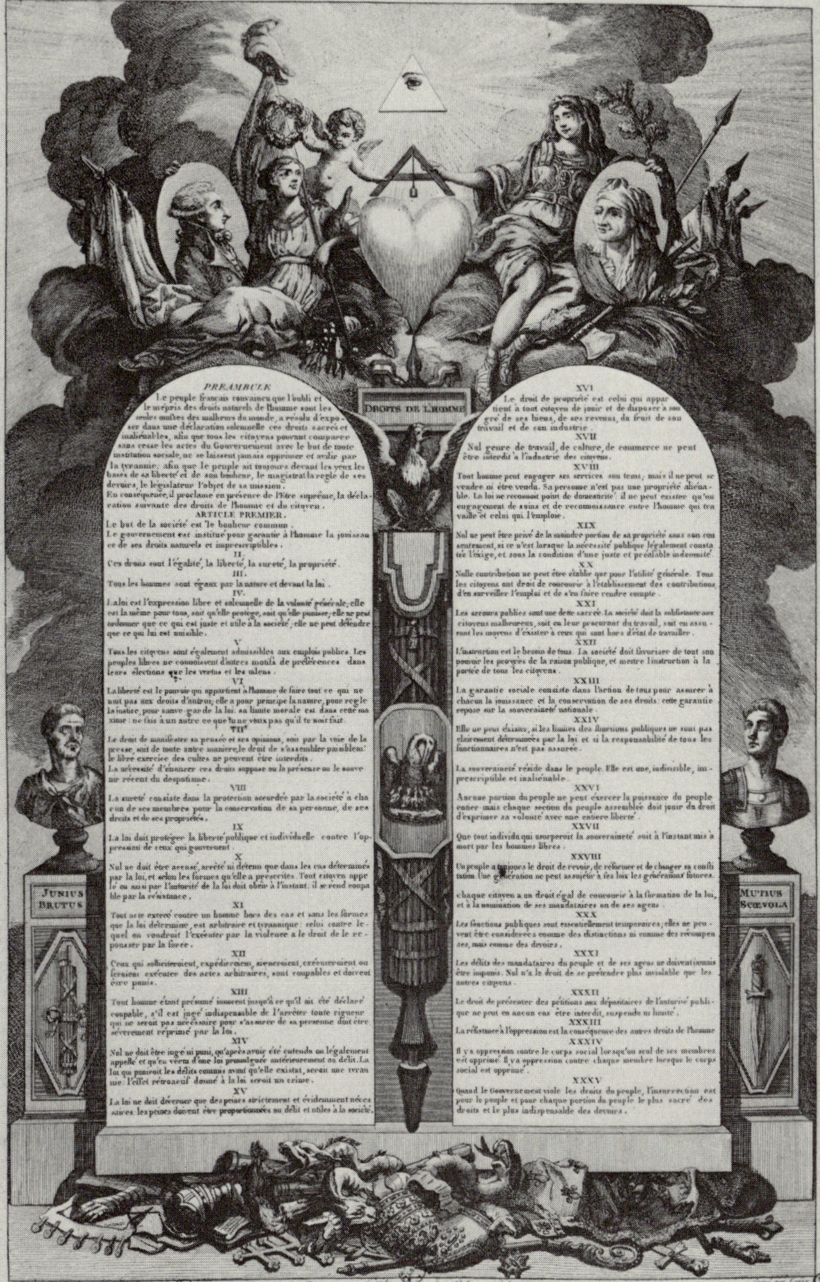
de Vinck
DROITS DE L'HOMME
PREAMBULE
Le peuple français convaincu que l'oubli et le mépris des droits naturels de l'homme sont les seules causes des malheurs du monde, a résolu d'exposer dans une déclaration solemnelle ces droits sacrés et inaliénables, afin que tous les citoyens pouvant comparer sans cesse les actes du Gouvernement avec le but de toute institution sociale, ne se laissent jamais opprimer et avilir par la tyrannie; afin que le peuple ait toujours devant les yeux les bases de sa liberté et de son bonheur, le magistrat la regle de ses devoirs, le législateur l'objet de sa mission.
En conséquence, il proclame en présence de l'Etre suprême, la déclaration suivante des droits de l'homme et du citoyen.
ARTICLE PREMIER.
Le but de la société est le bonheur commun.
Le gouvernement est institué pour garantir à l'homme la jouissance de ses droits naturels et imprescriptibles.
II.
Ces droits sont l'égalité, la liberté, la sureté, la propriété.
III.
Tous les hommes sont égaux par la nature et devant la loi.
IV.
La loi est l'expression libre et solemnelle de la volonté générale; elle est la même pour tous, soit qu'elle protége, soit qu'elle punisse; elle ne peut ordonner que ce qui est juste et utile à la société; elle ne peut défendre que ce qui lui est nuisible.
V
Tous les citoyens sont également admissibles aux emplois publics. Les peuples libres ne connoissent d'autres motifs de préférences dans leurs élections que les vertus et les talens.
VI
La liberté est le pouvoir qui appartient à l'homme de faire tout ce qui ne nuit pas aux droits d'autrui; elle a pour principe la nature, pour regle la justice, pour sauve-garde la loi: sa limite morale est dans cette maxime: ne fais à un autre ce que tu ne veux pas qu'il te soit fait.
VII
Le droit de manifester sa pensée et ses opinions, soit par la voie de la presse, soit de toute autre maniere, le droit de s'assembler paisiblement, le libre exercice des cultes ne peuvent être interdits.
La nécessité d'énoncer ces droits suppose ou la présence ou le souvenir récent du despotisme.
VIII
La sureté consiste dans la protection accordée par la société à chacun de ses membres pour la conservation de sa personne, de ses droits et de ses propriétés.
IX
La loi doit protéger la liberté publique et individuelle contre l'oppression de ceux qui gouvernent.
X
Nul ne doit être accusé, arrêté ni détenu que dans les cas déterminés par la loi, et selon les formes qu'elle a prescrites. Tout citoyen appelé ou saisi par l'autorité de la loi doit obéir à l'instant; il se rend coupable par la résistance.
XI
Tout acte exercé contre un homme hors des cas et sans les formes que la loi détermine, est arbitraire et tyrannique: celui contre lequel on voudroit l'exécuter par la violence a le droit de le repousser par la force.
XII
Ceux qui solliciteroient, expédieroient, signeroient, exécuteroient ou feroient exécuter des actes arbitraires, sont coupables et doivent être punis.
XIII
Tout homme étant présumé innocent jusqu'à ce qu'il ait été déclaré coupable, s'il est jugé indispensable de l'arrêter toute rigueur qui ne seroit pas nécessaire pour s'assurer de sa personne doit être sévérement réprimé par la loi.
XIV
Nul ne doit être jugé ni puni, qu'après avoir été entendu ou légalement appellé et qu'en vertu d'une loi promulguée antérieurement au délit. La loi qui puniroit les délits commis avant qu'elle existat, seroit une tyrannie: l'effet rétroactif donné à la loi seroit un crime.
XV
La loi ne doit décerner que des peines strictement et évidemment nécessaires, les peines doivent être proportionnées au délit et utiles à la société.
XVI
Le droit de propriété est celui qui appartient à tout citoyen de jouir et de disposer à son gré de ses biens, de ses revenus, du fruit de son travail et de son industrie.
XVII
Nul genre de travail, de culture, de commerce ne peut être interdit à l'industrie des citoyens.
XVIII
Tout homme peut engager ses services son tems; mais il ne peut se vendre ni être vendu. Sa personne n'est pas une propriété aliénable. La loi ne reconnoit point de domesticité; il ne peut exister qu'un engagement de soins et de reconnoissance entre l'homme qui travaille et celui qui l'emploie.
XIX
Nul ne peut être privé de la moindre portion de sa propriété sans son consentement, si ce n'est lorsque la nécessité publique légalement constatée l'exige, et sous la condition d'une juste et préalable indemnité.
XX
Nulle contribution ne peut être établie que pour l'utilité générale. Tous les citoyens ont droit de concourir à l'établissement des contributions d'en surveiller l'emploi et de s'en faire rendre compte.
XXI
Les secours publics sont une dette sacrée. La société doit la subsistance aux citoyens malheureux, soit en leur procurant du travail, soit en assurant les moyens d'exister à ceux qui sont hors d'état de travailler.
XXII
L'instruction est le besoin de tous. La société doit favoriser de tout son pouvoir les progrès de la raison publique, et mettre l'instruction à la portée de tous les citoyens.
XXIII
La garantie sociale consiste dans l'action de tous pour assurer à chacun la jouissance et la conservation de ses droits: cette garantie repose sur la souveraineté nationale.
XXIV
Elle ne peut exister, si les limites des fonctions publiques ne sont pas clairement déterminées par la loi et si la responsabilité de tous les fonctionnaires n'est pas assurée.
La souveraineté réside dans le peuple. Elle est une, indivisible, imprescriptible et inaliénable.
XXVI
Aucune portion du peuple ne peut exercer la puissance du peuple entier mais chaque section du peuple assemblée doit jouir du droit d'exprimer sa volonté avec une entiere liberté.
XXVII
Que tout individu qui usurperoit la souveraineté soit à l'instant mis à mort par les hommes libres.
XXVIII
Un peuple a toujours le droit de revoir, de réformer et de changer sa constitution. Une génération ne peut assujétir à ses loix les générations futures.
chaque citoyen a un droit égal de concourir à la formation de la loi, et à la nomination de ses mandataires ou de ses agens.
XXX
Les fonctions publiques sont essentiellement temporaires; elles ne peuvent être considerées comme des distinctions ni comme des récompenses, mais comme des devoirs.
XXXI
Les délits des mandataires du peuple et de ses agens ne doivent jamais être impunis. Nul n'a le droit de se prétendre plus inviolable que les autres citoyens.
XXXII
Le droit de présenter des pétitions aux dépositaires de l'autorité publique ne peut en aucun cas être interdit, suspendu ni limité.
XXXIII
La résistance à l'oppression est la conséquence des autres droits de l'homme
XXXIV
Il y a oppression contre le corps social lorsqu'un seul de ses membres est opprimé. Il y a oppression contre chaque membre lorsque le corps social est opprimé.
XXXV
Quand le Gouvernement viole les droits du peuple, l'insurrection est pour le peuple et pour chaque portion du peuple le plus sacré des droits et le plus indispensable des devoirs.
JUNIUS BRUTUS
MUTIUS SCŒVOLA
A PARIS, chez Villion et comp.ie M.ds papetiers. Rue S.t Jacques, à la Ville de Rouen N.o 2.
Gravé par Lerey

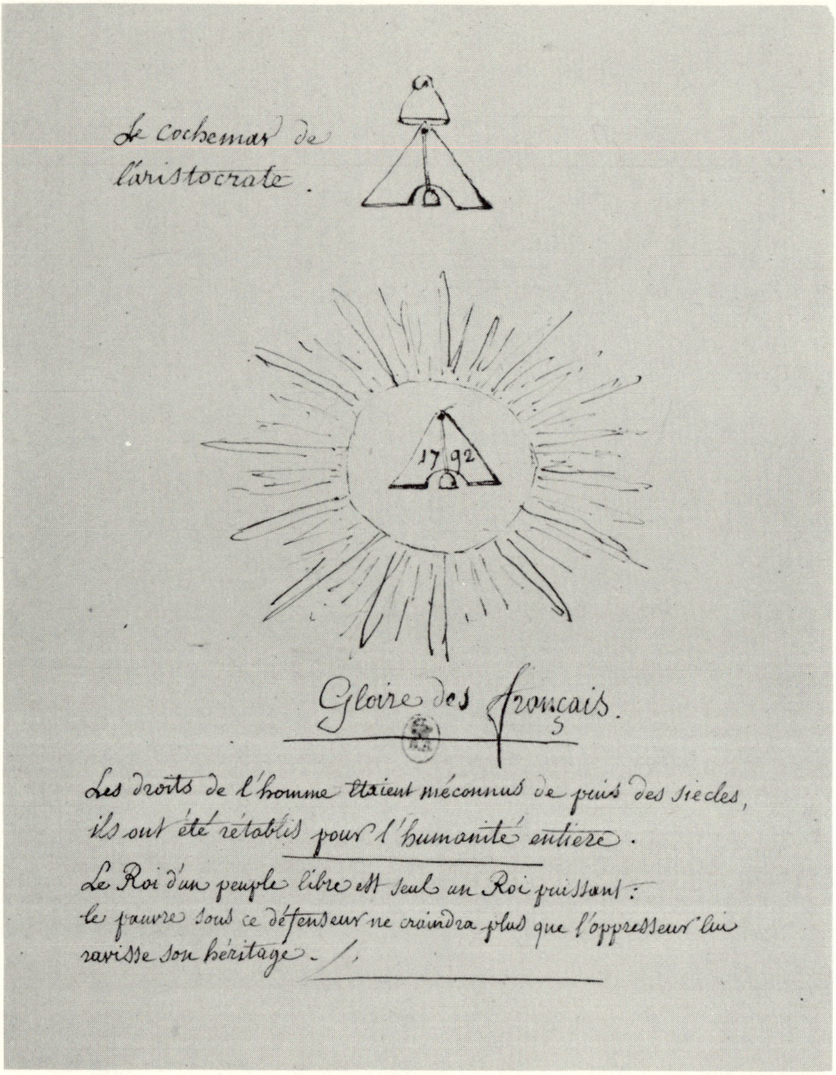

Le cochemar de l'aristocrate.

17 92

Gloire des Français

Les droits de l'homme étaient méconnus depuis des siecles, ils ont été rétablis pour l'humanité entiere.

Le Roi d'un peuple libre est seul un Roi puissant: le pauvre sous ce défenseur ne craindra plus que l'oppresseur lui ravisse son héritage. /.

Fig. 26 Jean-Jacques Lequeu, Level of Equality.
Bibliothèque Nationale, Estampes
(Photo: B.N. Service Photographique).

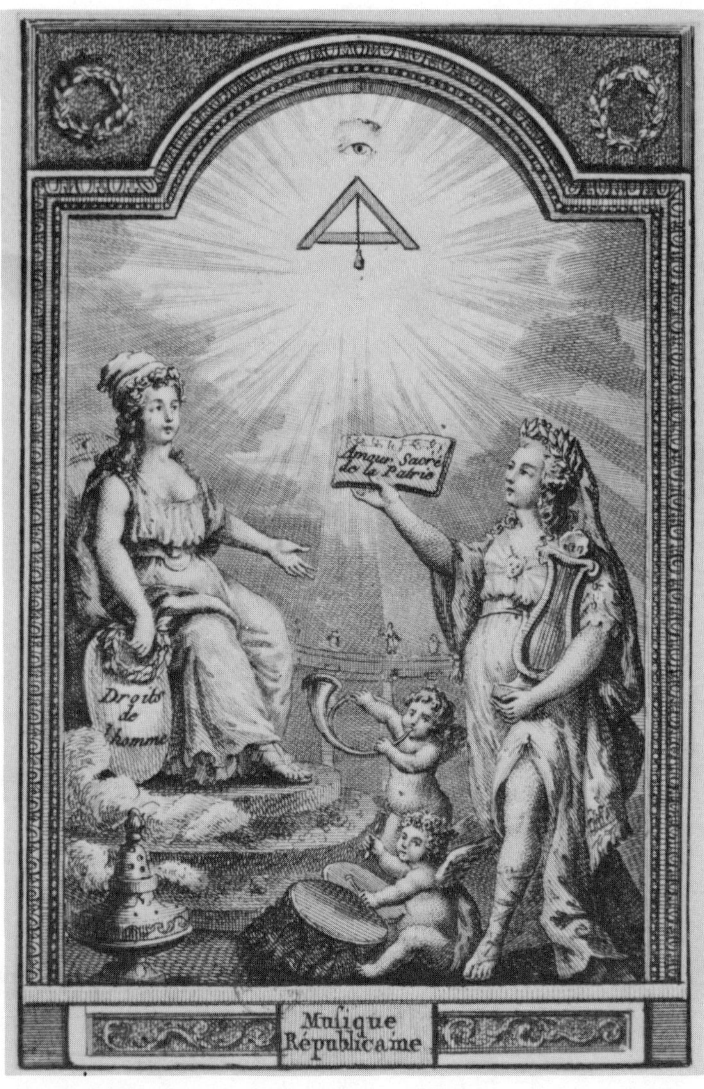

Fig. 27 "Musique Républicaine."
Bibliothèque Nationale, Estampes
(Photo: B.N. Service Photographique).

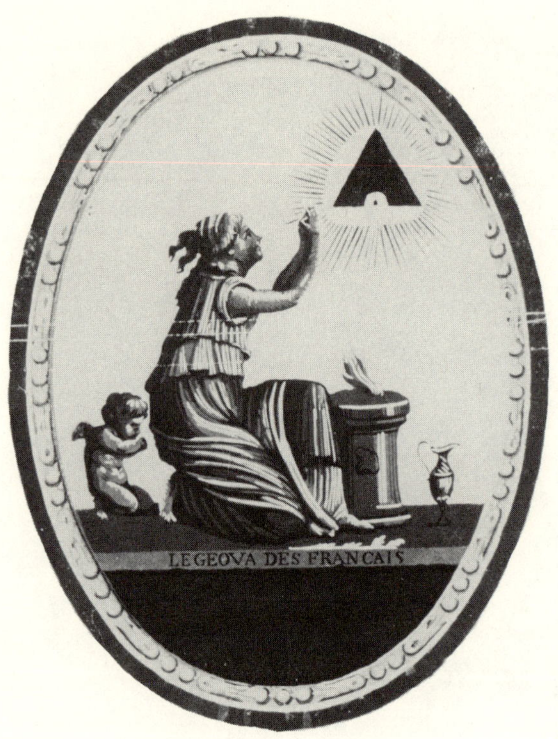

Fig. 28 "Le Geova des Français."
Bibliothèque Nationale, Estampes
(Photo: B.N. Service Photographique).

Fig. 29 Heading of the *Bulletin des lois*.
Archives Nationales (Photo: Josse).

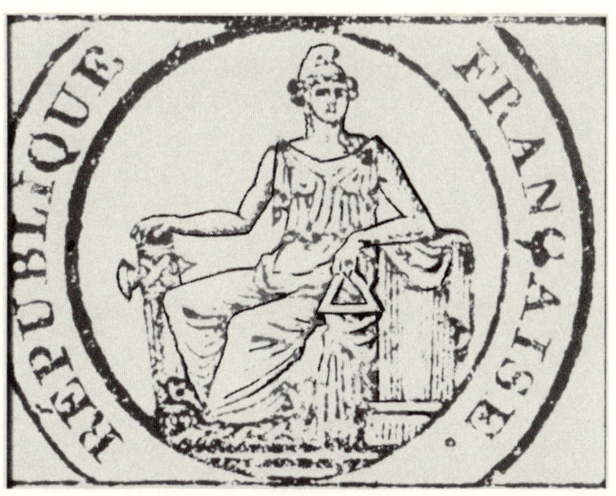

Fig. 30 Radicalized figure of Liberty in the heading of the *Bulletin des lois*. Archives Nationales (Photo: Josse).

Fig. 31 "Moi libre aussi." Bibliothèque Nationale, Estampes (Photo: B.N. Service Photographique).

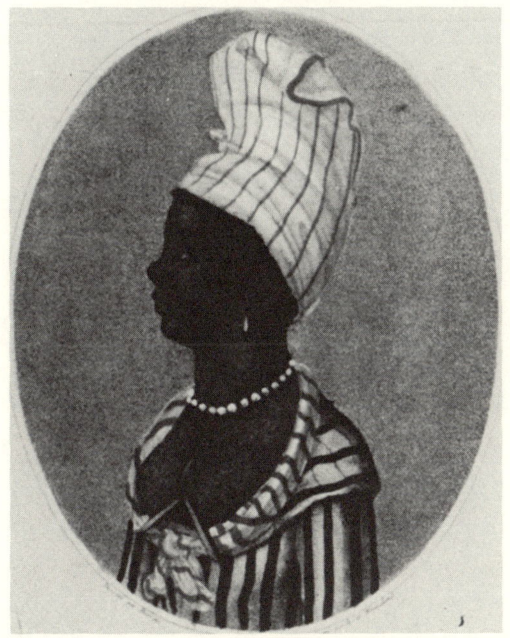

Fig. 32 François Delannoy,
Project for the Place du Carrousel.
Musée Carnavalet (Photo: Bulloz).

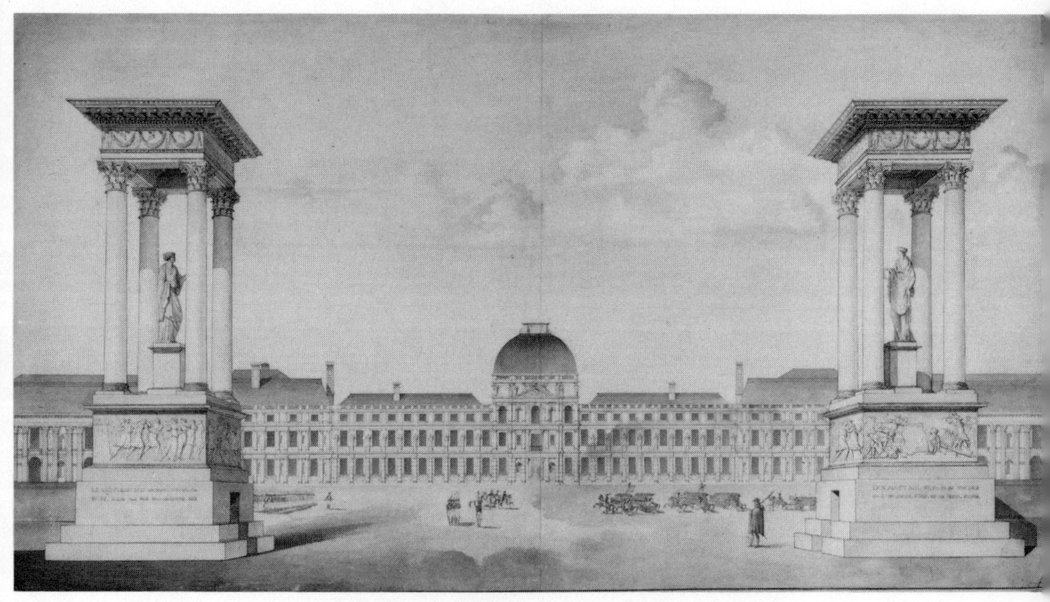

Fig. 33 François Delannoy,
Detail of the project for the Place du Carrousel
(Photo: Bulloz).

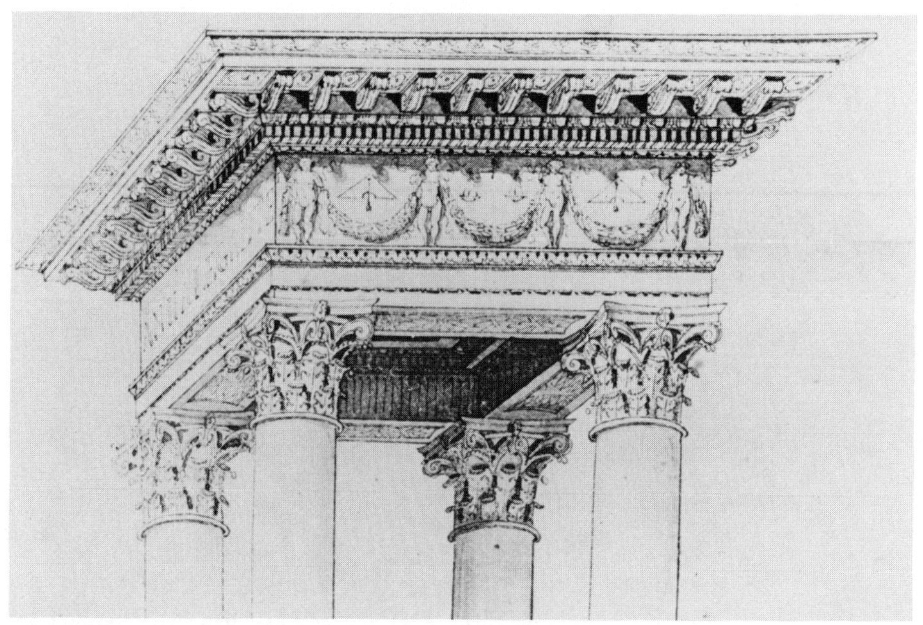

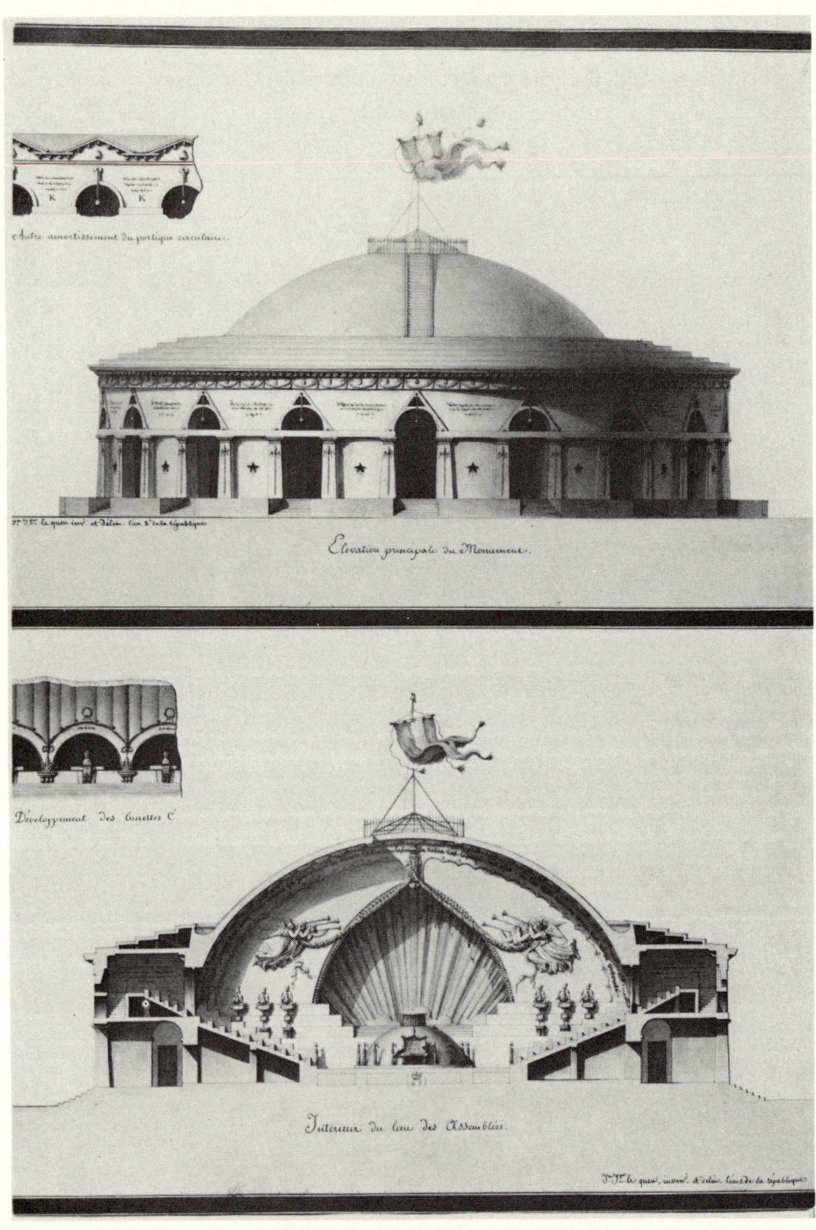

Fig. 34 Jean-Jacques Lequeu, Project for a Primary Assembly. Bibliothèque Nationale, Estampes (Photo: B.N. Service Photographique).

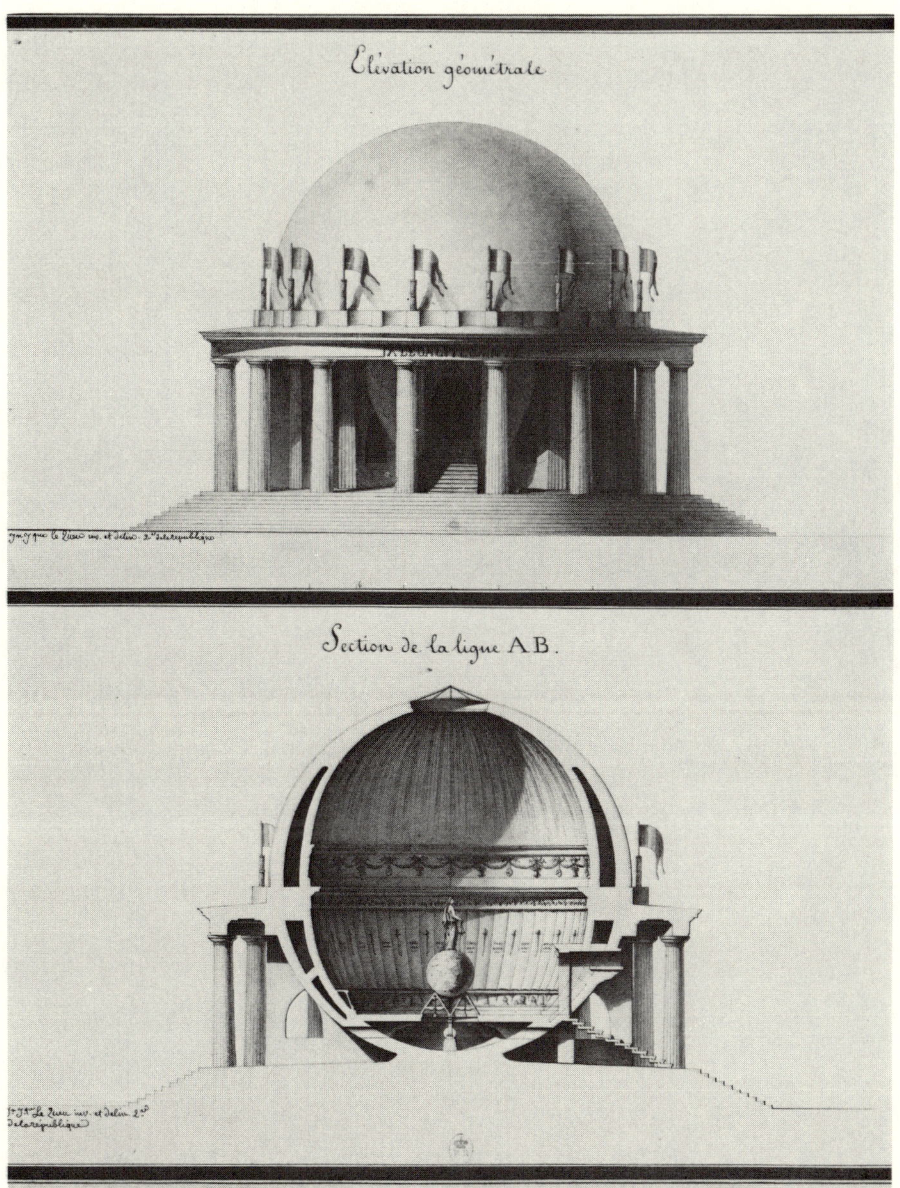

Fig. 35 Jean-Jacques Lequeu, Temple of Equality.
Bibliothèque Nationale, Estampes
(Photo: B.N. Service Photographique).

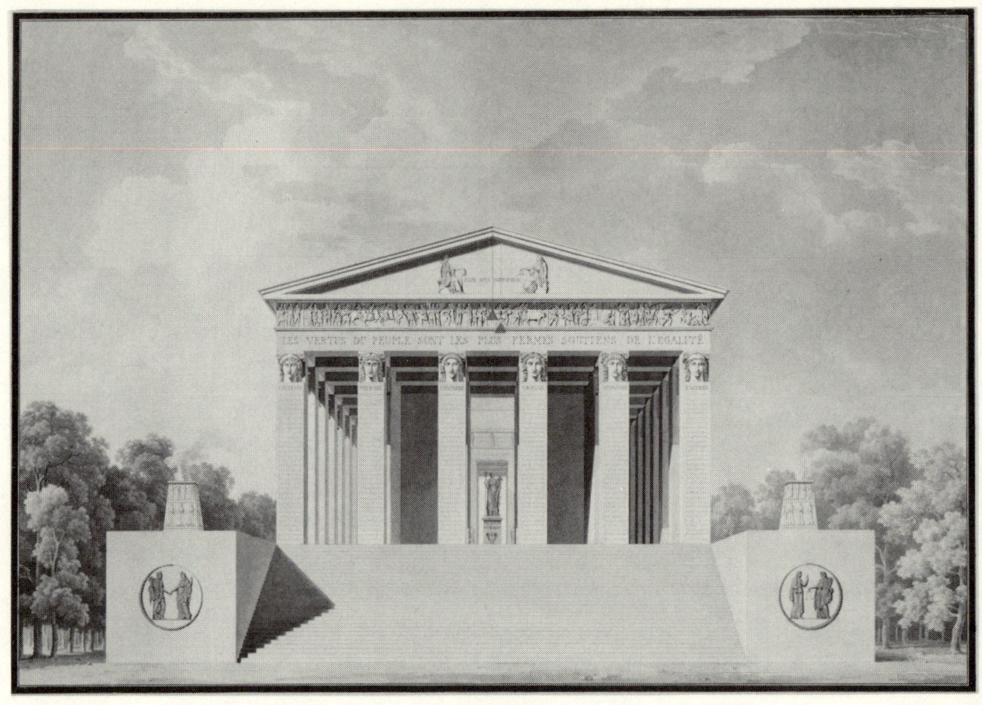

Fig. 36 Jean-Nicolas-Louis Durand and Jean-Thomas Thibault, Temple of Equality as copied by Leo von Klenze. Staatliche Graphische Sammlung, Munich (Photo: the Museum).

OPPOSITE

Fig. 37 New heading of the *Bulletin des lois*. Archives Nationales (Photo: Josse).

Fig. 38 François Cointeraux, Plan for Paris. Bibliothèque Nationale, Estampes (Photo: B.N. Service Photographique).

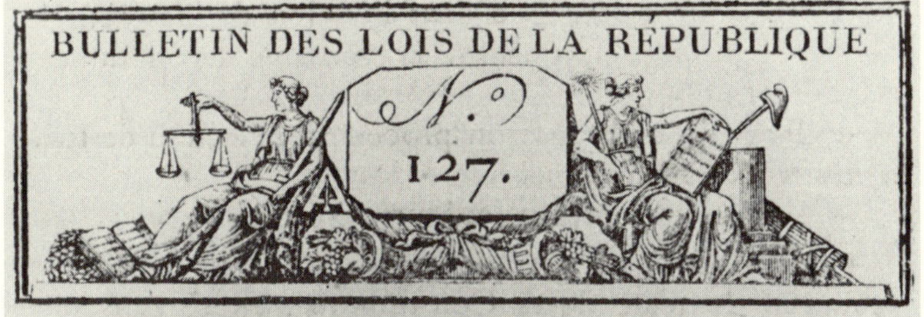

AU NOM DE LA RÉPUBLIQUE FRANÇAISE.

(N.° 1225.) *ARRÊTÉ du Directoire exécutif, contenant rectification d'erreurs dans le texte d'une édition originale de la Constitution française.*

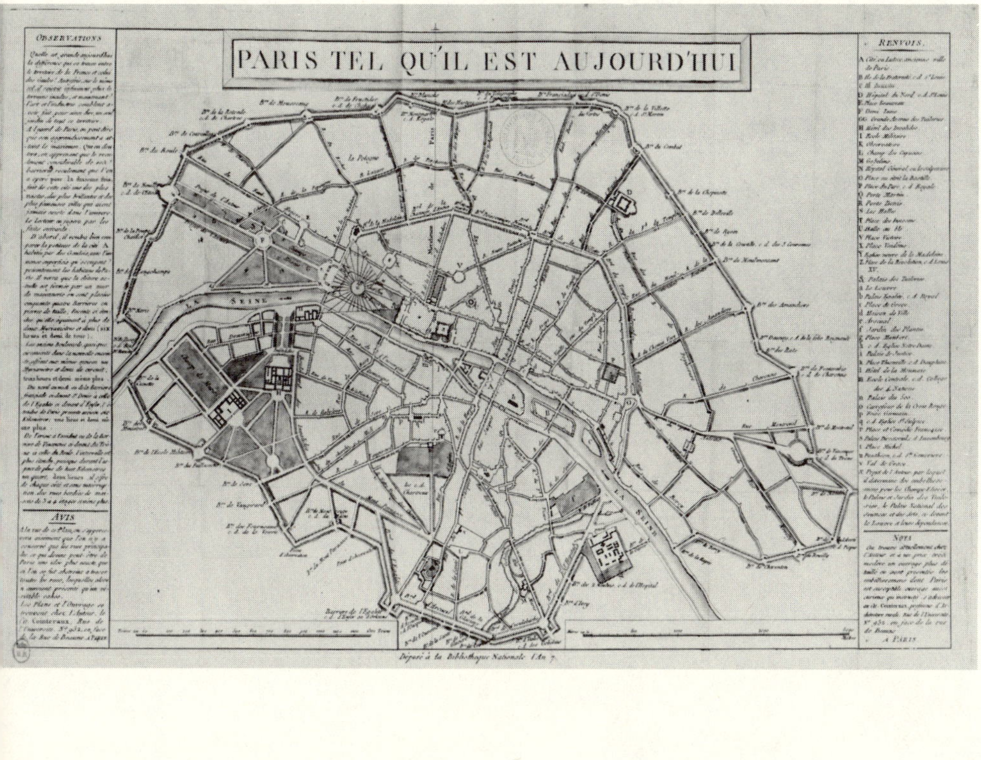

PARIS TEL QU'IL EST AUJOURD'HUI

Déposé à la Bibliothèque Nationale l'An 7.

Fig. 39 Detail of "Le Miroir du Passé pour Sauvegarde de l'Avenir."
Bibliothèque Nationale, Estampes
(Photo: B.N. Service Photographique).

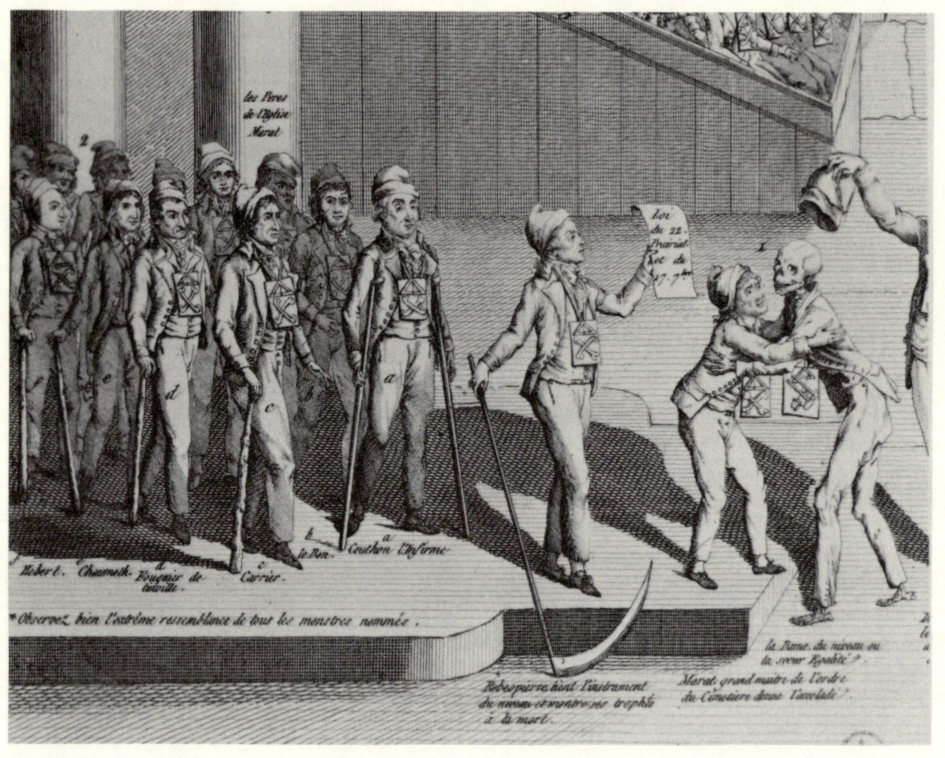

OPPOSITE

Fig. 40 "La Trinité Républicaine."
Bibliothèque Nationale, Estampes
(Photo: B.N. Service Photographique).

18. FRUCTIDOR AN V.

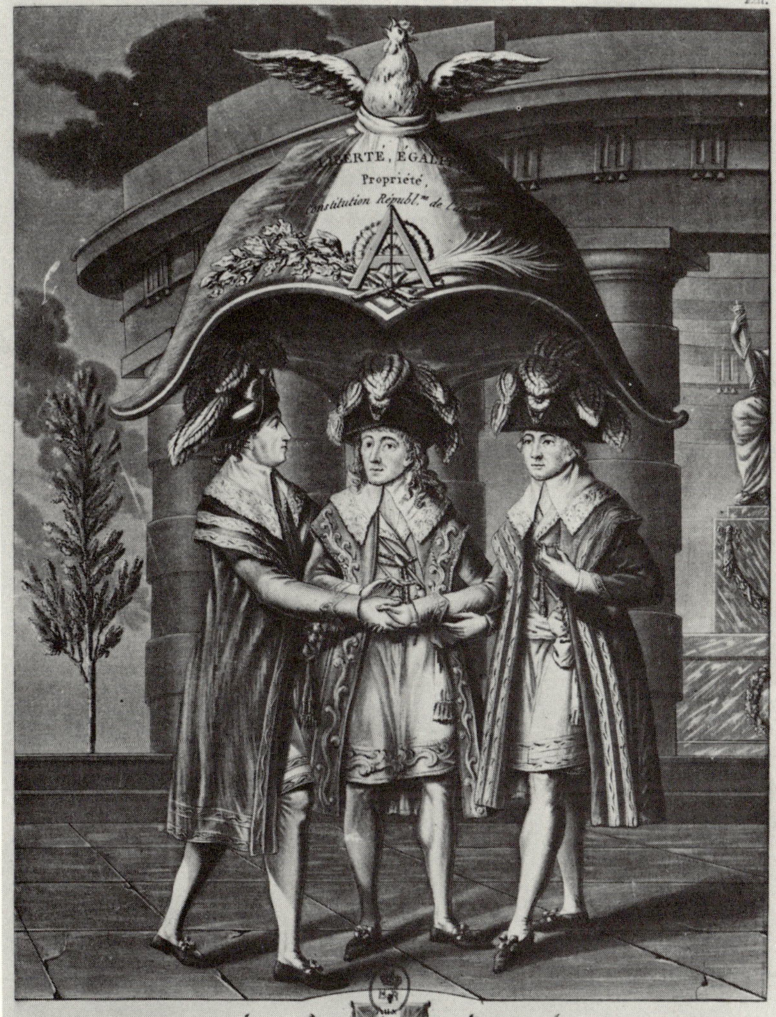

LA TRINITÉ RÉPUBLICAINE

Aux Mandataires Fidèles.

Que d'actions de graces les Républicains doivent aux trois Directeurs BARRAS, REWBEL, et REVELLIERE-LÉPAUX! qu'avec plaisir ils les proclament Sauveurs de la Patrie. C'est à leur union Courageuse et sacrée que nous devons la Constitution et la République.

Déposé à la Bibliothèque N.le

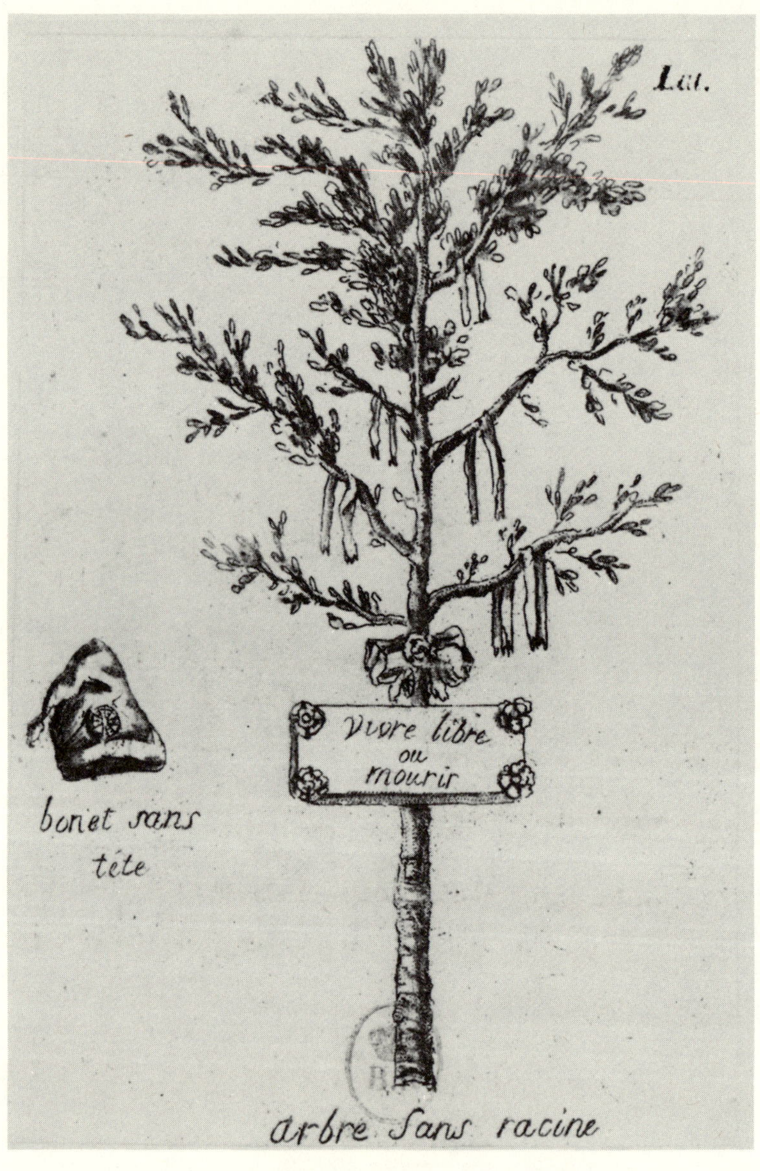

Fig. 41 "Vivre libre ou mourir."
Bibliothèque Nationale, Estampes
(Photo: B.N. Service Photographique).

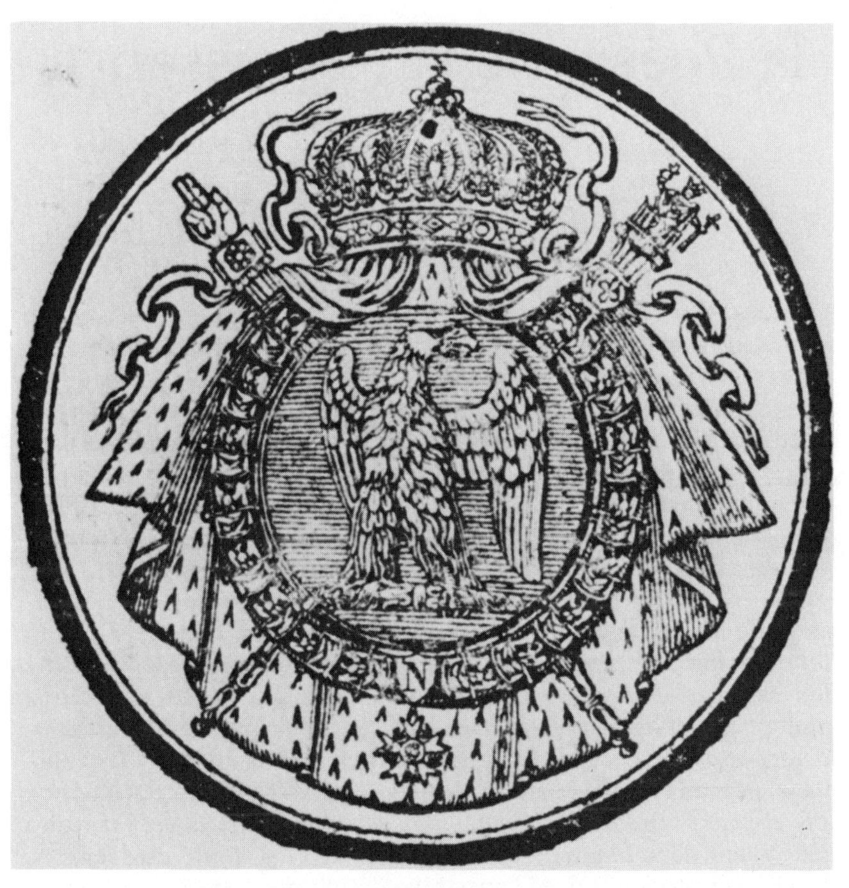

Fig. 42 Napoleonic Seal at the end of the *Bulletin des lois*. Archives Nationales (Photo: Josse).

EVA KUSHNER
McGill University

Le Statut du Symbole dans la Poésie de la Renaissance

L'étude des symboles en tant que structures de l'imaginaire est conçue, le plus souvent, en synchronie. Mais, précisément parce qu'elle est liée à des constantes du comportement humain, elle gagne également à être considérée d'un point de vue historique, ne serait-ce que dans le but de connaître, au travers des transformations, les permanences; les transformations, elles, illustrent, pour chaque coupe chronologique, ses traits spécifiques et le mode de leur rattachement aux réalités permanentes.

Au moment de ce qu'il est convenu d'appeler la Renaissance, il se produit dans le domaine de l'imaginaire comme dans bien d'autres une sorte de saut quantique, de ceux précisément qui témoignent d'un tournant historique. Il ne s'agit pas d'attribuer d'emblée à la notion de Renaissance une valeur par trop absolue, alors qu'elle naît d'une multiplicité de facteurs conjoncturaux et qu'elle connaît, d'un pays européen à l'autre, d'importants décalages. Il reste que s'accomplit en Italie, puis en France et dans la plupart des autres pays européens, aux xve et xvie siècles dans l'ensemble bien qu'il faille pousser beaucoup plus avant dans le temps pour les pays de l'Est, toute une série de fonctions historiques dont l'ensemble définit une Renaissance: retour philologique aux lettres antiques, en même temps qu'essor de la langue vernaculaire et forte impulsion vers la création littéraire dans cette langue par opposition aux langues anciennes; vision humaniste nouvelle, fondée à la fois sur la redécouverte de la littérature et de la pensée antiques; et, par contre-coup, sur une nouvelle prise de conscience de la religion chrétienne y compris (pensons à Léon l'Hébreu) de ses assises judaïques. Transformation, également, des formes littéraires, explosion d'activités artistiques et artisanales, expansion du monde connu, globe terrestre et cosmos. Ce n'est là qu'une liste imparfaite de tout ce qui sollicite alors l'imaginaire, et entre en interaction avec les mentalités; elle suffit toutefois pour nous permettre de poser notre question centrale: en quoi le statut du symbole diffère-t-il à une époque de transformation comme la Renaissance, en comparaison avec une époque de stabilité esthétique? Autrement dit, est-il concevable de penser en termes de systèmes symboliques plus ou moins ouverts (ou fermés) selon les moments historiques?

C'est à la poésie que nous emprunterons nos exemples car la poésie, plus encore que d'autres formes d'expression littéraire, peut être considérée comme action symbolique. Le symbole poétique continue-t-il, à la Renaissance, à être soumis à une codification rigide; ou est-il, comme nous aimerions le penser, objet de développement créateur à l'échelle individuelle, et de consensus, plutôt que de monologismes, à l'échelle collective? Ce questionnement implique naturellement que le statut, et les fonctions, des symboles comme véhicules de sens possèdent beaucoup de stabilité, mais sont susceptibles à certaines époques non seulement de devenir porteurs de sens additionnels, mais, à leur manière spécifique, d'innovation. C'est en tout cas le rôle que leur attribue Susanne Langer dans le vaste tableau de l'histoire des ères culturelles qu'elle trace au début de *Philosophy in a New Key*, et qui est peut-être l'énoncé le plus cohérent du post-modernisme en philosophie. "The formulation of experience which is contained within the intellectual horizon of an age and a society is determined … not so much by events and desires, as by the *basic concepts* at people's disposal for analyzing and describing their adventures to their own understanding."[1] Il est des "motive concepts," des notions motivantes qui caractérisent et font progresser la quête de vérité philosophique à une époque donnée; et, lorsque ces notions motivantes s'épuisent, c'est-à-dire perdent leur attrait, l'époque se termine. Les problèmes résiduels sont alors appelés problèmes métaphysiques, mais c'est – selon Langer – parce qu'ils ont déjà perdu tout intérêt.

Ainsi, la période philosophiquement créatrice du christianisme, celle qui commence avec les Pères de l'église et trouve son point culminant chez les grands maîtres scolastiques, finit par l'étouffement de la pensée scolastique lorsqu'elle se vide de tout élément émotif ou imaginatif et devient pure spéculation métaphysique.

Scholastic thought was gradually suffocating under the pressure of new interests, new emotions – the crowding modern ideas and artistic inspiration we call the Renaissance. After several centuries of sterile tradition, logic-chopping, and partisanship in philosophy, the wealth of nameless, heretical, often inconsistent notions born of the Renaissance crystallized into general and ultimate problems. A new outlook on life challenged the human mind to make sense out of its bewildering world; and the Cartesian age of "natural and mental philosophy" succeeded to the realm.[2]

La Renaissance apparaît donc comme une époque relativement brève d'ébullition, de "créativité" dans l'imaginaire, pour autant que celui-ci sert de moteur historique à la conceptualisation philosophique. Or, selon la pensée de Langer que nous faisons nôtre sur ce point, les symboles préparent le chemin du renouvellement par leur teneur en non-dit et même en indicible, en présupposé, en implicite indirectement suggéré. Ce qui est explicite est d'ores et déjà universellement admis, tandis que les voies du symbole, comme celles de son alliée l'idéologie, paraissent mystérieuses parce que liées au versant sombre de la conscience. Les symboles sont préfigurateurs ... On peut ne pas partager l'optimisme de Langer concernant l'étendue de leurs pouvoirs; mais ce qui est à coup sûr plausible dans sa théorie, c'est l'universalité et l'efficacité de leur fonctionnement.

In the fundamental notion of symbolization – mystical, practical or mathematical, it makes no difference – we have the keynote of all humanistic problems. In it lies a new conception of "mentality," that may illumine questions of life and consciousness, instead of obscuring them as traditional "scientific" methods have done... The philosophical study of symbols is not a technique borrowed from other disciplines, not even from mathematics; it has arisen in the fields that the great advance of learning has left fallow. Perhaps it holds a seed of new intellectual harvest, to be reaped in the next season of the human understanding.[3]

Or, c'est peut-être parce que, à la Renaissance, s'opérait cette éclosion secrète des systèmes intellectuels à venir, que la philosophie y voisine si harmonieusemenet avec la poésie, communiant avec elle, précisément, à travers les symboles.

Il est une autre raison pour laquelle, à la Renaissance, le symbolisme est particulièrement explicatif des mentalités: c'est le degré précis de son enracinement religieux. Selon Mircea Eliade, tout symbolisme est, au départ, religieux dans les sociétés archaïques.

Les symboles révèlent une modalité du réel ou une structure profonde du

Monde, et dans l'horizon spirituel de l'homme primitif, le réel se confond avec le *sacré*, et le monde est considéré la création des Dieux. Par conséquent, toute révélation portant sur la structure de l'Univers, ou sur les différents modes d'existence dans le Monde, et spécialement sur l'existence humaine, est en même temps une révélation de nature religieuse ...

Dès lors, le symbolisme religieux archaïque est

solidaire d'une ontologie. D'un certain point de vue, on peut même considérer le symbole comme un langage qui, bien que n'utilisant pas de concepts [mais peut-être faudrait-il dire: parce qu'il n'utilise pas de concepts] est néanmoins susceptible d'exprimer une pensée cohérente sur l'existence et le monde. Le symbole nous révèle une ontologie présystématique.[4]

Eliade suit un symbole à travers ses multiples valeurs: cosmologique, anthropocosmique, anthropologique, pour conclure à ce que nous connaissons comme polysémie des symboles; car chacune de ces valences est impliquée dans ou par les autres. Structures anthropologiques et structures cosmiques se représentent mutuellement, se substituant les unes aux autres; et ainsi l'homme accède par elles, graduellement, à l'universel, participant ainsi – Eliade insiste sur ce point – au sacré. Ce sens du sacré connaît ensuite des déplacements multiples, mais aussi des phases indirectes de resacralisation. A la Renaissance, l'imagination poétique sera stimulée, parce que l'homme en général est stimulé, bien que le poète le soit par définition davantage, par le contact défamiliarisant du symbolisme païen, dans le même temps que la symbolique chrétienne elle-même semblera s'absorber dans la fixité de ses significations. Il n'est d'ailleurs pas exact que tout l'imaginaire poétique occidental soit subjugué, à la Renaissance, par les symboles mythologiques de provenance païenne. Le poème le mieux connu de Saint-Jean de la Croix fait appel aux réalités les plus universelles: la nuit, l'amour humain – pour figurer la soif qu'a l'âme humaine de la présence divine:

En una noche oscura
Con ansías en amores inflamada,
¡Oh dichosa ventura!
Salí sin ser notada,
Estando ya mi casa sosegada.
¡Oh, noche, que guiaste
¡Oh noche amable, mas que la alborada!

¡Oh, noche que guiaste
Amado con amada,
Amada en el Amado transformada!

Rares sont les poèmes manifestant à un tel point la différence essentielle entre allégorie et symbole, l'allégorie comparant deux termes, idées ou images dans un but didactique, et le symbole relevant "d'une simple saisie de la réalité, antérieurement à tout raisonnement."[5] Le symbole est expression d'abord d'une simple image matérielle, intuitivement désignée, qui attire les significations destinées à se mirer en elle. Il constitue, en somme, sa propre évidence. La quête de Dieu, et l'union avec Dieu, sont ici figurées en termes d'une quête humaine: ce procédé reçoit sa garantie esthétique en même temps que théologique du fait qu'il se passe d'explication, de même que se passe d'explication le *Cantique des cantiques*, son modèle. "S'il est vrai que le symbole traduit la réalité, en tant qu'elle ne fait qu'un avec le moi qui l'expérimente, on conçoit que l'expression symbolique joue le rôle que le concept et le jugement jouent dans la connaissance ordinaire."[6]

Le symbole est moyen intuitif de transmission de l'expérience. Il n'est pas vrai que le croyant ou le mystique soit nécessairement doué d'expression symbolique. Il n'est pas vrai non plus que celui doué d'expression symbolique soit nécessairement croyant ou mystique. Mais il est des textes poétiques privilégiés constituant de tels points de rencontre. La poésie – si nous entendons par là la grande poésie de tous les temps – est alors à son maximum d'intensité parce qu'à travers, précisément, les symboles, elle organise un univers plus intense, plus concentré que l'univers familier. A l'intersection des choix les plus intimes du sujet lyrique et de l'inconscient collectif se constitue le réseau symbolique du poème. Il a ceci de particulier que les symboles y sont vivants (Wilfred Smith parlait hier de la vie et de la mort des symboles; une des particularités du symbole, surtout poétique, c'est précisément sa capacité de résurrection, galvanisé qu'il est par l'imagination créatrice, et rendu à sa force originelle dans le contexte du poème). Ecoutons sur ce point un grand poète récemment décédé, Pierre Emmanuel, en un texte de l'après-guerre immédiat intitulé *Poésie, raison ardente* ou il prédisait un grand essor de l'étude et de la compréhension des symboles grâce aux progrès de l'anthropologie. "Tout laisse prévoir ... qu'elle sera la science des rapports fondamentaux de l'univers, en même temps que du symbolisme moral qui constitue l'assise primitive de l'homme." Selon Emmanuel, les symboles "se développent en restant fidèles à leur être, poussant leurs images à l'assaut du ciel, selon la force qui les anime. Il arrive qu'un vocable, demeuré longtemps abstrait et comme artificiel, s'épanouisse brusquement au sein d'une oeuvre. ... Les constantes ne sont pas créées par le poète: simplement réinventées, d'un oubli parfois profond."[7]

En décrivant ainsi sa propre expérience ainsi que son expérience de lecteur des grands poètes du passé, Emmanuel mettait en oeuvre l'idée jungienne selon laquelle les symboles sont pris en charge par le psychisme, lequel s'en saisit et se les approprie, que ce soit dans le rêve ou dans l'art, selon ses propres exigences; par celles-ci, tel signe qui n'avait été qu'une simple image devient symbole. Or, selon Jung, le processus de sélection des symboles n'a rien de fortuit. Structurante, la pensée symbolique se saisit des signes qui satisfont à son appétit de figuration authentique de la vision du rêveur qu'est le poète ou artiste. Ce n'est qu'ainsi que l'on reconnaît les vrais symboles. "The sign," dit Jung, "is always less than the concept it represents, while a symbol always stands for something more than its obvious and immediate meaning. Symbols, moreover, are natural and spontaneous products."[8] Car les symboles ne sont pas créés à dessein, et qui le voudrait aboutirait à la métaphore et à l'allégorie, mais non au symbole. "No genius," dit encore Jung, "has ever sat down with a pen or a brush in his hand and said: 'Now I am going to invent a symbol.' No one can take a more or less rational thought, reached as a logical conclusion or by deliberate intent, and then give it a 'symbolic' form. ... It will remain a sign, linked to the conscious thought behind it, not a symbol that hints at something not yet known." Dans le rêve qui est le réservoir essentiel, mais non le seul, de l'activité symbolisante "symbols occur spontaneously, for dreams happen and are not invented; they are, therefore, the main source of our knowledge about symbolism."[9]

Il y a donc chez le poète individuel saisie sélective de signes issus de l'inconscient universel, mais qui dans sa propre configuration intérieure assument, tout à coup, ou graduellement, un sens personnel original; ce qui expliquerait le jaillissement des symboles dans l'oeuvre individuelle. Pour ce qui est de l'acceptation collective, souvent ou toujours religieuse à l'origine, des symboles, il y a de même des périodes d'affleurement des symboles essentiels dont l'évidence éclate, ou éclate à nouveau, au moment favorable; car il y a non seulement vie et mort mais résurrection de symboles, selon les mouvements, et les appropriations, des mentalités. Lorsqu'on dit que les symboles jaillissent de l'inconscient collectif, on n'a encore indiqué qu'une hypothèse quant à leur source commune; ce qu'il reste à expliquer, c'est l'émergence et la cristallisation de *configurations* de symboles fondateurs. En d'autres termes, les symboles ont une présence constante, sinon éternelle, coextensive avec le langage et son contenu en images concrètes. Ce qui évolue, ce qui fait que les symboles s'individualisent chez tel poète, et chez les peuples se constituent en visions collectives et participent donc au devenir d'une époque donnée et non d'une autre, ce sont les processus de l'imaginaire. Les symboles ne sont-ils pas les matériaux préhensiles de l'imaginaire?

Le poète, l'artiste individuel dont nous parle Pierre Emmanuel

> ne fait jamais qu'utiliser, de manière singulière, l'éternelle énergie des symboles communs. Par-delà les satisfactions apparentes ... que procure tel poème isolé, c'est aux sources même de l'affect humain que veulent atteindre le lecteur et l'artiste qui choisissent la poésie comme chemin vers l'unité. Est-il hasardeux de penser que l'opération du langage, chez un poète soucieux de progresser à l'intérieur de son art, présente en raccourci la même croissance de symboles que l'anthropologie tente de saisir dans le déroulement des civilisations?[10]

La conclusion essentielle de Pierre Emmanuel est celle que je souhaitais incorporer à cet exposé car elle me paraît parmi les plus fructueuses; c'est que la pensée poétique est pensée symbolique – ce qui suggère que l'inverse est également vrai. L'imagination symbolisante explore le réel, scrute l'expérience en quête des images les plus illuminantes. "Cette imagination," ajoute encore Pierre Emmanuel,

> qui saisit dans chaque élément la présence des autres, possède un clavier de métamorphoses plus vaste ... Or le ton d'une oeuvre lui vient de la hardiesse avec laquelle elle saisit certaines images, de l'assurance qui les transforme, sans détruire leur unité substantielle. *Est poète celui qui pense symboliquement*; toute altération, toute interférence d'une autre forme de pensée nuit à l'équilibre spirituel de l'oeuvre, donc à sa beauté qui en est le reflet ...[11]

En matière d'activité symbolisante, il existe entre les poètes du XVIe siècle, et un poète moderne tel que Pierre Emmanuel, une réelle continuité: les poètes de la Renaissance ne parlent guère de symboles, mais la symbolisation joue dans leur théorie et leur pratique un rôle séminal. Il n'est que de se rappeler la différence fondamentale établie par du Bellay et Ronsard entre "poète" et "versificateur," que ce soit dans la *Deffence et illustration de la langue françoyse* (1549) ou l'*Abrégé de l'art poétique* de Ronsard (1565), ou encore dans certains poèmes des *Quatre premiers livres des odes* du même Ronsard (1550) ou dans l'opuscule de Thomas Sébillet, *L'Art poétique françoys* (1548) qui s'attira la réaction coléreuse de la Pléiade ou encore le *Solitaire premier* de Pontus de Tyard (1552) et l'*Art poétique françoys* de Jacques Peletier du Mans (1555). Essentiellement tous ces petits traités, et leurs homologues dans d'autres pays d'Europe, en Italie avant la France, en Angleterre et en Allemagne après elle, contiennent certaines notions parfaitement compatibles avec les théories modernes du symbole dont je viens d'évoquer quelques-unes. Mentionnons d'abord la notion d'invention, issue de la rhétorique ancienne et ressuscitée par la poétique renaissante aux côtés de l'*elocutio* et de la *dispositio. Invenire* veut dire trouver, et le poète au sens souverain de ce vocable (par opposition au versificateur) est un inventeur d'images. Ces images, il doit les chercher d'une manière prédominante dans l'Antiquité païenne, c'est-à-dire chez les poètes de la Grèce et de Rome.

On peut se demander à ce propos si les poètes de la Renaissance étaient eux-mêmes, dans toute leur ardeur de néophytes, conscients du degré auquel les trésors symboliques de la mythologie gréco-latine ont été fertilisants, individuellement et collectivement, pour leur imaginaire; si bien que ce qu'ils voyaient assez naïvement comme une volonté obstinée, quasi ascétique, d'imitation des "exemplaires grecs," fut en réalité la porte d'accès, le choc défamiliarisant, la libération psychique indispensable pour sortir des ornières d'une rhétorique usée. Sur le plan esthétique survient le travail des symboles dont parlait dans le domaine philosophique Susanne Langer (cf. ci-dessus). Les poètes utilisent un symbolisme païen pour figurer des vérités chrétiennes, ce qui non seulement enrichit leur vision sur le plan esthétique mais ravive leur christianisme en déracinant ce que l'allégorisme antérieur pouvait avoir de trop automatique.

Les *Antiquitez de Rome* de du Bellay sont une exploration poétique et humaniste des ruines de la Rome ancienne qui est aussi le berceau de la chrétienté catholique romaine au XVIe siècle. Ce qui frappe, c'est que dans ce mince recueil du Bellay a encodé toute une philosophie chrétienne de l'histoire, sans que Dieu y soit nommé une seule fois. Toujours, il se cache et se révèle à la fois sous le *fatum* ou les divinités païennes. Le sonnet XII des *Antiquitez,* lequel oppose la grandeur de Rome à sa décadence, compare les Romains aux Géants ou Titans qui ayant escaladé le Ciel en furent précipités par les Dieux jaloux de leurs prérogatives. Déjà l'axe sémantique grandeur/décadence est lui-même symbolisé par l'axe vertical escalade/chute, narrativisé en mythologie sous forme de l'histoire de Titans:

Tels que l'on vid jadis les enfans de la Terre
Plantez dessuz les monts pour escheller les cieux,

Combattre main à main la puissance des Dieux
Et Jupiter contre eulx, qui les fouldres desserre:

Puis tout soudainement renversez du tonnerre
Tumber deça dela ces squadrons furieux,
La Terre gémissante, et le Ciel glorieux
D'avoir à son honneur achevé cette guerre:

Tel encor' on a veu par dessus les humains
Le front audacieux des sept costaux Romains
Lever contre le ciel son orgueilleuse face:

Et telz ores on void ces champs deshonnorez
Regretter leur ruine, et les Dieux asseurez
Ne craindre plus là hault si effroyable audace.

Ce qui se profile ici dans la polysémie du symbole c'est, sous l'échelle gravie per les "enfants de la terre," la construction de la tour de Babel. Contamination ou plutôt combinatoire du matériau symbolique et mythique, figurant sur l'axe de la verticalité l'agressivité ascendante de l'orgueil humain allant dangereusement à la rencontre de l'absolu divin exerçant sa dominance du haut vers le bas. En complémentarité avec ces symboles axés sur la verticalité, et par opposition à eux, il y a l'humanité, horizontale, dans son rôle de soumission à la transcendance; avant l'attaque contre le ciel, et après la chute des orgueilleux géants, le plan horizontal, sur lequel sont distribués les sept côteaux romains figurant une silhouette humaine, incarnait donc la situation humaine en une vision commune à l'Antiquité gréco-latine et au christianisme. Dans la densité poétique du sonnet, tout signifie. C'est ainsi que la locution adverbiale "tout soudainement" figure le déclic de la volonté innommée par quoi l'homme est précipité du plan vertical vers le plan horizontal.

On pourrait superposer à la manière de Mauron un grand nombre d'autre sonnets des *Antiquitez de Rome* ainsi que les quinze sonnets du *Songe* qui leur font suite; le mythe qui s'en dégage est remarquablement stable: le sommet de la transgression appelle en retour le moment du châtiment. C'est par l'entremise d'un mythe grec que le poète laisse entendre ce qui ne saurait être dit directement sans perdre le pouvoir de l'expression poétique. L'élément caché que recèle le "tout soudainement," c'est l'intervention du Dieu de la Bible qui est aussi le Dieu de l'Eglise, indirectement désigné par le pluriel mythologique "les Dieux."

En outre, l'ensemble du syntagme narratif qu'est ce sonnet est à son tour symbolique d'un événement psychologique qui est la face intérieure, intemporelle, de l'histoire de la chute de Rome, la fatalité psychique au travers de laquelle la transcendance affronte et châtie l'orgueil humain.

C'est ainsi que l'imaginaire renaissant pratique "l'invention" pour parer les croyances chrétiennes des prestiges, plus mystérieux parce que moins familiers alors, de la mythologie païenne.

Mais l'art poétique recouvre ici une profonde réflexion sur les aspirations communes à toutes les religions, et sur les concordances symboliques de leurs formes d'expression. Bien entendu, il s'agit, à l'époque, de rapports hiérarchisés: les autres religions ne font que préfigurer le christianisme, mais du moins, il est admis qu'elles le préfigurent. Ainsi se trouve illustrée, pour l'époque de la Renaissance, l'intuition hindoue rapportée par Wilfred Smith hier, et selon laquelle toutes formulations théologiques, et notamment toutes personnalisations de la transcendance, renvoient les unes aux autres tant sur le plan cosmique que sur le plan anthropologique et spirituel; et, en dernière analyse, à une même réalité spirituelle.

Dans la tradition occidentale où s'élabore la Renaissance il survient un moment où, parmi les penseurs du xve siècle, des attitudes semblables à celle-ci se préparent. Dans le *De pace fidei* (1453) de Nicolas de Cuse, qui suit le modèle d'un dialogue des morts et met en scène le Verbe lui-même, les apôtres Pierre et Paul ainsi que des tenants de plusieurs religions dont la judaïque et la musulmane, il est admis que toutes ces religions ont un fond spirituel commun; et que d'une manière ou d'une autre tout en elles préfigure ou annonce la vérité chrétienne. Même la notion de la Trinité serait opérante, selon le Cusain, dans plusieurs religions.

Chez Marcile Ficin et Pic de la Mirandole, toutes les sagesses antérieures au christianisme préfigurent la sagesse de celui-ci, notamment la pensée d'Orphée, Pythagore, Platon, Zoroastre, Moïse. (Ainsi que nous le disions à propos du Cusain, la dominance du christianisme sur le plan dogmatique ne fait aucun doute; c'est au niveau du rêve symbolique que s'ouvre la série des vérités possibles, et la conscience de leur interdépendance.) Ficin va très loin dans sa conciliation de Platon avec Aristote d'une part, et avec la doctrine chrétienne d'autre part; mais pas au point où la spécificité chrétienne serait obscurcie. Dans la *Theologia platonica* l'âme reste individuelle jusque dans son immortalité, et le platonisme est voie d'accès à la vérité chrétienne et non lui-même vérité. "Philosophica ingenia," écrit Ficin à un ami, "ad Christum perveniunt per Platonem."

En attendant, quelle riche mine de symboles pour les poètes que les mythes des religions préfiguratrices véhiculés par leurs théologiens, *prisci theologi*. La lyre d'Orphée est chez Ronsard un symbole séminal; elle se transmue parfois en "luc" ou "guiterre." Dans l'élégie consacrée à Orphée (1563) il est clair que Ronsard s'identifie au créateur mythique de la poésie et de la musique. Au cours de l'expédition argonautique, Orphée se tient aux côtés de Jason qui incarne le souverain, pour protéger l'expédition des blandices des Sirènes, et la mener à bien; entendons par là que le souverain ne saurait se passer du poète comme conseiller; que le pouvoir royal est moindre que celui de la lyre, laquelle l'éternisera aux yeux de la postérité. Mais cet aspect social n'est qu'un premier niveau de signification. La lyre d'Orphée, dans la vie du héros comme à la Renaissance, incarne le pouvoir de la poésie et de la musique sur les esprits, et les effets théurgiques de l'alliance harmonieuse de la poésie et de la musique. Au sein de l'humanisme musical, la musique en tant qu'image vivante de l'harmonie morale (*musica humana*, liée au microcosme), est à son tour figure de l'harmonie cosmique (*musica mundana*, liée au macrocosme). "La musique des sphères" était symboliquement, donc réellement pour qui savait l'entendre – et entendre signifie aussi comprendre – l'expression de cette harmonie universelle où l'homme était englobé. Etre poète, être saisi de la fureur poétique, elle-même important élément symbolique de la vision platonicienne du monde, c'est savoir retraduire le chant de l'univers dans les *nombres* de la poésie, faite de mots, c'est-à-dire de signes eux-mêmes en relation symbolique avec le monde à la fois par leur face matérielle (phonologique et rythmique) et leur face sémantique.

N'oublions pas non plus que chez Ronsard et d'autres poètes la lyre d'Orphée a pour équivalent paradigmatique la flûte d'Amphion qui bâtit la cité (la cité elle-même suscitant dans l'espace une autre configuration symbolique de l'harmonie, ou de la désharmonie universelles). Mais surtout, il y a passage symbolique entre Orphée, et David dansant devant l'arche, entre poésie au sens le plus inspiré et psalmodie. C'est ainsi qu'au début des années 1560, lorsque s'aggravent les conflits religieux, la Pléiade n'a aucune peine à montrer que la mythologie païenne qui a tant enrichi sa poésie des années 1550 fut alors et peut rester un "fabuleux manteau" rendant le poème moins facilement accessible, mais par là plus fidèle à la stricte vérité chrétienne.

Afin de percevoir l'entière encyclopédie du savoir dans son réseau d'interrelations symboliques, il fallait remplir une condition à la fois psychologique et ontologique qui était, nous l'avons dit, la fureur poétique, notion issue du *Phèdre* et de l'*Ion* de Platon. Vulgarisée par les poètes de la Renaissance dans plusieurs pays, cette notion leur servit surtout à souligner l'importance du caractère inné de la poésie, en comparaison avec le travail et en particulier l'imitation poétique, bien que l'"art" fût inséparable de la "nature." Pour pouvoir "inventer" des symboles à bon escient il fallait connaître, donc étudier, les grandes visions du passé. Mais cela ne suffisait pas sans l'inspiration créatrice. Or, ce que nous avons dit précédemment concernant certaines théories modernes du symbole et de l'activité symbolique aide à comprendre de quelle manière les doctrines qui avaient cours à l'époque de la Renaissance figurent d'une manière symbolique la symbolisation elle-même, et l'affleurement du fond lyrique personnel alors qu'il entre en contact, et parfois en collision, avec l'ensemble du fond culturel, et les symboles de tous. A cet égard, les quatre "fureurs" décrivent en fait quatre façons de sortir de l'emprise de la matière, et de percevoir l'univers dans toutes ses interrelations, c'est-à-dire en une vision symbolique unifiée et susceptible de s'exprimer à différents niveaux.

C'est de cette fonction symbolique que parle Edmund Wilson lorsqu'il dit dans *Axel's Castle* que la grande poésie est celle qui cherche un langage nouveau, c'est-à-dire une représentativité nouvelle du langage; et qu'alors la cohérence symbolique de la poésie est comparable à celle des mathématiques et d'autres systèmes. Mais cela nécessite une présence extraordinaire du poète à la fonction symbolisante du langage et au contenu anthropologique et psychologique de celui-ci. Je pense aux interprétations structuralistes selon lesquelles les mythes collectifs sont aussi des langages, et le devenir personnel dont parlaient Freud et Jung en est un autre. De son côté, Gilbert Durand décrit la "fonction fantastique" de la poésie, capable d'infuser la plus-value symbolique au monde moderne, qui pourtant lui résiste. L'imaginaire, selon lui, est le "recours suprême de la conscience"; il est "supplément d'âme," "le contrepoint axiologique de l'action," lestant "d'un poids ontologique le vide sémiologique des phénomènes."[12] Mais les poètes de la Renaissance avaient-ils accès à cette vision intériorisée et, pour tout dire, symbolique de l'imaginaire lui-même? Oui, dans la mesure où ils étaient platoniciens et où Platon bien avant, par exemple, Cassirer, avait perçu l'universelle représentativité des formes, c'est-à-dire l'interdépendance des langages, même ceux des arts et des sciences.

Le problème immédiat du poète de la Renaissance était d'une nature beaucoup plus concrète, tout en débouchant sur cette problématique universelle. Dans l'art chrétien primitif dont les symboles lui étaient transmis par l'église médiévale, les sens étaient codifiés, attachés aux formes. Animaux, oiseaux et insectes, fleurs, arbres et plantes possédaient des significations connues; et le monde animal et végétal entrait en relations symboliques fortement codifiées avec certains passages de l'Ancien et du Nouveau Testament. L'amande, par example, est symbole de la Vierge Marie à cause de Nombres 17:1 – 8 où Aaron est choisi comme prêtre de l'Eternel après le miracle de la baguette qui fleurit et produit des amandes. Le soleil a toute une histoire platonicienne et néo-platonicienne; mais dans la symbolique chrétienne plus spécifiquement, il en vient à représenter le Christ (Malachie 4:2). Il est par ailleurs intéressant de voir la teneur en sacralité religieuse du symbole du soleil lorsque dans la poésie pétrarquisante il signifie la Dame. Voyons-le chez Scève, où déjà le saut quantique entre sens fixe et sens véritablement symbolique, c'est-à-dire riche de connotations et doué de plusieurs niveaux de signification, a eu lieu:

> Ce lyen d'or raiz de toy mon Soleil
> Qui par le bras t'asservit Ame et vie
> Detient si fort avec la veue l'oeil
> Que ma pensée il t'a toute ravie …
>
> Heureux service en libre servitude
> Tu m'apprends donc estre trop plus de gloire,
> Souffrir pour une en sa mansuetude
> Que d'avoir eu de toute autre victoire.[13]

Notons la résonance paulinienne de "libre servitude," oxymore dont toute la force ici provient de ce qu'il est sevré de son contexte théologique. En général, il semble que dans la poésie de la Renaissance la symbolisation commence à se détacher des sens codifiés (ceux de la symbolique chrétienne primitive; ceux des quatre niveaux de l'exégèse médiévale). Cette libération du sens éclate lorsque l'on compare les sonnets du *Songe* de du Bellay déjà mentionnés aux sonnets des *Antiquitez de Rome*. Le songe est par définition un genre allégorique; les quinze poèmes suivent exactement le même modèle figurant la ruine de Rome déclanchée par un événement catastrophique. Le sonnet XIV du *Songe*, par exemple, voit une cité aussi somptueuse que celle de l'Apocalypse, et bâtie sur le sable, détruite, comme l'on pouvait s'y attendre, par un puissant orage. De même, aucune des autres représentations allégoriques du pouvoir de Rome (l'Aigle, le Torrent, l'Arc, etc.) ne vit d'une vie véritablement symbolique, tant leur sort est immédiatement réduisible au même commun dénominateur: le soudain châtiment rencontré par l'orgueil. La Rome des *Antiquitez* est au contraire parée de toutes les richesses symboliques, pour une multiplicité de raisons, dont la moindre n'est pas la pluralité des strates de connotations évoquées d'emblée par son seul nom: ville ancienne traçant, entre sa naissance et son déclin en passant par sa période d'immense grandeur, une courbe historique idéale et en elle-même symbolique; ville moderne; centre de la chrétienté catholique romaine, et par là intersection du pouvoir spirituel et du pouvoir temporel de la papauté et de l'église ... Le nom même de Rome, comme par exemple, *mutatis mutandis*, celui de Babylone, se charge de valeurs archétypales; elle devient LA ville, et de multiples valences symboliques s'organisent autour d'elle et en elle: "Rome fut tout le monde, et tout le monde est Rome."[14] Aucun poème des *Antiquitez* n'est construit autour d'un symbole isolé; plutôt, chacun englobe un réseau de symboles aux fonctions convergentes (par exemple, le raz-de-marée, l'orage et le feu du sonnet XVI); et à l'échelle du recueil, et de la vision poétique de du Bellay, ces réseaux se lient les uns aux autres paradigmatiquement jusqu'à former une seule et saisissante représentation de l'espace humain vaincu par le temps de l'histoire.

Cette liberté d'association des symboles entre eux aurait été impossible sans ce que nous avons appelé la libération des sens symboliques, c'est-à-dire des signifiés par rapport aux signifiants, corrélative de la pensée et de l'esthétique de la Renaissance. Essor fragile dans la mesure où le baroque et le classicisme poétiques tendront à maîtriser davantage le symbole, sans pour autant qu'il y ait retour absolu à la codification antérieure. En prenant pour exemple le symbole de l'eau on peut le trouver, chez un La Céppède, à l'état de comparaison asservie à sa place exacte dans un grand tableau religieux:

Cette rouge sueur goutte à goutte roulante
Du corps de cet Athlète en ce rude combat
Peut être comparée à cette eau douce et lente
Qui la sainte montagne en silence rebat.[15]

Mais on rencontre l'eau dans tel poème de Sponde comme maître-symbole de la résistance impassible au temps:

Je contemplais un jour le dormant de ce fleuve
Qui traine lentement les ondes dans la mer,

Sans que les Aquilons le facent escumer
Ni bondir, ravageur, sur les bords qu'il abreuve.[16]

Il faudra attendre les grands mouvements symbolistes modernes pour voir s'accomplir la libération du sens qui s'était annoncée à la Renaissance.

NOTES

1 Susanne Langer, *Philosophy in a New Key* (Cambridge, Mass., 1960), 6.
2 Ibid., 11–12.
3 Ibid., 25.
4 Mircea Eliade, "Le symbolisme des ténèbres dans les religions archaïques," dans *Polarité du symbole* (Paris, 1960), 15.
5 Lucien-Marie de Saint-Joseph, OCD, "Expérience mystique et expression symbolique chez Saint-Jean de la Croix," ibid., 33.
6 Ibid., 37.
7 Pierre Emmanuel, *Poésie, raison ardente* (Paris, 1948), 122.
8 *Man and His Symbols*, ed. Carl Jung *et al.* (New York, 1964), 41.
9 Ibid.
10 Pierre Emmanuel, *Poésie*, 123.
11 Ibid.
12 Gilbert Durand, *Les Structures anthropologiques de l'imaginaire* (Paris, 1963), 467.
13 *Délie*, dizain XII, éd. Eugène Parturier (Paris, 1916), 13.
14 *Les Antiquitez de Rome*, éd. H. Chamard (Paris, 1961).
15 *Les Théorèmes* (Paris, 1593), 118.
16 *Poésies* (Genève, 1949), 191.

NORMAN H. MACKENZIE
Queen's University

Reflections

For my own contribution, rounding out this ambitious colloquium on "Symbols in Life and Art," our chairman Dr Jim Leith has chosen the symbolic and significant title "Reflections." In the larger university Installation symposium which so nearly overlapped and overwhelmed us, a rather different role was assigned to people who, under organizers less sensitive to language, were denominated "Discussants." For this audience, a select interdisciplinary group, I need hardly paraphrase the laws of physics which explain why reflections glancing off a plane unruffled surface are always less brilliant than the light falling on it.

Dr Leith tried to arrange for all the conference papers to be available to me weeks before their presentation, so that I could bring you a considered synthesis, reconciling conflicting points of view and filling in omissions, but up to the day before our proceedings began I had seen only three out of the eight. I propose therefore to concentrate upon the special relevance of what has been said to my own field of English literature, while emphasizing one dimension which has been less prominent in the contributions made in English – the profound antiquity of some symbols commonly encountered in poetry and the modernity of others. It will be obvious to you that lectures which took some eight hours to deliver and two more to discuss cannot be adequately summarized, harmonized, and supplemented in less than one.

Northrop Frye was a true prophet in his key-note address when he warned us that the word "symbol" is of such elusiveness that he always tries to avoid it whenever possible. It has been, predictably, used in a variety of ways by our speakers; nevertheless, we could not possibly have dispensed with it. The broadest interpretation was suggested by Dr Frye himself when he argued that every word is in effect a symbol for some object or emotion or action. But from this definition, which might be thought to equate symbolism with language itself, he went on to consider narrower categories, commending the definitions advanced by George Whalley, in whose memory this colloquium has been held. The ninth chapter of Whalley's *Poetic Process* is entitled "Symbol and Myth." Let me quote a few brief passages from it: "metaphor is the means to express whatever cannot be clearly conveyed in a logical or technical manner ... the symbol proves to be a special kind of metaphor and the myth proves to be a cluster of symbols brought into resonance in the process of metaphor."[1] Dr Whalley then cites from W.B. Yeats a statement which reads like a manifesto against realism: "True art is expressive and symbolic, and makes every form, every sound, every colour, every gesture a signature of some unanalysable essence."[2] Symbolic form we have been examining in the architecture of the French Revolution and the images in dreams, symbolic colour in Van Gogh, symbolic sounds in music and poetry, symbolic gestures in the statues of a Buddha or of Liberty. Dr Frye reminded us of George Whalley's compressed definition of a symbol as "a focus of relationships." To this we might add Dr Kushner: "One of the fascinations of symbols is their function as nodes, linking the universal and the particular by combining in their concreteness timeless and timebound meanings." *The Princeton Encyclopedia of Poetry and Poetics* has useful articles on such confusing and confused terms as Symbol, Symbolism, Allegory (Dr Kushner was again very helpful there), Myth, and Metaphor, some of them by Northrop Frye, and some signed "N. Frie" (i.e., Norman Friedman). Frye's own *Anatomy of Criticism* (1957) deals at length with "The Theory of Symbols" and "The Theory of Myths."

The second paper, "Symbols and the Search for Wholeness," was by an eminent psychologist, Dr Anthony Storr. In a delightfully simple and appealing illustration, Dr Storr contrasted with man the unreflective consciousness of an animal perfectly adjusted to a limited environment, with plenty of food and mates, no enemies. Upset its food supply, however, and it may perish (like koala bears deprived of their favourite type of eucalyptus) – I wish ants, mosquitoes, and bacteria were as easily brought to the fringe of extinction. Man, said Dr Storr, is almost infinitely adaptable, but only at the psychic cost of living in a certain state of dissatisfaction with his environment. He is always seeking new conquests, new territories. I immediately thought of John Donne, who in his "Second Anniversary," published as long ago as 1612, imagined the soul as a sort of spacecraft speeding to heaven in a minute, flashing past the planets and beyond the realm of the stars; while Van Gogh, as Dr Welsh reminded us, thought of death as a swift train into the starry regions. The human imagination forms an inner world which is quite distinct from the external world, and one of the functions of symbols is to form bridges between the imagination and the reality around us.

The symbol to which Dr Storr gave prominence was the *mandala*, which I have often used in dealing in graduate seminars with the theory of symbols. The *mandala* is a perfect circle, often with a square or triangle inside it. In dreams it reflects in various contradictory ways the impulse towards self-unity in the psyche. Dr Storr illustrated the desire for wholeness by means of a Platonic myth frequently alluded to in poetry, of how human beings were at first created as rounded, self-contented spheres, hermaphrodite, the two sexes in a single body. But they behaved towards Zeus with such *hubris* that he cut them in two, and ever since then each half has had a restless desire to find its lost mate. I was delighted with this reference to Plato's *Symposium*, having assumed that Plato would be on everyone's lips, but in fact for the most part, except for Dr Kushner and Dr Moles, we have rather taken Platonic origins for granted.

We do not have leisure enough to develop Dr Storr's references to music as "the symbolic activity *par excellence*" because it is a temporal art, existing in time, and like life itself is constantly changing. The development of a theme to its final resolution symbolizes typical patterns in human experience. In Western diatonic music the melody's return to the tonic – half-fulfilled (we may feel) by a modulation on the dominant or an interrupted cadence – when it eventually arrives seems like a return home. Of the composers he instanced I derive this satisfaction more from Bach. Beethoven seems to gyrate with such irresolution, indefinitely postponing the final fulfilling chords, that I have sometimes felt like sticking my head (metaphorically speaking) out of the front door and yelling, "Ludwig! Stop playing around now and come on home!"

Carl Jung, in the introduction to a collection of his essays called *Psyche and Symbols*, relates how a patient who was a rationalist and a highly intelligent man was being driven to the brink of insanity by the images which rose in his mind, generally in the form of dramatic dreams. He was calmed and reassured when Jung took down from his shelves a volume 400 years old, and showed him a woodcut which almost exactly mirrored a particularly vivid dream he had endured.[3] While I was running the multi-racial English Department in Natal about thirty years ago, I was able to discuss with social anthropologists in our university some striking discoveries about Zulu dreams. Whenever they dreamed of cattle or sheep being tended, the herder was always a woman, whereas among Bantu tribes south of the Zambesi, for as many centuries as records carry us, only men were allowed to handle cattle. North of the Zambesi, whence the Zulus and other tribes had migrated, the reverse is often found. The dream content seems therefore to belong to a time before the dreamers themselves were born. Still more curious was the fact that the symbolic stone-lined graves which figured in Zulu dreams were completely different from any in contemporary Zulu culture. To match them the anthropologists had to go back (if I remember rightly from so long ago) at least a thousand years to Stone Age burial customs in other parts of Africa. This appeared to me a dramatic confirmation of Jungian theory of a "Collective Unconscious" which transcends political and geographic boundaries, giving us access (as Yeats also believed) to a timeless reservoir of symbols.[4]

Yeats, being scientifically inclined, carried out practical experiments even with the symbols which he found in the carefully guarded lore of the Theosophists under Madame Blavatsky and the ritual of such occult societies as the Golden Dawn, to which he and many of his friends belonged. The Theosophists found his experiments rather disruptive. One important nucleus of symbols can be met in ancient India, Tattwa symbols concerning five-fold streams of energy (the Hindu Pranas), currents of what Theosophists called the Astral Light.[5] Each of these forces – spirit, air, fire, water, and earth – had its own visual symbol, distinct in shape and colour: it is interesting that Plato in his *Timaeus*, ca. 350 BC, assigns the same shapes to some of them (55d, ff). Using a highly technical word with a long history in mysticism, Yeats reasoned that if there was a profound "correspondence" between the spiritual world of the Anima Mundi and our own,[6] then showing the correct visual symbols to uninitiated but responsive people ought to evoke in them relevant visions. With an uncle whom he trained to become sensitive to cabbalistic symbols, Yeats, merely by concentrating hard but silently on one of them as he walked along the seashore at Rosses Point, could evoke appropriate visions in his uncle who was striding along a low cliff above him.[7] I myself, when our graduate seminars reached the topic of symbolism, used to arrive early and draw one of the Tattwa shapes on the board, and then listen to the general chatter before the paper was read to see if the symbol had affected their gossip. One year I had some success with the symbol for fire (an upward-pointing red triangle), but my satisfaction was doused when I remembered that since we had last met a prominent building in the centre of Kingston had burned down spectacularly!

It was through my attempts to interpret Yeats's poetry that my own special interest in Symbolism arose. Soon after the end of the war with Japan, I was appointed to the staff of the University of Melbourne just as a new Head of the English Department took office. He decided to concentrate part of our first-year poetry courses on Hopkins, Yeats, and Eliot – a formidable array which few students on this continent could enjoy so early. Nobody else was willing to tackle the intricacies of Yeats, to whom I was devoted, and so I found myself, straight out of the army, with my books and lecture notes lost in the fall of Hong Kong, facing not only serried tiers of about 500 students, but the Head of Department himself in the front row, along with, quite often, five or six of my colleagues, all senior to me. My strong background of Biblical and theological typology and symbolism was of small help with Yeats, though invaluable with Eliot and Hopkins. At that stage there were extremely few books on any aspects of Yeats: out of more than 160 studies of his work on my shelves today perhaps half a dozen pre-date 1946. My only recourse was to devour all his prose writings, and to follow up every clue in them to his own reading, in a frantic effort to become an instant expert for my expectant audience.

To study Yeats thoroughly a completely interdisciplinary approach is necessary. He began his career as an art student and never lost his responsiveness to visual forms. I was reminded of this a few months ago when I spent an evening in Anne Yeats's Dublin home – she is herself an artist with a solid reputation; across the room from me hung twenty-one etchings from Blake which she had inherited from her father. Yeats, in collaboration with E.J. Ellis, wrote a three-volume exposition of William Blake's symbolism.[8] Nearly everyone before Yeats's time had dismissed Blake's prophetic poems as the confused visions of a simple-minded poet, teetering on the verge of insanity. Though Yeats made plenty of mistakes in his scholarship, it was he who discovered that Blake's prophecies and visions belong to a system going back into the remote past, far beyond immediate predecessors such as the eighteenth-century Swedish scientist and mystic, Swedenborg, and even the sixteenth-century German-Swiss alchemist Paracelsus.[9]

Yeats picked up ideas in the most unexpected places, as I realized most vividly years later when a special privilege came my way. After

Yeats's widow Georgie died, his library was bequeathed to his daughter Anne. By good fortune I happened to be working in the National Library of Ireland in 1969, and Anne readily accepted my offer to help her unpack the many boxes of her father's books (which he had kept in no discoverable order), and arrange them systematically on her shelves. His books on art, particularly Blake's, were numerous and costly, dating from his more prosperous years. There was volume after volume of Swedenborg, with marginal marks and occasional annotations. There was *The Tibetan Book of the Dead*: it turned out to be AE's personal copy for which Yeats had apparently felt he had greater call than its owner, George Russell; books on the Tarot (Michael Yeats had already shown me Yeats's packs of Tarot cards with which he had practised divination); a collection of legendary Welsh stories, the *Mabinogion*; selections from Plotinus, edited by Taylor; works on the history of Magic, on Alchemy, Astrology, the Rosicrucian philosophers of the Middle Ages, Psychical Research, on Indian philosophy, especially the Veda and the Upanishads (Yeats was profoundly influenced by the East); and a strong collection of Irish literature and mythology. Although I have since then worked in Yeats's library several times, I have no recollection of books on psychology or any standard Biblical or Christian expositions.[10]

One fact which I have come to realize is that however universally a symbol may be found, in different countries it is liable to be given subtly varying national colourings. To interpret Yeats with any security it is essential to be well grounded in early Irish mythology and modern Irish history. Let me take as an instance the symbolism of stone. Ancient Irish rituals revered four sacred talismans – the sword, the stone, the spear, and the cauldron. Each stood for a particular quality, the stone symbolizing power.[11] In his poems and stories Yeats sought to marry the Irish race to cold Clare and Galway rock.[12] Then there was the neo-Platonic tradition which reached Yeats through Porphyry, a philosopher of the third century AD. Porphyry wrote a detailed exposition of Homer's "Cave of the Nymphs," described in the thirteenth book of the *Odyssey*, where the looms of stone on which the nymphs weave purple webs are interpreted as the bones and veins of the human body which clothe spirits as they become reincarnated.[13] The discovery of fossilized human bones may lie behind this belief.

Though stone has thus been associated with life, it has (in accord with the contradictoriness of symbols and dream images) been linked with its opposite, death: "dead as a stone" is frequent in Chaucer. During the ruthless struggle for Irish independence, still raging today,

Yeats came to view the nationalist fanatics, some of his friends among them, as imbued with "hearts of stone," dead to normal human sympathy and remorse.[14] I wonder whether Dr Cantwell Smith has encountered the equivalent symbol among the heart images he referred to in the East.

Hearts with one purpose alone
Through summer and winter seem
Enchanted to a stone
To trouble the living stream

– a rock which splits the flowing water and buffets it. But though the symbol has strong Irish overtones, the reference to hearts being "Enchanted to a stone" awakens memories of the classical Gorgons, one glimpse of whose snake-writhing heads could turn victims to stone.

When we look at the poetry of Hopkins we find his use of stone on occasion reflecting the somewhat stereotyped interpretations imposed or discovered by the Middle Ages, about which Dr Kushner has spoken. To the Middle Ages, stone stood for the element earth. Each element had its own natural movement – fire upwards, stone downwards.

As kingfishers catch fire, dragonflies draw flame;
As tumbled over rim in roundy wells
Stones ring …[15]

– there go the stones, symbolically tinkling downwards, while the kingfishers rise from the river, like gleaming flames.

Let me interject at this point how pleasurable an indulgence it has been to me to hear experts in so many different fields, all prepared to venture outside them – such as Dr Cantwell Smith, one of this continent's leading Christian theologians who is also profoundly read on Islam and Hinduism. Last night, after seeing him demonstrate a Buddha's elephant-stopping gesture, I took down from my theatre shelves a volume on *Elizabethan Acting*,[16] which reproduced page after page of similarly expressive hand signs from John Bulwer's *Chirologia* and *Chironomia* (1644), the "Language of the Hand" and the "Law of the Hand," traditional on the stage. There are counterparts in Chinese and Japanese theatre, where the sleeve is especially signifciant. But because each particular conformation of the fingers stands for an arbitrarily specified emotion, these should really be classified as signs rather than symbols.

University work frequently invites, and sometimes compels, excursions into areas beyond our specialist training. I turn now to architecture. Dr Whalley found himself called upon to play a major part in the design of a large University block, a fate which I suffered in Rhodesia when our Faculty of Arts rejected the plans submitted by our official architect. Dr James Leith, in his investigation of French Revolutionary symbolism, carried out pioneer research among long-forgotten building plans in Paris. He was too modest to reveal that these symbolic designs, such as those fascinating triangular structures we viewed this morning, were completely unknown to modern French historians before he coaxed and bullied the dusty sheets out of their official archive and library custodians. Their patterns throw light on the shifting ideologies of the National Assembly and the Directory. His illustrations are too fresh and vivid in our minds to need repeating. As I watched, a minor parallel occurred to me. My mind went back to a time when I was responsible for a course in eighteenth-century poetry, and, since there was no faculty of architecture, I showed my students slides of an architectural style which mirrored the tendency towards symmetry found in the verse of the period. The careful balance of a favourite verse form, the heroic couplet, has its counterpart in the Italianate, classical architecture which poised one wing of a building against the other. Country gentlemen even had their sprawling mansions remodeled to match the new fashion. Similarly, as my slides also established, the great eighteenth-century landscape gardeners such as Repton and Capability Brown turned rich estates into living demonstrations of the belief held by many contemporary philosophers and poets that art can improve upon Nature. Both these art forms embody symbolically the Augustan belief in restraint.

Triangles are not common in poetry – though George Canning wrote *The Loves of the Triangles*[17] in satiric response to Erasmus Darwin's *The Loves of the Plants* (1789), and old Irish poets rejoiced in composing *Triads*. The analysis of geometric forms in verse can be either rewarding or stultifying, depending on whether the investigator avoids contracting a fever worse than double pneumonia, *Monomania symbolorum*. A friend is convinced that Gerard Manley Hopkins cunningly concealed symbolic circles, the theologically resonant Greek *omega*, in poem after poem. With some pieces he may be right. But in "The Sea and the Skylark" Hopkins described two sounds, that of the tide ("low lull-off or all roar") and the song of the skylark which zig-zags up into the air, and after singing aloft spirals down and finally drops to its nest. Neither the pulsing tide nor the lark's flight pattern would strike a mathematician as describing circles, but my friend writes: "The fluctuating, horizontal activity of the ocean is contrasted with the lark's vertical flight, singing as it ascends. The geometric pattern of both is circular and perfect."[18]

Even the most eminent scholars who wade deeply into the mighty stream of symbolism may be swept off their feet. I was once external examiner for a PHD thesis at an excellent university on the most important geometric symbol in Yeats, the gyre or spiral. Yeats used it as a vibrant symbol for the way a concept, or a nation, may curve out from its point of origin, circling it at an ever increasing distance, now on one side of it and presently on its opposite side, but never traversing exactly the same ground twice.[19] Most of the thesis was convincing. But I objected when he included circular mazes or labyrinths (also found in Yeats's poetry) as gyres. I pointed out the contrast both in construction and intention between them : the bewildered wanderer in the maze is never allowed to complete a single circuit: he is continually brought up by a blank wall where the track doubles back on itself to left and right. The candidate was shocked by my criticism, because – or so he claimed – he had found spirals and circular labyrinths treated as equivalent symbols by Northrop Frye. However, the most careful cultivator may overlook in his treasured plot a few stinging nettles: those who venture outside it (and today I am compelled into half-a-dozen specialist preserves) will inevitably confuse some weeds with herbs.

Dr Bogomila Welsh-Ovcharov's visual and verbal demonstration of symbolism in Van Gogh was the work of an eminent expert in that field. It brought back happy memories of the splendid exhibition she arranged and expounded in the Art Gallery of Ontario in 1980. I could spend half-an-hour happily following up in literature the symbols found in this artist – the reaper, the sower, the sun (an image which Dr Leith also showed us in the France of the preceding century). Parallels between the symbolism in a man's paintings and those in his poetry are sometimes elusive. I was baffled for years in my attempts to reconcile pre-Raphaelite pictures and poems. George Landow has recently suggested that each obtrusive typological detail in a Holman Hunt has to be interpreted separately, before the painting can be seen as a whole.[20] Blake's illustrations, however, generally help us to handle the delusive simplicity of his verse, though they may, as symbols are wont to do, suggest subtly different reaches of association. When lecturing on Blake I have often arranged for an art historian to present his etchings.[21] I have usually made one proviso: "Please don't show my students his illustration of the 'Tiger.' I prefer to let the poem itself strike them with all its imaginative power."

Tyger, tyger, burning bright
In the forests of the night,
What immortal hand and eye
Dare frame thy fearful symmetry?

But the plate on which these mystic words are engraved shows a plump, surely non-symbolic, striped cat in full daylight, under a tree, gazing off to the left with a rather beery, bemused expression, as though the poet's awkward questions had left him thoroughly befuddled. The poem itself haunts us because its symbolism is from such varied depths – including the great myth alluded to by Dr Moles, the theft of fire by Prometheus, with which the tiger's eyes seem to blaze.

Ever since hearing Dr Welsh's paper my mind has been ringing with another Blake poem, causing me to wonder whether the symbolism of the sunflower was the same in Van Gogh's paintings – as Dr Welsh told us he repeats it tirelessly – and Blake's "Songs of Experience." The sunflower myth goes back to the Greek legend of Clytie, a nymph who fell in love with Apollo the sun-god and pined away when he would not respond; she was transformed into a sunflower. Blake uses the symbol in one of his most beautiful lyrics:

Ah, sunflower, weary of time,
Who countest the steps of the sun,
Seeking after that sweet golden clime
Where the traveller's journey is done;

Where the youth pined away with desire
And the pale virgin shrouded in snow
Arise from their graves and aspire
Where my sunflower wishes to go.

This seems to be a Platonic poem, showing the soul in its human grave, gazing towards the sun, the source of life. Note the way in which Blake identifies himself with the plant, "*my* sunflower," because he felt himself possessed of the solar Los, the imagination. At a lower level, Blake's sunflower is a symbol of frustrated desire. Van Gogh's life story was also one of aspiration and frustration, since his spiritual vision was not shared by the leaders of his own church; like Blake's, his art was often met with condescension.

But were the two men using the same flower as symbol? The *Oxford English Dictionary* implies doubt: Blake's first two lines are cited under a paragraph which deals with the heliotrope (usually purple), and other flowers which turn so as to follow the sun, while the common sunflower (*Helianthus*) is described as earning its name because its yellow disc and rays make it look like the sun. Blake's illustration is inconclusive: the deeply rooted stem seems to me to be surmounted by a tiny human figure couched in the calyx, but from his illustrations elsewhere we can be sure that he knew the yellow sunflower.[22] Most species of this sun-like plant also turn their leaves and flowers to follow the sun across the heavens. With that curious and sometimes exasperating ambiguity familiar in dream images and poetic symbols alike, the sunflower may stand either for faithfulness or unreliability. In Chinese symbolism it represents longevity and magical powers, but why this should be so my *Illustrated Encyclopaedia of Traditional Symbols* has no space to conjucture.[23]

I am particularly glad that Dr Abraham Moles brought into our discussions the nature of myth, and suggested that universal myths such as we find embodied in Greek and Latin poetry are still the secret driving forces behind man's most characteristic patterns of behaviour. He mentioned among the twenty-five most "dynamic" myths the story of Icarus, symbolizing the impulse towards the conquest of the air which has reached its climax this century: man has been able to fly to the moon, and to send exploratory spacecraft to the most distant planets in the solar system. Dr Storr also found this yearning for new fields to conquer highly typical of the human race.

Myths are defined in contradictory ways by various schools of thought. Even the latest supplement to the thirteen-volume *Oxford English Dictionary* offers no definition which covers its uses in modern anthropology, psychiatry, and social studies. I take a myth as being symbolism expressed in the form of a compressed narrative, in which the characters and events mirror a certain set of desires and impulses deep in our "collective unconscious." One of the forces at work in the change-over from mediaeval literature to the Renaissance, a topic which Dr Kushner so ably handled an hour ago, was the discovery of the myths and allegories of ancient Greece and Egypt. Dr Moles is convinced that these myths enshrine human aspirations and drives which are still current sociological factors. He made the interesting proposal that they should be collected on a global scale, analysed, and put on a computer, so that they could be compared and studied. He argued an excellent case for their relevance to our own times. Thus we are today, with our worship of Energy, as eagerly in search of sources of warmth and heat as the legendary Prometheus. Since Dr Moles accepts the concept of Jungian psychiatrists that such myths surge out of the unconcious, he exemplifies the multi-disciplinary scholar – a sociologist using ancient and modern literary creations, and interpreting them in the light of analytical psychology to explain social behaviour, with a view to modifying it into more desirable forms.

Not all myths, of course, are in keeping with modern sociological theory as springs of action to be encouraged. The myths of the Greek and Roman gods and goddesses, as Hopkins complained,[24] include some ignoble conceptions and objectionable symbolism. We might call them a licentious galaxy of hedonists: I wondered last night whether Dr Cantwell Smith, in building up his concept of divinity from all religions, would allow elements from these debased deities to contaminate his synthesis. Then there is the myth of the Fall of Adam and Eve, used for thousands of years to reinforce the stereotype of woman as morally weaker than man, the too readily unlatched gateway through which sin entered the world.

But many myths and symbols encountered in modern literature do not have a lineage lost in antiquity: they have been created in our own time and have yet to prove by their powers of survival whether they reflect modern man's profound desires and emotions. In his paper on the railroad as symbol in Canadian poetry and culture, Dr Douglas Jones illustrated the precarious symbolic niche which a comparatively recent human artifact may occupy in poetry. His was a poet's vision equally sensitive to Anglophone and Francophone literature. I admired the scholarly restraint and critical honesty with which Dr Jones analysed his examples, refusing to force the evidence. He expressed surprise that in the century and a half since railroads began to criss-cross our civilized world, they have contributed so little to the imaginative life of British and American poetry. Even in Canada, where they figure more prominently, their effect is found in English literature more than in French. He advanced several interesting explanations: French Canada thinks rather in the dimension of time, dwelling on her cultural past and on dreams projected into the future, whereas English Canada is concerned predominantly with the dimension of space – in earlier eras the conversion of trackless solitudes into regions of habitation.

The great Canadian Pacific Railway forged a tenuous double steel band across an entire continent, a triumph of human enterprise in the face of opposition from men and natural forces. E.J. Pratt celebrates the physical achievements and obsessive visions which urged on the enterprise till the driving of the last spike. But the imperialist motives soured other poets and to some, such as John Ford, the railroad stood not for the dawn of a new national life, but for death. Ford's "Night Train" is our human life rushing us towards "a discovery that is not / a destination" – a train from which we cannot dismount without being cut to pieces. His train is redolent of Death.

This seems to have been one of its earliest significances in English literature. We remember in Charles Dickens's *Dombey and Son*, written in 1846, the chapter (20) describing the journey by train taken by the grief-burdened Mr. Dombey, whose hard-gathered wealth had suddenly become meaningless to him because Paul, his only son and heir, had sickened and died.

> He found no pleasure or relief in the journey. Tortured by these thoughts he carried monotony with him, through the rushing landscape, and hurried headlong, not through a rich and varied country, but a wilderness of blighted plans and gnawing jealousies. The very speed at which the train was whirled along, mocked the swift course of the young life that had been borne away so steadily and so inexorably to its foredoomed end. The power that forced itself upon its iron way – its own – defiant of all paths and roads, piercing through the heart of every obstacle, and dragging living creatures of all classes, ages, and degrees behind it, was a type of the triumphant monster, Death.

In poetry the impact of a new man-made symbol usually depends on the voltage imparted to it by its context. It may at first be accompanied by an ancient symbol in which associations accumulated during many hundreds or even thousands of years have created vortexes of universal significance. Dr Leith gave us an excellent example this morning when he showed us the new Revolutionary symbol of the mason's triangular level placed side by side with an equilateral triangle – though the geometric shape was also a symbol not only of a trinity but of perfection, and in that particular instance contained within it another symbol of plentiude, a circle with "God" inscribed in Hebrew. A poetic example of the juxtaposition of old and new symbols is offered by Hopkins. In his great ode, "The Wreck of the Deutschland," Part the Second, the poet prefaces an account of the voyage of that doomed ship into the treachery and fury of the storm-tormented sandbanks of the

North Sea, with a stanza full of symbols redolent of the ancient Hebrew Psalmists and prophets.[25] This stanza drapes the emigrant vessel with emblems of fatality, though it was carrying passengers full of hope from the depressed cities of Euorpe to the promised land of America. We hear Death boasting of his many agents and disguises.

> "Some find me a sword; some
> The flange and the rail; flame,
> Fang, or flood" goes Death on drum,
> And storms bugle his fame.
> But wé dream we are rooted in earth – Dust!
> Flesh falls within sight of us: we, though our flower the same,
> Wave with the meadow, forget that there must
> The sour scythe cringe, and the blear share come.

Readers may be jolted by the sudden transition from "flesh" to "flower," but this is designed to evoke (if we know our Bibles) the Old Testament prophecy of Isaiah (40:6): "What shall I cry? All flesh is grass, and all the goodliness thereof is as the flower of the field: / The grass withereth, the flower fadeth: because the spirit of the Lord bloweth upon it." The symbolism of the Bible has supplied the whole Christian world, in all languages, with an international currency of exchange, as Northrop Frye has explained in his books and papers. The image of Death with a drum almost certainly comes from Holbein's series of woodcuts, *The Dance of Death*. The stanza ends with Death the Reaper, an age-old image which, as Dr Welsh-Ovcharov proved from one of Vincent Van Gogh's letters, he was consciously using when he painted a picture of a reaper to balance one of a sower in his St Rémy period.

But my main reason for quoting this stanza was to show Hopkins adding to the time-honoured list of death-dealers – sword, flame, and flood – a modern one, symbolic of man's lethal demand for speed, "The flange and the rail." When I studied *The Times* of London, to read the proceedings of the official enquiry into how the "Deutschland" came to be wrecked, I found on another page of the issue for 22 December 1875 an analysis of the causes of railway accidents in Britain during the first nine months of that year. These had brought 900 deaths and over 4,000 injuries. In seventy cases broken *rails* were at fault, and in 194 the *flanges* of the wheels had led to derailment and injury. The central part of the wheel, with its spokes and inner rim, used I believe to be cast, and the forged outer rim and flange were later secured to it by various patent methods. Out of a mundane technical report which disclosed that twenty-seven wheels made by the Gibson patent had failed, fourteen by the Beattie, and so forth, Hopkins created a new symbol, "The flange and the rail."

Let me draw to a conclusion by quoting from T.S. Eliot a poem which also echoes that same verse in Isaiah underlying Hopkins's stanza. Eliot's "Difficulties of a Statesman" is the second part of a work called "Coriolan" (1931–2).[26] The first part shows the "Triumphal March" of the war hero, and the second sees him battling the still more resistant bureaucracy and electorate. Eliot uses a clever device to indicate the perennial nature of this problem (as familiar to the Roman Coriolanus as in the twentieth century): he oscillates his images between past and present, leaping from ancient Hebrew prophecies to modern telephone operators.

Cry what shall I cry?
All flesh is grass: comprehending
The Companions of the Bath, the Knights of the British Empire, the Cavaliers,
O Cavaliers! of the Legion of Honour ...

Cry cry what shall I cry?
The first thing to do is to form the committees:
The consultative councils, the standing committees, select committees and sub-committees.
One secretary will do for several committees.

No wonder that, entangled in the verbal meshes of administration, the statesman feels too weary to carry on.

I refer to the poem because the symbolism, particularly in the first part, is so complex that critics have been somewhat at a loss to interpret it. I was convinced from some of the imagery that Eliot felt a measure of sympathy for the hero, while nearly every other critic viewed the portrait as purely negative. I was therefore grateful to be able to discuss the matter with Eliot himself one afternoon in Natal when I took him bird-watching to see his first flamingoes. These spectacularly beautiful birds, if only they'd had the wit to realize it, were that day being given their own opportunity of poetic immortality – Eliot was very eager to see them. In the morning, scouting on my own, I had located them wading in a picturesque lagoon close to a quiet road, against a background of mangrove trees swarming with chattering monkeys. What a symbolic poem Eliot could have made of the scene! But the wretched birds traded in the chance of a lifetime for a sea-food lunch. By the afternoon, when I drove Eliot to see them, they had flapped their way to a sandbank in the middle of Durban Harbour, where they remained inaccessibly remote, shrimping. We could inspect them only by means of a telescope (which the poet had some difficulty in focusing), gazing through a gap between a moored dredger and its dirty barge. Any poem which had emerged from so improbable a combination would have depended upon private symbols, meaningful only to Eliot and his host.

As we refreshed ourselves on the wharfside after this disappointing outcome, I recited lines from "Triumphal March" for his verdict. The same mingling of symbols ancient and modern directs us away from any time-anchored identification. We begin with Roman legionaries tramping stone streets, followed by the cavalry.

Stone, bronze, stone, steel, stone, oakleaves, horses' heels
Over the paving ...
This is the way to the temple, and we so many crowding the way.

We remember the Oriental emphasis upon the temple entrance, alluded to in Dr Cantwell Smith's paper. We have time only for snatches of the poem:

What comes first? Can you see? Tell us. It is
5,800,000 rifles and carbines ...
53,000 field and heavy guns ...
13,000 aeroplanes ...
11,000 field kitchens
1,150 field bakeries ...
Look
There he is now, look:
There is no interrogation in his eyes
Or in the hands, quiet over the horse's neck,
And the eyes watchful, waiting, perceiving, indifferent.
O hidden under the dove's wing, hidden in the turtle's breast,
Under the palmtree at noon, under the running water
At the still point of the turning world. O hidden.

These final symbols, as they occur elsewhere in Eliot, carry very positive overtones, relating to someone close to the heart of reality, secure from trivial distractions and triumphs. This I suggested to the author himself.

Eliot agreed that a degree of approval could be deduced, but he was reluctant to dismiss the impressions of other critics that the portrayal conveyed a hidden menace, the hint of a potential dictator. A poem, he said, emerges from depths in the memory where images from his personal experience of reading have become saturated with complex feelings such as the poet himself cannot fathom. What the poem means to an author and his emotions while he was writing it do not exhaust its meanings. Each sensitive reader may make of a poem something different, something personal.[27]

This was a wise answer which I have never forgotten. What Eliot said about poems applies *a fortiori* to symbols. The context in which a symbol is placed reacts upon it to form a new compound. It is like the dream images of which Dr Storr spoke, familiar in psychoanalysis, possessing positive aspects as well as negative ones, all of which the patient and analyst must explore little by little; "no symbol," said Yeats, "tells all its meaning to any generation."[28] The eight speakers whom it has been our privilege to hear during this colloquium have given us material for months, indeed years, of exploration. To them all I pay my warm tribute of appreciation.

NOTES

1 *Poetic Process* (London, 1953; rpt. Westport, Conn., 1973), 164–6.

2 These ideas are most fully developed in Yeats's essays on "Symbolism in Painting" (1898) and "The Symbolism of Poetry" (1900), rpt. in *Essays and Introductions* (London, 1961), 146–64.

3 *Psyche and Symbol: A Selection from the Writings of C.G. Jung*, ed. Violet S. de Laszlo (New York, 1958), xiv-xv.

4 See W.B. Yeats, "Magic" (1901), rpt. in *Essays and Introductions*, 44–5. See also 28.

5 Israel Regardie, *The Golden Dawn: An Account of the Teachings, Rites and Ceremonies of the Order of the Golden Dawn*, 4 vols. (rpt. Saint Paul, Minn., 1971), IV, 11–14.

6 Northrop Frye in his keynote address quoted from Andrew Marvell's "The Garden," stanza 6 (1681), his anticipation of Swedenborg's Doctrine of Correspondence: "Meanwhile the Mind, from Pleasure less, / Withdraws into its happiness: / The Mind, that ocean where each kind / Does straight its own resemblance find." Marvell emphasizes the symbolism of the colour green.

7 *The Trembling of the Veil* (London, 1922); rpt. in *Autobiographies* (London, 1956), 258–9.

8 *The Works of William Blake*, ed. with a memoir and interpretation by Edwin John Ellis and William Butler Yeats, 3 vols. (London, 1893).

9 See Deborah Dorfman, *Blake in the Nineteenth Century* (New Haven, 1969), ch. 8.

10 That Yeats was aware of early psychoanalytical interpretations, however, is clear from such passages as *Per Amica Silentia Lunae* (1918), sect. xii; rpt. in *Mythologies* (London, 1962), 341.

11 *Mythologies*, 220–1; cf. his *Memoirs*, ed. Denis Donoghue (London, 1972), 125.

12 *Autobiographies*, 194; *Collected Poems* (London, 1950), 149–50; *Essays and Introductions*, 97.

13 See Yeats's discussion of the symbolism of the Cave of the Nymphs, *Essays and Introductions*, 81ff. He used Thomas Taylor's translation from the Greek of Plotinus and Porphyry. A useful reprint of Porphyry's essay "On the Cave of the Nymphs" is appended to Robert Snukal's *High Talk: The Philosophical Poetry of W.B. Yeats* (Cambridge, 1973), 240–62. The typesetters and proofreaders being ignorant of Greek script, however, the Greek passages in the footnotes are often unintelligible.

14 *Collected Poems*, 204, 249; *Essays and Introductions*, 314.

15 *The Poems of Gerard Manley Hopkins*, ed. W.H. Gardner and Norman H. MacKenzie, 4th ed. (London 1967), 90.

16 B.L. Joseph, *Elizabethan Acting* (London, 1951), 2–4, 40–8.

17 Published in the *Anti-Jacobin* (London, 1799).

18 James Finn Cotter, *Inscape: The Christology and Poetry of Gerard Manley Hopkins* (Pittsburg, 1972), 176.

19 The most detailed general study known to me is T.A. Cook's *Spirals in Nature and Art* (London, 1903). The mandala circles mentioned by Dr Storr often have spirals coiling out from their centres, usually in serpent form: see C.G. Jung, *Mandala Symbolism*, trans. R.G.C. Hull (Princeton, 1959), figs. 4, 16–18, 21, 34.

20 *William Holman Hunt and Typological Symbolism* (New Haven, 1979).

21 In the Far East, however, struggling to expound to Oriental students Hazlitt's essays with their incessant references to European paintings, I had to take on myself the presentation of five illustrated lectures on the development of Western art, which is in general much less symbolic than the art of China and Japan.

22 Blake's etching combines on one plate this poem with two others among the *Songs of Experience*. Some critics are not sure whether the marginal sketch applies to the sunflower lyric. For his yellow sunflower and sunflower symbolism see Kathleen Raine, *Blake and Tradition*, 2 vols. (Princeton, 1968), I, 218–22. She quotes Ovid and Proclus to explain the myth.

23 Ed. J.C. Cooper (London, 1978), 164.

24 *The Letters of Gerard Manley Hopkins to Robert Bridges*, ed. C.C. Abbott (London, 1955), 217.

25 *Poems*, 55.

26 T.S. Eliot, *Collected Poems, 1909–35* (London, 1936), 133–9.

27 Cf. T.S. Eliot, *On Poetry and Poets* (London, 1957), 112–14; *The Use of Poetry and the Use of Criticism* (London, 1933), 145ff.

28 "Symbolism in Painting," in *Essays and Introductions*, 148.

ORGANIZING COMMITTEE–COMITE D'ORGANIZATION

Clifford Hospital, Queen's University

James A. Leith, Queen's University

Norman MacKenzie, Queen's University

Lorne Maclachlan, Queen's University

Anthony Riley, Queen's University

John Stedmond, Queen's University

Clive Thomson, Queen's University